· Siliconnections ·

·Siliconnections·

COMING OF AGE
IN THE ELECTRONIC ERA

Forrest M. Mims, III

McGraw-Hill Book Company
New York · St. Louis · San Francisco
Hamburg · Mexico · Toronto

ISBN 0-07-042411-X

1 2 3 4 5 6 7 8 9 DOC DOC 8 7 6 5

LIBRARY OF CONGRESS CATALOGING IN PUBLICATION DATA

Mims, Forrest M.
  Siliconnections; coming of age in the electronic era.
  Includes index.
  1. Microelectronics—Popular works. I. Title.
TK7874.M528   1986   621.381'7   85-13223
ISBN 0-07-042411-X

Book Design by Laura Ferguson

In memory of Professor Alexander Graham Bell, 1847–1922, teacher of the deaf, inventor of the photophone and telephone, enthusiastic experimenter, and consummate gentleman

Acknowledgments

At the Winter Consumer Electronics Show in January 1984 Harold Crawford and Jeff McCartney of the McGraw-Hill Book Company were kind enough to allow me to describe a proposed book to be called *Siliconnections*. Jeff delivered a copy of my written proposal to Tom Quinn of McGraw-Hill's General Books Division, who issued a contract. For their siliconfidence in *Siliconnections* when it was merely a proposal I'm indebted to these editors. And I'm particularly appreciative of Tom Quinn's frequent and wise counsel during the preparation of the manuscript.

My personal files and records were the source of most of the facts and dates in *Siliconnections*. For assistance in reconstructing the mood at the time of some of the siliconnected happenings related in the book, I relied on telephone discussions with some of the principals. For their assistance in this regard I am especially grateful to my former MITS partners, H. Edward Roberts and Stan Cagle, and a former Air Force Colleague, Dr. Roger G. Mark. Several silicon press friends were also very helpful, especially David Gunzel and Harry Helms, as was the old *Popular Electronics* editorial team of Arthur Salsberg, Leslie Solomon, John McVeigh, and Alexander Burawa. For some helpful shop-talk sessions with fellow siliconnected writers, I'm indebted to William Barden, Jr., Steve Ciarcia, and Don Lancaster. Ted Lee and Mark Miller, the sharp attorneys who were willing to tackle the largest corporation in the United States, provided their usual expert counsel. I would also like to be able to thank Michael Urbano, a Bell Labs patent attorney, for his explanation of why he and his cohorts became camera shy during my deposition in 1980. However, that is not possible, since Mike said it would be a violation of the Canons of Professional Ethics to discuss the matter.

Finally, *Siliconnections* would not have been possible without the loving patience of a former Air Force Weapons Lab colleague, my wife Minnie. She put up with everything from living on a parking attendant's income and all-night sessions at MITS to my frequent bouts with that siliconfounded occupational malady known as HTS. Practically everything that matters in *Siliconnections* was discussed with Minnie, and the manuscript reflects her wise suggestions. For her help I am deeply appreciative, and promise never again to allow lawyers from Bell Labs to search our home.

Contents

· Siliconnections ·

Coming of Age in the Silicon Era

Previews

FUTURISTS ARE FOND of saying we're living in the Information Age. Or the Space Age or the Computer Age. They're right, of course, but these "ages" are connected by and dependent on a common link with a silvery-gray crystal called silicon.

The silicon connection is a solid-state electronic network that to some extent has influenced, or soon will, every person on earth. Digital watches, portable stereos, electronic calculators, transistor radios, pocket televisions, and home computers are *silicontraptions*. If you possess any of these products, then you're a *siliconsumer*. And simply by reading these words, you and I have established a *siliconnection*, for they were typed into the keyboard of a *siliconcocted* microcomputer.

Though silicon is simultaneously fueling a second industrial revolution and creating an extension of the human intellect having more fundamental importance than the invention of printing, most people haven't the slightest idea how the microelectronic devices made from silicon work. Nor do they fully realize the overall impact silicon now has on their lives. Certainly one need not understand the inner workings of a television, calculator, or digital watch to effectively use these devices. But those who have this knowledge possess magical, siliconnected glasses through which they can get a glimpse of what's to come in the Silicon Era.

Since first seeing a photograph of a transistor in 1954, I've followed the silicon industry, awestruck by its pioneers and mesmerized by its gadgetry. *Siliconnections* is a Cook's tour of what I've experienced and observed. Included is the story of how I met Ed

Roberts, and we and two friends formed MITS, Inc., the company through which Ed altered the course of history when he developed the Altair 8800, the world's first successful personal computer. Also included is a behind-the-scenes account about the bright scientists and crazy happenings at the top-secret Air Force laser laboratory in New Mexico where Ed and I first met. *Siliconnections* contains descriptions of firsthand experiences involving siliconnected secrets and spies, both real and otherwise. And it gives an insider's perspective on the topsy-turvy, boom-bust world of the silicon press, the influential information industry that has provided my livelihood since 1970. After all, *Popular Electronics*, a magazine for electronics experimenters and hobbyists, played the role of midwife at the birth of the multi-billion-dollar personal computer industry when it published a construction article about Ed Roberts's Altair in its January 1975 issue.

My siliconnected career has been greatly influenced by the engineers and editors you'll meet in the pages that follow. But my mentor was Professor Alexander Graham Bell, a consummate experimenter, inventor, teacher, and gentleman. Though known best for his invention of the first practical telephone, Bell viewed the discovery of speaking over beams of light as his greatest invention. To accomplish this triumph, nearly a century before it found widespread use, he turned to selenium, an element that shares the semiconducting properties of silicon. Bell thus became one of the first solid-state researchers and, incidentally, the umbilical (seleniumbilical?) cord that established and nourished my lifelong obsession with solid-state electronics. *Siliconnections* includes accounts of Bell's invention of lightwave communications and the link I established with him through his grandson at *National Geographic*.

The telephone company that Bell founded is now the world's largest utility. From the laboratory that bears his name sprang the transistor, the semiconductor switch with no moving parts that is the cornerstone of today's solid-state electronics industry. Bell Laboratories is one of the world's most productive and respected research institutions. That's why an experimenter in New Mexico submitted to Bell Labs in 1973 an invention disclosure for a more efficient method of communicating over beams of light carried by optical fibers. Five years later, amid a great deal of fanfare, Bell Labs demonstrated an experimental fiberoptic telephone that incorporated the principle submitted by the experimenter. Dozens of magazines and newspapers carried stories about the new phone. *Business Week*, for instance, proclaimed it ". . . so radically different it may eventually transform American Telephone and Telegraph Co. and the entire telephone industry . . . and dramatically alter the basic nature of the phone network" (Dec. 4, 1978). What the press didn't know was that Bell Labs refused to honor its contract with the lone experimenter from the hinterlands, and pay him for his "radically different" invention disclosure.

Mark Miller, one of the lawyers who represented the experimenter in his little-guy-versus-big-guy battle with Bell Labs, recently reflected on the significance of the event: "Joe Blow, just minding his own business, not a hero, not looking for a fight, but at a very important place at the right/wrong time and too pigheaded to know enough to get out of the way of a herd of stampeding elephants, unintentionally became the focus of a battle of truly vast implications and won simply because he refused to give ground or acknowledge he was outgunned. It was Luke Skywalker versus the Evil Empire." Mark Miller was my lawyer; I was that pigheaded experimenter. *Siliconnections* includes the highlights of that duel with the corporate legacy of the man who so profoundly influenced my life.

Though *Siliconnections* is about high-tech things, events, and people, it is not a technical tome for scientists and engineers. That wouldn't be possible anyway, for I am neither a scientist nor an engineer. Although physics was initially my major at Texas A&M University in 1962, I quickly switched to government after nearly failing freshman algebra. Because of my active pursuit of various electronic projects, well-meaning counselors tried to persuade me to switch from government to electrical engineering. Graduating with a degree in liberal arts, I told them, was better than flunking out with a major in engineering. Nevertheless, I once mustered up the courage to visit an electronics lab where students worked with test equipment far beyond the level of anything on the primitive electronics workbench in my dormitory room. For a few minutes that scene proved tempting. But on spotting endless strings of meaningless (to me) equations scrawled across a green chalkboard, I fled the lab and never returned.

My inability to grasp the principles of higher mathematics beyond Ohm's simple law (E = IR, or voltage equals current times resistance) didn't squelch my ambition eventually to perform productive work in electronics. "Within ten years I'll be able to afford a mathematics consultant," I naïvely told a skeptical father properly concerned that his befuddled son was taking the easy way out. Little did either of us realize that the hoped-for consultant would arrive ahead of schedule. It came neatly packaged inside a black plastic box studded with push buttons, which slipped into a pocket and demanded only that its batteries be recharged every few weeks. It was a programmable scientific calculator, and it was made possible by a silicon microchip imprinted with a microscopic network of thousands of transistors.

The microchip was about to overtake electronic circuits made from individual transistors. This transition had consequences far more sweeping than the switch from vacuum tubes to transistors in the 1950s, and it was a window of opportunity for a college student whose high-tech aspirations were jeopordized by higher-math phobias. While engineering students were struggling to master a technology that would be largely obsolete in five years, I was designing a miniature guidance system for small rockets, devising sensors that could detect the light from a match at the far end of a dark dormitory hall, and sending a voice and music superimposed on flickering beams of light projected thousands of feet along dark rural roads or across the Texas A&M campus.

Among the most interesting experiments during those college years were those which used infrared-emitting diodes, state-of-the-art semiconductor devices that were largely unknown to engineering students learning about transistors. These $365 devices were provided by Dr. Edwin Bonin, a scientist at Texas Instruments whose work with infrared diodes had been described in 1965 in *Electronics*, an industry trade magazine. After reading the article I hitchhiked to Dallas to visit Dr. Bonin, who seemed rather surprised that anyone would go to such trouble. During our first meeting Dr. Bonin plucked from his desk drawer a penlight that emitted a soft red glow. Instead of a conventional lamp, the penlight was equipped with a glass-windowed, miniature metal can similar to those in which transistors were installed. Inside was a speck of glowing semiconductor, a light-emitting diode. Though that red diode was fascinating, it produced very little light. Much more powerful infrared-emitting diodes were my objective, for I had concluded that a pulsating beam from a single diode could be used to make a handheld infrared "radar" that would warn blind persons about objects in their path. The inspiration for this project was my great-grandfather, who had been blinded by a dynamite explosion when he was a young railroad worker.

Dr. Bonin agreed to provide one of the costly diodes if I would first build a transistorized circuit that would perform the task I envisioned, and send it to him for his evaluation. Within two days of my return to Texas A&M, the circuit was ready and mailed special delivery to Dr. Bonin. Not having access to a real infrared-emitting diode, there was no way for me to know whether the circuit would function properly. But it did work, and ten days later a package arrived from Dr. Bonin containing the circuit plus three of the coveted diodes. Within a few weeks I had constructed several experimental handheld travel aids. This project led directly to many of the siliconnected happenings related in the chapters that follow.

The Star Wars Set

Now that siliconnected appliances have become a commonplace and accepted part of life, those of us past forty envy the younger generation. If only we had had access to personal computers and programmable calculators when we were their age. If only we could be around to experience the high-tech times in their future.

Today's high-tech generation was born with a silicon spoon in its mouth. It has become so accustomed to an ever-expanding galaxy of siliconnected gizmos and gadgets that it takes for granted what was once the stuff of dreams. Those of us who came of age in the early days of the silicon era, however, were imprinted with a life-long ability to become exhilarated by reports of a soon-to-be-announced high-tech development. Remembering the pre-Sputnik era of $90 silicon transistors, we can scarcely contain our excitement over an announcement of the latest integrated circuit containing hundreds of thousands of transistors intricately interconnected atop a silicon chip smaller than the head of a thumbtack. And we become downright euphoric when we learn of the arrival of a new semiconductor laser smaller than a grain of sand, which emits a beam of coherent red light while consuming only a tenth the power of a penlight. Meanwhile, the high-tech generation yawns and wonders why the daffy engineers in the research labs are taking so long to develop holographic television and voice-activated type-writers. Will the silicon spoon society ever fully appreciate the significance of the engineering triumphs it takes for granted?

Consider two marvels of siliconnected engineering at my finger-tips as these words are typed: a portable computer and its liquid-crystal readout panel. Who would have predicted that only ten years after the clumsy Altair, writers would type manuscripts into portable computers the size of a notebook? As for the computer's readout panel, though I've experimented with liquid crystals since 1968, I am still amazed by the phenomenon through which infor-mation appears as if by magic on the displays of digital watches, pocket calculators, and portable computers. That's because I clearly remember when the most complicated liquid-crystal "dis-play" was a do-it-yourself light shutter made by sandwiching a greasy fluid between two sheets of electrically conductive glass. When a voltage was applied to the opposing glass plates, the clear fluid became turbid, thus blocking the passage of light. The liquid-crystal display of the computer into which this book was typed contains 15,360 such shutters that can be individually switched on or off to form numbers, letters, graphs, and designs. The liquid-crystal displays of some portable computers contain an incredible 128,000 light shutters, and displays having a far greater capacity are undergoing development. My high-tech-generation son is not especially surprised by these developments for he can't remember when flat-screen display devices were only a dream. Liquid-crystal displays are as old as he is.

I first encountered the high-technology generation gap back in the early 1970s while presenting seminars on solid-state electronics at a summer program for gifted high-school students at the Univer-sity of New Mexico. The program was organized by James P. Miller, a mathematics teacher and fellow science-fair veteran and model rocketry enthusiast. It involved a rigorous dose of computer programming and individual projects in which each student had to devise a program to predict the downrange impact point of a model rocket. Admission to the program was highly selective, and the students weren't easily impressed by demonstrations of silicon-nected gadgets like lightwave communicators and miniature electronic instruments designed to be launched in model rockets. Hoping to liven up a particularly nerdy class, I demonstrated a helium-neon gas laser, a device the size of a loaf of bread, which emitted a pencil-thin, highly parallel beam of coherent light. Though they were all aware of lasers, only a few of the students had actually seen one in operation. For the first time they seemed genuinely enthusiastic.

The laser demonstration was an effective means of raising the high-tech consciousness of bright kids jaded by an overdose of computers, rockets, and electronics. It became a permanent fixture of these summer programs. One of the more memorable sessions with the laser occurred when a group of students from New York City asked me to conduct a laser demonstration from the roof of a seven-story building at the university. The previous night we had attached a telescope to the laser to narrow its beam. We then rigidly mounted the laser atop Albuquerque's First National Bank, and pointed its slender beam at a special reflector previously concealed near the base of the Sandia Mountain tramway nine miles away. We drove to the tramway where we found the reflector amid a fifty-foot-wide patch of cactus and granite gravel bathed in shimmering crimson. Looking back at the city we were awestruck by the brilliance of the red laser beam. Though it was much less powerful than a penlight, it far outshone the lights of Albuquerque and even the airport beacon. When the same skyline was viewed from outside the dimly illuminated area surrounding the reflector, the brilliant spotlight effect disappeared entirely.

I assumed that the students had this spectacular demonstration in mind the next night when they asked to go up to the roof of the tall building in which we met. But they had a much more creative idea. Five or six of them had stationed themselves just below the building around an open plaza that fronts the university library. When the laser battles in *Star Wars* were still a gleam in George Lucas's eye, their plan was to startle the campus by pretending to be zapped by a ray gun that silently knifed through the warm summer air and nailed its victims with a deadly red beam. Not wishing to dissuade the newly enthusiastic students who had previously seemed so underawed, I agreed to participate in their unrehearsed scheme by serving as the ray-gun sniper. The scene that followed was reminiscent of the public's reaction to Orson Welles's 1938 radio dramatization of H. G. Wells's "The War of the Worlds."

Those of us on the roof prepared for the attack by mounting the laser on an easily adjusted, heavy-duty tripod. We removed the telescope to broaden the beam, thus removing any possible eye hazard. At a prearranged signal the first "victim" gave out an ear-splitting scream and crumpled onto the plaza, his chest drilled through by the deadly beam from the harmless laser. Curious students raced to the scene, only to be shooed away from the body by a couple of soon-to-be "victims" who stirred up the gathering crowd with diabolical rumors about ray guns and U.F.O. sightings. Terrified coeds screamed for help and shrieked at passersby, warning them to stay away from the area. Meanwhile, one by one the summer-program earthlings bravely marched out to face the death ray. Finally, the last student raced courageously through the maze of bodies sprawled on the plaza, ran into the glass-walled foyer of the library, and approached an armed campus policeman who had rushed to the book checkout counters to check out the disturbance outside. By this time I was thoroughly enjoying the spectacle below, and was even becoming rather good at zapping the victims. A chorus of "Do it! Do it! Do it!" from the hysterical students on the roof quickly vaporized what was left of my better judgment. I took careful aim through the library's big plate-glass window, and fired on the heroic earthling next to the policeman. Pandemonium broke out as he collapsed to the floor clutching his throat and screaming, the mysterious red spot shimmering on his chest. Those of us on the roof would have laughed until it hurt, but we didn't have time. The outnumbered and outgunned campus cop called the real cops and within minutes three or four cruisers, sirens sounding, roared into the library parking lot.

When Pat Miller moved the summer program to the University of California at Los Angeles a few years later, another class tried to duplicate the legendary laser massacre staged by their predecessors. Alas, the apparently laser-wise U.C.L.A. students either ignored or were bored by our death-ray demonstration. Perhaps they were veterans of previous laser sniper attacks. We reluctantly removed the laser death-ray demonstration from the summer student program. Any novelty effect it may have retained was dispatched a few months later by the fake but spectacular laser ray guns in *Star Wars*. I've yet to observe a demonstration of high-technology with such frenzy-inducing properties as the laser death-ray sniping incident at the University of New Mexico. But there's a siliconnected happening that comes close. It's the high-tech carnival for silicon-crazed merchants called the Consumer Electronics Show.

·2·

The Consumer Electronics Show

High-Tech Highs

MOST PEOPLE HAVE never heard of the largest trade show in the world, too big to fit under one roof. It's the Consumer Electronics Show, a twice-a-year megaconvention where tens of thousands gather to touch, hear, see, and write millions of dollars in orders for the latest in microelectronic gizmos and gadgetry.

CES happens in Las Vegas in January, and Chicago in June, and both are must events in the consumer electronics industry. The winter 1984 happening was among the biggest ever. For four days an excited horde of 85,000 sales representatives, exhibitors, buyers, and reporters elbowed its way through a maze of more than 1,200 high-tech exhibits stuffed into the cavernous Las Vegas Convention Center and three nearby hotels. Some 7,500 attendees came from 72 countries. Altogether, visitors' centers, press room, concessions and exhibits, many of them as big as houses, covered nearly seventeen acres.

As for the press, 1,500 writers, photographers, and editors showed up, some to combine work with a vacation in Las Vegas but most to ferret out industry gossip and rumors, sell advertising space, and see firsthand the latest electronic goodies pouring from the siliconsumer foundries of the United States, Taiwan, Hong Kong, Korea, and Japan, Inc.

It's name notwithstanding, the *Consumer* Electronics Show is definitely *not* for the general public. "For the Trade Only" its brochures announced. Further, "Minors Under 18 Years of Age Will Not be Admitted," although the officials did bend the rules and admit some teenage entrepreneurs who had developed some bestselling computer software. The attendance restrictions made sense; with 85,000 people crowding its halls, there wasn't room to admit everyone who wanted to attend. Who wouldn't like to see a live demonstration of the latest digital stereo, the newest home computers, the smallest pocket TV's, the fanciest digital watch, and maybe pick up a couple of confidential "dealer price lists"?

Besides, who wants customers around when you're talking business? Would a home computer company executive tell people thinking about buying one of his firm's machines that, "We will walk away from any customer who does not agree" with Atari's new return policy? That's what one told a meeting of financial analysts at CES. And would the folks at "The New Tech Times," public television's popular series about consumer electronic products, want viewers to see the brochure that reveals their hidden agenda? "THE NEW TECH TIMES pre-sells today's electronics," reads the copy below the photo of a smiling Nicholas Johnson, former Commissioner of the Federal Communications Commission and host of the PBS series. "It brings people into your store. It makes the product so appealing that price becomes secondary. This means you can stop discounting and sell at full price. Sales come easier because customers are more knowledgeable. And the more they know, the more they'll buy!"

For years friends in the consumer electronics industry had portrayed CES as the quintessential focus of high-tech siliconsumerism, and urged me to make the pilgrimage. The opportunity arrived when Arthur Goldsmith, editor of *Popular Photography*, and Norman Goldberg, the magazine's technical director, asked me to accompany them and some of their writers to Las Vegas. They wanted someone to advise them about the silicon connection behind late-breaking developments in video cameras with self-contained recorders (so-called *camcorders*).

Long familiar with my interest in anything electronic that creates or senses light, Norman arranged the invitation. He describes himself as "just a camera mechanic," and I believed him until I asked what he did with the remains of the discombobulated cameras he meticulously disassembles, unsolders, and dissects each month to be photographed for his famous "stripdown" report in *Popular Photography*. "I reassemble them and send them back to the company," he replied. Take a look at a picture of a brand new, disemboweled camera body whose delicate electronic, optical, and mechanical innards are carefully laid out for display, and you'll understand why Norman is not your average camera mechanic.

It didn't take long to discover that Norman and some of the other PopPhoto people knew far more than I'll ever know about portable videotape systems. Freed from their assignment, but still wearing the magic "this-will-get-you-anywhere-in-the-show" press badge, I set forth on a coveted tour of the Las Vegas Convention Center. For three busy days, fueled by a free ticket to the VIP dining room, and equipped with notepad, camera, and microcassette recorder, I wandered through the exhibits, collecting press kits and racing away from panting sales people attracted like magnets to that magical press badge. Though I was determined to identify truly significant high-tech developments and trends, the carnivallike atmosphere of flashing lights, jostling crowds, miles of aisles, and the incessant cacophony of bleeps, sirens, and periodic fanfares kept getting in the way. It was like being inside a giant Pac-Man game.

Lowbrow High Tech

My first stop was Japan, Inc.'s enormous and very busy Sanyo exhibit. There a snappily dressed woman, her voice amplified by a portable public address system, lectured onlookers about the latest advances in digital high-fidelity sound systems. She must have given the lecture a hundred times; at one point she caught herself saying "*b*igital *d*its." In any event, her presentation was quite good. Ten years ago it would have been unusual for a woman to give a technical presentation. In those bygone days women, often wearing hot pants or bathing suits, served primarily as bait to lure prospective customers and clients to the exhibits. That still occurs, but today many of the women staffing the booths have degrees in electrical engineering or computer science.

Though digital audio was big news at the 1984 Winter CES, camcorders—those compact video cameras which captivated the *Popular Photography* staffers—were bigger news. Kodak had announced two weeks earlier that they would be showing their Japanese-developed camcorders at CES, so Sanyo decided to unveil ahead of schedule its entry in the new field. With its collection of colorful macaws and free blank videocassettes, the Kodak camcorder exhibit was much fancier than Sanyo's. But Sanyo's unexpected exhibit took the video world by complete surprise, and its lone prototype, displayed inside a clear exhibit case, was surrounded by a mob of pushing and shoving onlookers. Never mind the fact that no one from Sanyo, despite repeated requests, would disclose technical details about the machine, much less its introduction date and price.

If Sanyo's exhibit was a show-stealer, SpectraVideo's was a sideshow. SpectraVideo, which makes low-cost home computers, had apparently decided the best way to beat the competition was to poke fun at its products. A man and woman took turns every half hour or so panning competing home computers, some of which were stuffed in a porcelain toilet at one end of a table. Meanwhile, across the aisle, Coleco played host to enormous crowds. Their exhibit was noteworthy for its size alone—it measured about 6,750 square feet. Most of this space was taken by aisles lined with Adam computers and video games. In recessed cubicles, pretty young women wearing short black dresses and bright red hose demonstrated Adam's features. A hall at the back of the exhibit, guarded by a phalanx of uniformed Coleco women, led to secret offices for press briefings and deal making.

The Nonstop Shakeout

Now that the home computer is an established consumer product, it's easy to forget that only a few years ago cavernous exhibits like Coleco's and comic spectacles like SpectraVideo's didn't exist at CES. Back then computer companies were sandwiched between the calculator and watch exhibits. At this CES some 275 computer hardware and software companies occupied a third of the main hall plus the entire West Hall, a nearby annex to the Convention Center. In terms of exhibition space, computer products and software were second only to audio products.

Of course computers were only one of the beneficiaries of the ongoing revolution in solid-state electronics on display. More than 300 telephone, watch, and calculator companies, and several hundred audio equipment manufacturers also exhibited their wares.

Nevertheless, although camcorder developments attracted the most attention on the surface, the 1984 Winter CES will be remembered for marking a major turning point in the highly competitive home computer industry. Some of the decisions made by the major home computer makers just before, during and shortly after the show were particularly momentous.

Consider the Texas Instruments home computer debacle. IBM wasn't even present at this CES. But rumors about their PCjr, a low-cost complement to IBM's industry-standard personal computer, were believed by some industry watchers to have contributed to Texas Instruments' announcement shortly before the show that it was abandoning the home computer market. In view of the hundreds of millions of dollars TI was losing on the machine long before reports about the PCjr began appearing, the IBM theory didn't make much sense.

TI invented the first integrated circuit back in 1958, and was at one time the biggest home computer company of them all. But its battle to dominate the market through repeated cycles of cost cutting had backfired. Originally introduced at $1,150 in 1979, the price of its Model 99/4 home computer was about $200 by the end of 1982. At each price cut and rebate offer, TI's competitors fought back, offering newer and better machines for even less money. But the TI assembly lines kept turning out 5,000 99/4's a day. By the summer of 1983 a slightly revised version of the 99/4, the 99/4A, was selling for only about $100, and the company was losing money on each machine it sold.

TI had planned to recapture its lead by introducing a new computer, the 99/8. Instead, in October 1983 the company formally announced its withdrawal from the home computer market. TI became the first major victim of the price war it had started. At the 1984 Winter CES TI retreated to its line of calculators and microprocessor-based learning machines like the popular "Speak 'n Spell." But without the 99/4 and its plethora of associated products and software, the TI exhibit looked strangely barren.

Like TI, Atari's problems in the home computer and video-game field were widely publicized prior to and during the show, and with good reason. The company lost a whopping $538.6 million in 1983. Nevertheless, Atari was at CES with a huge exhibit bordered on one side by a row of some twenty video games, each equipped with a different game cartridge. Unfortunately there wasn't much excitement about new Atari merchandise since the company didn't introduce any significant new products at the show.

What was new was a handout in which James Morgan, Atari's chairman, repented of past sins by promising that his company would no longer announce new products ". . . unless we can ship them almost immediately." Morgan also claimed Atari had "bottomed out" and was now on its way back up. Skeptics, however, noted Atari's enormous losses and layoffs, and predicted the worst. Little did they or anyone else know about the post-CES bombshell that was to emerge from Commodore International, one of Atari's biggest competitors.

Commodore International, Ltd. was founded in 1959 by Jack Tramiel. Originally a typewriter importer, Commodore eventually got into the adding machine business. In the early 1970s the company entered the silicon business, and introduced a popular line of handheld business and scientific calculators. In late 1977 Commodore unveiled the PET, its first entry in the new personal computer market, and by 1983 Commodore was the leading manufacturer of low-cost home computers.

Jack Tramiel almost single-handedly led Commodore to the pinnacle of success. Aptly described by *The Wall Street Journal* as having a reputation "as an intense and sometimes tyrannical leader," Tramiel's hard-driving manner resulted in a musical chairs style of management wherein top executives came and went on a regular basis. His management style notwithstanding, Tramiel's marketing skills often commanded the respect of even those he fired. Indeed, four top executives, including the company's acting president of United States operations, agreed to return to Commodore after having been fired by Tramiel.

At a big press conference at the MGM Grand Hotel Tramiel announced that his company had sold more than a billion dollars of home computers and software in 1983, more than twice the 1982 sales. He then revealed Commodore's goal of becoming a five-billion-dollar company by 1990. Tramiel also announced two new computers. A few days after returning from CES, however, Tramiel stunned both his stockholders and his competitors by abruptly resigning as Commodore's president, chief executive officer, and director. *The Wall Street Journal* reported company insiders as having said Commodore's chairman, Irving Gould, had opposed Tramiel's plans to place his two sons in management slots.

"I was absolutely shocked," John Roach, Tandy Corporation's chairman, told *Business Week*. Since Tandy's Radio Shack division is a major Commodore competitor in the low-cost computer field, Roach's shock probably escalated into terminal giddiness a few weeks later when Commodore dropped a new pair of bombshells. This time the company confirmed reports that the new computers announced amid the hoopla of CES would *not* be introduced, at least not yet. Moreover, four of the firm's top executives resigned to join Tramiel in a new venture. (No one imagined that within six months, with cash from the sale of Commodore stock, Tramiel would buy Atari, his arch-rival, from its parent corporation, Warner Communications, and begin a siliconnected war against the company he founded.)

Though the startling developments at Commodore had their origin during a three-hour meeting between Tramiel and Gould during CES, no one was the wiser during the show, and Commodore remained untainted by the concerns of an across-the-board home computer shakeout caused by the huge losses at TI and Atari. Coleco wasn't as fortunate, even though the toy and video-game maker's ranch-sized exhibit was one of the most crowded. Serious questions lurked behind the excitement over the company's new Adam family computer system, the first to include both a letter-quality printer and a built-in, high-speed tape data storage system. Why did Coleco produce only a third of the half-million Adams it had promised to have ready by the preceding Christmas? Why were there persistent reports about reliability problems with the machine? Though Coleco officials attempted to ease the doubts about Adam, one couldn't help wondering whether the company's wildly successful Cabbage Patch doll was propping up the balance sheet. (This suspicion was confirmed just before the 1985 Winter CES when Coleco dropped the Adam.)

While touring CES, I met friends and acquaintances from siliconnected companies and electronics magazines. The conversation inevitably turned to computers, and some of them commented on how the long-expected "shakeout" had finally arrived. Finally? Sure, some very big home computer companies were losing not just millions but *hundreds of millions* of dollars. But personal computer companies have been coming and going and booming and busting since the industry was begun in 1975.

Heaping Hype

Four adjoining rooms near the entrance to the convention center floor were reserved for the press. One of the rooms was lined with more than a hundred shelves stacked high with colorful press kits. Just as I walked in, a shelf loaded with press kits crashed to the floor. Several people helped replace the shelf and its stacks of glossy brochures, envelopes, folders and photographs. Two other shelves were less fortunate, for their loads were still scattered where they had fallen earlier. I never knew hot air could be so heavy. A young reporter revealed his inexperience as he sorted through the reams of siliconnected propaganda. "There's so much hyperbole," he complained. "Everything's either revolutionary or a breakthrough." Nodding in agreement, I stuffed another sheaf of papers into my bulging shopping bag.

Later, I thought about the reporter's remarks. Sure, the press kits were full of hype. But the solid-state marvels they described were indeed revolutionary breakthroughs. Have we become so accustomed to high-tech life that we've forgotten just how far electronics has come in the past quarter century? The tiny microcassette recorder in my shirt pocket is smaller than a 1950's microphone. The sophisticated electronics in my fully programmable camera automatically and instantly calculated proper exposure times and aperture settings. And, in addition to the standard stopwatch, timer, calendar, and alarm functions, the calculator watch on my wrist featured four memories, twenty mathematical functions, and six metric conversion operations, all made possible by a microscopic network of thousands of transistors etched on the surface of a tiny flake of crystallized beach sand.

If any of these high-tech gadgets isn't a technological breakthrough, what is? Imagine the reaction of Galileo, Newton, or Leonardo da Vinci to a five-dollar solar-powered calculator, much less one of the three home computers in my son's bedroom. Thoughts like these lingered throughout the evening as I remembered how remarkably far solid-state electronics has advanced since

I first experienced the thrill of hearing voice and music emerge from the earphone of a homemade one-transistor radio thirty years ago.

In those days expensive hearing aids were the only consumer devices that used transistors. Only experimenters and do-it-your-selfers, working alone or guided by project articles in hobby electronics magazines, had discovered the magical, solid-state world of transistor radios, solar batteries, and relay circuits triggered by flashlight beams. I discovered these magazines shortly after learning about the transistor in a fascinating article by Robert Leslie Conly in the July 1954 issue of *National Geographic*. Conly described the transistor as "a tiny speck of silvery-gray metal, coated in plastic" and "the 'electronic' midget that makes cautious physicists and sober businessmen talk like science fiction writers."

Conly described the transistor as "miraculous," and the photos accompanying his article supplied ample proof: a television set the size of a hatbox made possible by pea-sized transistors; a telephone with a transistor amplifier for the hard of hearing; a tiny transistorized radio transmitter powered by magical silicon wafers that converted sunlight directly into electricity.

These early siliconnected gadgets were still in the prototype stage, but they were nothing less than spectacular to a pre-*Sputnik*-era ten-year-old boy. Imagine the contrast if that 1954 article were updated to include the siliconnected technology on display at the 1984 Winter Consumer Electronics Show. The article would describe color camcorders the size of a shoebox, television receivers that fit in a shirt pocket, and a clever calculator watch operated by a finger tracing invisible numbers and signs on its face. As for the *Geographic*'s miraculous silicon transistors, which sold for $50 or more each in the mid-1950s, the high-tech gadgets that accompanied me to Las Vegas, all of which could be carried in one hand, incorporated tens of thousands of transistors integrated on several silicon chips smaller than a baby's fingernail.

Dreaming and Doing

One evening while looking for a restaurant I was reminded that the convention center wasn't the only place in Las Vegas replete with the latest silicontraptions and gadgets. Back in 1976 when I attended a big personal communications show in Las Vegas, old-fashioned slot machines dominated the casinos. Now the casinos have been invaded by noisy rows of chortling, beeping, flashing, and even talking video gaming machines that play everything from poker and keno to re-created horse races. Already more than 90,000 gaming machines have been siliconized.

Even the traditional one-armed bandits aren't immune to silicon's impact. While an elderly woman, oblivious to my presence, fed coins to a slot machine, I inspected the inner workings housed in its transparent cabinet. Amid the rows of spinning gears and wheels I spotted a familiar looking rainbow-colored ribbon of wires that led to a card festooned with transistors and integrated circuits. As my eyes adjusted to the dim light, I found more wires, two other circuit boards, and some motors and solenoids.

Some of the CES attendees spent their evenings poring money into such machines. Others congregated in small groups around restaurant tables, sometimes with a trade reporter present, to share siliconnected gossip, reveal secrets about undisclosed products, conclude deals, and exchange jobs. I sat in on a few such meetings, but none was as memorable as the few minutes of conversation I overheard while waiting to pay for dinner at the Castaways on my final evening in Las Vegas. As I stood in line at the cash register, I couldn't help noticing five men engaged in a heated discussion at a nearby table.

The most common business discussions at CES were multisided, with representatives of different companies arguing the merits of their respective products or trying to strike deals with customers. But this discussion was different; everyone at the table was with the same company. Apparently it was a small company, and these five agitated men probably constituted the entire professional staff. Maybe they doubled as secretaries and janitors too.

One slightly balding man, fortyish and with glasses perched on his nose, looked like a printed circuit board designer. Another, around 35 or so, fit my mental picture of the typical electrical engineer, as did the young man who looked only a year or two past college. At the head of the table was a fairly handsome, sharply dressed fellow of about 30, apparently the company's president. At his right sat an older man whose words revealed experience in public relations, sales, and marketing.

The man who looked like a salesman jumped into the fray and said, "The best slogan I've seen at the show was at General Electric's exhibit: 'If you can dream it, you can do it.' That ought to be our slogan!" Suddenly harmony prevailed as they all nodded and looked toward the apparent leader at the head of the table, the man with the ideas, the entrepreneur. For the first time he spoke.

"Fellows, I want to be part of a successful company," he began. "But it's going to take cooperation, everybody working together. . . ." The sound of the cash register drowned out his voice, but from the serious looks on their faces it was obvious they were again unified in purpose. The conversation continued in a subdued, serious tone. Someone asked if a bank loan had been approved. Another attributed poor sales to the post-Christmas slowdown.

I wanted to stop by their table and find out about their company. Were they an up and coming computer firm? Had they developed a new computer peripheral? Perhaps they were developing something entirely new, one of those yet-to-be-introduced silicontraptions one reads about in the trade literature long before it's disclosed to the general public.

Whoever they were and whatever they were developing, I detected the potential of success, for their conversation reminded me of four men of equally diverse backgrounds who held a similar discussion around a kitchen table in Albuquerque, New Mexico, fifteen years earlier. Those men founded MITS, Inc., the company that in 1974 started a solid-state revolution when it developed the Altair 8800, the first successful microcomputer ever offered to the general public.

Sure, personal computing would have eventually arrived without MITS, but more than two years before Apple, Commodore, and Radio Shack, MITS pioneered the industry that occupied a substantial percentage of the Las Vegas Convention Center floor in 1984. Six months after the Altair was announced, the world's first computer store, stocked with MITS equipment, opened in California. MITS organized the first convention for computer hobbyists, and stimulated the formation of computer clubs, newsletters, and user groups across the country. Steve Wozniak, the young engineer who would later design the Apple, became a member of one of those clubs.

Purchased by a larger computer company in 1977, MITS and its Altair vanished from the personal computing scene a microgeneration ago. Today, comparatively few computer users have even heard of the company, its visionary president, or its pioneering machine. Many think Apple was the first to develop the personal computer, but MITS was first, and its pioneering contribution to personal computing cannot be diminished by the advertising claims of today's personal computer makers. Moreover, MITS had a major impact on the careers of the computer veterans who bought Altairs. It especially influenced my career, for I was one of the company's four founders.

·3·

The Silicon Garage

High-Tech Recipes for Silicon Gourmets

IN THE EARLY 1970s the leather-holstered slide rules hanging from engineers' belts were replaced almost overnight by scientific calculators in zippered vinyl pouches. These wondrously powerful number machines were made possible by a radically new kind of integrated circuit, a problem-solving chip that used methods borrowed from digital computer technology. But whereas computers have endless applications, calculators only calculate.

Marcian "Ted" Hoff, one of the engineers at Intel, Inc., assigned to develop a new calculator chip for a Japanese company, realized that a more elegant approach would be an integrated circuit that in addition to numbers would process information. This new kind of chip came to be known as the *microprocessor*.

Intel was a California semiconductor firm that made integrated memory chips used by the thousands in the electronic systems built and sold by other companies. They introduced the first microprocessor chip in 1971, and called it the 4004. From the outside, the 4004's buglike housing bordered by two parallel rows of eight stubby legs was indistinguishable from hundreds of much simpler integrated circuits. Inside was a thin silicon sliver a little more than a tenth of an inch square containing 2,250 transistors. Today simple microprocessors like the 4004 control the timing in our car engines, calculate our taxi fares, add our taxes, and control our appliances. More complicated ones form the nerve centers of video games and personal computers. We take them for granted.

Microprocessors and the massive industry that they spawned would not have been possible without the invention in 1958 of the integrated circuit by Jack Kilby, a silicon gourmet at Texas Instruments. Consider the alternative had Intel's Ted Hoff been forced to build his 4004 microprocessor from 2,250 individual transistors. The contraption would have required something like a hundred electronic circuit boards, each the size of a business envelope and each sprouting 20 or more individual transistors. The transistor is Bell Labs' solid-state switch that forms the basic building block of digital electronic circuits ranging from quartz watches to microprocessors and computers. Kilby's idea eliminated the need to install individual transistors on circuit boards. Instead, all the transistors and other components necessary for an electronic circuit are formed or *integrated* on a single silicon chip, and electrically connected to one another by a network of microscopic aluminum conductors deposited directly over the chip. The 4004 was primitive by today's standards, merely a solid-state *hors d'oeuvre* that provided a hint of the vast array of siliconcocted *entrees* to come. Nevertheless, the 4004 was functionally equivalent to the central processing unit of a simple digital computer. All that was necessary to obtain a working computer was a memory chip and a simple circuit called a clock. Instructions that told the 4004 what to do were stored in the memory chip. Like a metronome, the clock delivered a continuous string of electronic pulses that cycled the instructions through the 4004. Since the 4004 could perform the control and processing functions of a real computer, the proper sequence of instructions stored in the memory chip could turn the 4004 into the brain of a calculator. Simply by changing the instructions (the program) and nothing else, the same 4004 could also control a taxi cab meter, traffic signal, elevator, digital scale, or a piece of electronic test equipment.

No, there was nothing radically new about the operating principles behind the 4004. Its significance was its tiny size which, for the first time, permitted the power of a computer to be added to everyday gadgets and appliances. And if an important limitation could be overcome, the 4004 concept would lead to even more powerful microprocessors.

Remember, the transistors that form digital circuits, from simple light flashers to microprocessors like the 4004, work like switches: at any instant they are either on or off. By designating off as *0* and on as *1*, digital circuits can represent numbers in the two-digit or binary number system: 0 is 0, 1 is 1, 2 is 10, 3 is 11, 4 is 100, 5 is 101, and so on.

The major limitation of Intel's 4004 was that it could process only four binary digits, or *bits*, at a time, those from 0000 to 1111. Since this corresponds to the decimal numbers from 0 to 15, the 4004 was ideally suited for manipulating numbers. Information like letters of the alphabet, however, is represented by a pattern of eight bits popularly known as a *byte*.

The only way the 4004 could process bytes was by splitting them in half and digesting them in four-bit gulps. This complicated the program instructions and slowed down the processing time. Intel's people realized this early on, and within months of introducing the 4004 they announced an 8-bit microprocessor called the 8008. Compared to the 4004, the 8008 was difficult to use since it required several additional chips. Nevertheless, for nearly two years the 8008 was the only 8-bit microprocessor.

In 1973 Intel released a greatly improved 8-bit chip, the 8080. Though the company hyped this new chip as a *microcomputer*, the 8080 required external memory and support chips and was, in fact, a *microprocessor*. But with the ability to understand 30 more instructions than the 48 of the 8008, and the speed to process them ten times faster, the 8080 caught the attention of thousands of engineers. One of them was H. Edward Roberts.

Engineers knew that the 8080 could be used as the nerve center of a compact digital computer much like the powerful minicomputers that then sold for thousands of dollars. A few electronics experimenters who found out about the 8080 dreamed of using it in homebrew computers, but who could afford the $360 Intel wanted for a single chip? A former electronics experimenter himself, Ed Roberts was the only entrepreneur who thought hobbyists would buy an 8080 computer in volume if the price were right. If his nearly bankrupt company was to survive, they would have to.

H. Edward Roberts

As a teenager in Miami in the late 1950s Ed Roberts's driving ambition was to become a doctor. When he was only seventeen, he was performing open-heart surgery on dogs at a research laboratory. There he began learning about electronics, not because of a consuming interest but better to understand the biomedical instrumentation used at the lab.

I first met Ed in the summer of 1968 at the Air Force Weapons Laboratory at Kirtland Air Force Base in Albuquerque. He had just received a degree in electrical engineering at Oklahoma State University and I was just back from a year in Vietnam. A big man with a no-nonsense style, Ed was two years older than I and seemed more like a seasoned master sergeant than a new lieutenant. The fact that I was a first lieutenant didn't impress him in the least. We were both assigned to the Effects Branch of the Weapons Lab. The principal role of the branch was to simulate and study some of the little publicized, nonblast effects of nuclear explosions. These ominous effects were triggered by invisible electromagnetic waves like powerful X-ray bursts and the much feared electromagnetic pulse phenomenon that promised to wipe out power lines and radio communications over thousands of square miles. Ed and I worked in the Laser Group, a special organization assigned to develop various kinds of solid-state laser systems, and to study the biological hazards of laser radiation. Much of the work was highly classified.

One of Ed's first assignments was to purchase Hewlett-Packard's new, state-of-the-art desktop programmable calculator, the HP-9100. Ed was attracted to that machine like a magnet and, within a few days of its arrival, he proudly showed me a program he had written for it that calculated the values of the components used in a transistor amplifier. In those pre–pocket calculator days, the HP-9100 stimulated long discussions about computers, Ed often saying he wanted to build a digital computer in his garage workshop. Sure, I thought.

Actually, both of us had prior experience as do-it-yourself computer hobbyists. In high school I had built a series of *analog* computers that multiplied and divided numbers dialed into a couple of knobs on a panel, displaying the results on a volt meter. By 1961 these simple machines had culminated in a considerably more complicated machine that included twenty memory elements and automatically translated twenty words of Russian into English. Ed, too, had built analog computers in the late 1950s. He had also built simple digital machines that used electromechanical relays, a method popular with experimenters who couldn't afford the parts for more advanced vacuum tube or transistor logic circuits. As for integrated circuits, they weren't yet available.

Raising a family on an Air Force enlisted man's pay was no simple matter when Ed was stationed at Lackland Air Force Base in San Antonio in the mid-1960s. Ed's need to supplement his income, and his entrepreneurial instincts, culminated in not one but two one-man companies, Reliable Radio and TV and Reliance Engineering. The Reliance Engineering job of which he was most proud was the electronic systems that controlled the movements of the animated Christmas characters in the windows of the Joskes' store across from the Alamo.

Though we shared a common interest in computers, our technical backgrounds were very different. Ed was a first-class electrical engineer, skilled at designing circuits that used transistors as either digital switches or amplifiers, their two primary roles. I, on the other hand, with my degree in government, had no formal electronics training. However, I had learned a good deal about optoelectronics when I designed and built the miniature infrared travel aids for the blind. This difference in backgrounds led to an ongoing competition to impress or outsmart each other.

Once Ed called me over to his side of the big lab space we shared with another officer to announce he had just built a transistor circuit that switched on and off in a few tenths of a *millionth* of a second. I smugly reminded him about a circuit I'd recently built to switch on a semiconductor laser in only a few *billionths* of a second. Another time the discussion turned to optoelectronics, and I triumphed again when we differed over the sensitivity of silicon solar cells to visible light. With barely concealed glee, I proved my claim with a graph from a reference book.

Ed won his share of these contests. One time, hoping he would be impressed, I proudly showed him my latest infrared travel aid for the blind, a handheld device weighing a few ounces. After looking the device over with the indifferent air of a customer in a flea market, Ed asked to see a diagram of its electronic circuitry. He quickly finished me off by patiently explaining how a simple revision of the circuit would increase the distance over which it could detect objects.

If I bragged that I'd built analog computers before Ed, he'd remind me of his teenage open-heart surgery. When Ed boasted about the electronic fish counter he'd once designed, I'd bounce back with tales about the experiments with miniature guided rockets that resulted in my Weapons Lab assignment. Ed's favorite word at times like these was *trivial*. "That's a trivial engineering problem," he might say. I knew he really admired a circuit or project when he pronounced it *nontrivial*.

I relate these incidents, and there were dozens more, to give some idea of the yin-yang aspect of the relationship Ed and I developed. Our frequent differences of opinion, which extended to matters of religion, politics, and even whose camera was better designed, stimulated as rich and varied a cross-current of ideas as I've ever experienced. And though our discussions sometimes erupted in subdued shouting matches, we never held a grudge. Instead, we developed a strong sense of mutual respect and friendship.

When Ed and I weren't debating the philosophy of Ayn Rand or the relative merits of screw-mount versus bayonet-mount camera lenses, we sometimes talked about the future. My goal was to become a freelance writer. His were to learn to fly, own his own airplane, live on a large farm, and graduate from a medical school. How did he plan to accomplish all this? First he'd earn a million dollars; the rest would be easy.

Launching MITS, Inc.

By 1969 the Laser Group had been incorporated into the new well-funded and highly classified Laser Division at the Weapons Lab. Since Ed and I worked long hours at the lab exploring super-secret applications for state-of-the-art laser technology, we devoted evenings and weekends to our families. Well, not completely. Our wives, who would have preferred that we limit our projects to those at the Weapons Lab, eventually found themselves involved too.

Ed's off-duty projects were strictly business. Putting his dormant Reliance Engineering back in operation, he teamed with Glen Doughty, an Air Force captain in the Laser Group, to build an infrared intrusion alarm for his uncle's fish farm in Florida. A few months later Ed and Stan Cagle began work on a power supply they planned to sell. Ed had met Stan, who worked for an Air Force contractor, when they were both electrical engineering students at Oklahoma State. Ed and Stan never completed their power supply, for one of my off-duty projects got in the way.

That spring, when Ed and Glen were building the burglar alarm, I continued work on a miniaturized, siliconnected guidance and control system that steered a small rocket to light. (The idea for the guided rocket had popped into my mind one morning in the spring of 1959 as I daydreamed about model rockets instead of paying attention to my seventh-grade teacher.) Most rockets are controlled by movable vanes or steerable rocket nozzles. My idea was to equip a rocket with a nosecone having a forward-facing hole. Air entering the hole would be directed out one of a series of ports around the nose, thereby providing the necessary force to steer the missile. Gathering data for the project, which I had begun in earnest in my off-duty hours shortly after entering the Air Force in 1966, required extensive wind-tunnel tests and dozens of flights of small test rockets. After preliminary tests with a homemade wind tunnel strapped onto the passenger side of a 1966 Chevelle, I borrowed the wind-tunnel facility at the University of New Mexico. A group of cadets at the Air Force Academy volunteered to help, and performed a series of more sophisticated tests in a much better wind tunnel. Once when I needed help launching a series of test rockets Ed pressed the launch switch while I photographed the smoke trail of each flight.

Grateful for Ed's help, I especially enjoyed discussing rocketry with someone older than the kids in the model rocket club I had organized. Soon Ed and I began to discuss the possibility of making and selling the light flashers, radio transmitters, and other gadgets I flew a thousand or so feet above the mesas around Albuquerque.

Things began falling into place when *Model Rocketry* magazine paid me $93.50 for an article, the first I'd ever written, about how to build a miniature light flasher to track and recover model rockets flown at night. Would rocket hobbyists also pay real money to buy flashers and other electronic payloads to fly in their paper and balsa missiles?

In the summer of 1969 we arranged to meet with Stan Cagle at Ed's home to discuss forming a company to make and sell electronic instruments for model rocket hobbyists. We also invited Bob Zaller, another officer from the Weapons Lab. Most of that first meeting around the bar in Joan Roberts's kitchen was spent in a serious discussion of what to develop and how to finance our first production run. Stan, still single and making more money than the rest of us, volunteered to advance some of the necessary capital. We also attended to our first order of business, unanimously electing Ed president of our nameless venture. Before closing the meeting, Ed attempted to seal our loyalties to the new venture by emphasizing the importance of everyone contributing equal time to the company. Repeating an admonition learned somewhere in his past, he insisted that the company wouldn't survive if it were loaded down with a burden of "silent partners."

At the next meeting we selected a name for our new company: MITS. Actually, Ed wanted to call the company Reliance Engineering. After all, he maintained, his former company had a track record, and even some leftover stationery. Ed's point about his company's record was good. But since some of the best model rocketry research in the country was then taking place at the Massachusetts Institute of Technology, I suggested we form an acronym around the letters MIT. With a bemused expression on his big face, Ed silently watched while Stan and I began thinking of words to match the letters in the acronym. I mentioned micro for the M, and telemetry for the T. Within a minute or so Stan responded with *Micro Instrumentation and Telemetry Systems.*

Though we all agreed the name was too long, I insisted the MIT connection was important. To appease Ed's sympathies for his former company, I said we could call MITS a subsidiary of Reliance Engineering. But wouldn't people call us *mits*, Ed chuckled? I confidently claimed they would refer to us as *M-I-T-S* just as MIT is referred to as *M-I-T.* This time Ed was right; within days we tired of saying *M-I-T-S* and reverted to *mits*. Later we capitalized on the name by labeling as MITS KITS some of our model rocket telemetry kits.

Like hundreds of other start-up entrepreneurships, MITS was then what is commonly referred to as a garage operation. To the uninitiated, the phrase probably seems disparaging at best and insulting at worst. Actually, starting new electronics companies in garages is a noble tradition; Hewlett-Packard, one of the most successful and respected electronics companies in the world, was born in a garage in the 1930s. Ideally, of course, the garage phase should be brief. As is probably the case with most other similar operations, during our garage phase we were also a closet operation, a kitchen operation, and a bedroom operation. Ed and Bob designed circuits and built prototypes on the two wood workbenches in Ed's garage workshop. Stan laid out the black-tape patterns for the printed circuit boards at his apartment. He used his closet and bathroom to make photographic negatives of the patterns and transfer them to copper-clad circuit boards coated with light-sensitive photoresist. When Stan was mixing developer and fixer and soaking boards in copper etchant, his apartment smelled like a chemical factory. I wrote instruction manuals, advertising copy, a catalog, and *The Booklet of Model Rocket Telemetry* on my kitchen table. Our countless midnight meetings were held in Ed's kitchen and front bedroom.

By October most of the circuit designs were complete, and parts for the first production run had been ordered. I drafted MITS's first press release:

"Reliance Engineering in Albuquerque, New Mexico, has announced the formation of a subsidiary company for the manufacture of miniaturized electronic and telemetry systems for model rockets. The company is called Micro Instrumentation and Telemetry Systems (MITS). Reliance Engineering president Henry Roberts announced that 'MITS is presently conducting an intensive research program involving high quality miniature telemetry systems.'

"The first commercially available model rocket telemetry transmitter is among the first items to be offered by MITS. Accessory modules, including a tone beacon, temperature sensor, and a roll rate sensor, as well as tracking lights, ground systems for data reduction, and light weight, water-activated batteries will soon be available.

"MITS has prepared *The Booklet of Model Rocket Telemetry* to introduce rocketeers to their telemetry equipment. Copies of the booklet are available at 25 cents. . . ."

We sent the release to *Model Rocketry*. While waiting for it to appear, Ed, Stan, and Bob assembled hundreds of modules while I designed an order form and mimeographed hundreds of copies of our handbook. In December we incorporated.

Soon after the news release appeared, hundreds of quarters began to arrive, and our already heavy workload was increased. Ed and I went to work each morning at the Weapons Lab only half awake, with bloodshot eyes. We soon recruited our wives to help assemble telemetry modules and package them, insert the boxes in clear vinyl sleeves, staple them to the operating instructions, and type dozens of stencils for the mimeograph machine.

Meanwhile, with the help of the boys in the rocket club I launched several missiles equipped with those beautifully designed telemetry systems. In February 1970 one of the instrumented payloads crashed to the ground, its parachute tangled in the transmitter's 18-inch-long trailing wire antenna. Even though the impact pushed the three modules connected to the transmitter through the payload tube, they still worked. I happily took a full roll of photographs of the thoroughly demolished but fully functional payload to help spread the word about the crashworthiness of MITS equipment.

Those MITS model rocket modules were reasonably priced, superbly designed, and they worked well. But by May 1970 we had sold only a hundred or so light flashers, transmitters, and modules. We managed to lower prices by converting some of the more popular items into MITS KITS, but sales remained slow. Worse, an omen of what was to hound MITS throughout its existence appeared. A couple of other silicon garages sprang up to sell similar products for slightly less money. These imitators boldly advertised their telemetry gear in *Model Rocketry*. Even though our modules were far more professional in design and performance, sales never took off like we had hoped. The market was so highly specialized it was practically saturated by the products we'd already sold. MITS could not survive on a trickle of orders from a handful of precocious teenagers, college students, and professors of aeronautical engineering. We needed a new product idea.

By summer, Bob Zaller decided to leave MITS. (He returned several years later.) I also made a big change. After four years in the Air Force I left to become a freelance writer while continuing to work for MITS and taking a job as the night attendant at the parking lot of Albuquerque's airport, the Sunport. Ed, Stan, and I held endless meetings in the attendant's booth to discuss possible new products. A few months earlier I had sold a feature article about solid-state diodes that emit light to *Popular Electronics* magazine, then the largest circulation magazine for electronics hobbyists and experimenters. Several small companies, among them Southwest Technical Products of San Antonio, published project construction articles in *Popular Electronics* and sold printed circuit boards and kits of parts to interested readers. Why couldn't we do the same? The articles would provide free advertising, and the magazine would even pay us for the privilege of printing them.

But what should we select for our first project? We had no information about which of the projects that appeared in *Popular Electronics* were the most successful. We therefore did what Ed and I did best—we engaged in a series of brainstorming sessions in an attempt to identify a winning project. Ed had received from a friend at Motorola, a major semiconductor company, a big bag full of amplifying integrated circuits that had been rejected for such reasons as too high a noise level or smudged part numbers. Most of these chips worked as well as new ones, and we seriously toyed with the idea of using them to develop an analog computer kit. Finally, drawing on my experience with devices for transmitting voice over beams of light, I suggested we design an infrared voice communicator.

In retrospect, we probably should have selected the analog computer, but instead we agreed that the infrared communicator project would probably have more appeal to the readers of an electronics magazine. I queried *Popular Electronics*, and they agreed to consider the article. During the summer of 1970, while we continued to fill the trickle of orders for our model rocketry gear, Ed and Stan began designing the communicator, which I dubbed the Opticom.

The Siliconnected Editor from New York

In late July, before the Opticom was ready, Leslie Solomon, *Popular Electronics*'s technical editor, called. He was planning to visit Albuquerque while on vacation. Could he stop by? This was the moment I had been waiting for. *Model Rocketry*, for which I was then writing a monthly column called "Experimenter's Notebook," was showing signs of folding, and Solomon's visit would be my chance to meet a big-time editor. Moreover, maybe Solomon could meet Ed and Stan so we could tell him about our kit ideas and get his opinion on which had the best commercial possibilities.

The Solomons arrived at my mobile home on August 3, 1970. Self-conscious about our surroundings, we were apprehensive about the upcoming visit from the distinguished New York City magazine editor. We had worried needlessly, for in real life Les turned out to be a gregarious, cigar-smoking, stand-up comic who told amazingly far-fetched tales, some of them, one never knew which, apparently true.

In one of my miniature bedrooms I had installed an electronics workshop that doubled as an office. While Les and I talked electronics in the workshop, he inspected with some interest my notebooks, rocketry gear, miniature travel aids for the blind, and other siliconcoctions. That evening we joined the Robertses for dinner at a restaurant where Les told incredible stories between puffs on a smelly cigar, while Ed and I silently wondered how we would ever manage to pay the bill. After the meal, our wives visited and the kids fidgeted while Les, Ed and I spent a couple of hours discussing all our ideas, especially the Opticom project. We wanted desperately to know how many kits we could expect to sell after the article appeared, but Les said there was no way of knowing. Perhaps one or two hundred, he said, maybe a thousand. He gave us some fragmentary statistics about kit sales at companies like Southwest Technical Products, but they provided no obvious pattern. He also gave us lots of advice, such as suggesting we preserve peace and harmony by avoiding projects that infringed on territory staked out by the other companies selling kits through *Popular Electronics.* Southwest Technical Products, for example, had the monopoly on audio projects. As the meeting ended the ever-cheerful Les, having detected my optimism about becoming a full time freelance writer, became serious and offered a bit of advice. He said it was next to impossible to make a living from freelance writing outside of New York City.

Les's gloomy warning was personally discouraging, especially later that night when I reported to work at the parking lot. However, his visit was a milestone for MITS since it encouraged us to complete work on the Opticom. Ed and Stan installed the prototype transmitter and receiver in attractive metal cabinets, in Ed's garage, and I tested the units in a big field. The transmitter included a switch which, when pressed, caused the unit to send a tone over its invisible, infrared beam. I placed the transmitter on a concrete block and pointed it toward the field. I then walked into the field, pointing the receiver unit toward the transmitter. Keeping the two units aligned by pointing the receiver directly at the transmitter while staying within the transmitter's narrow beam proved tedious, but with practice and patience I was able to detect the transmitted tone at night at a distance of more than 1,000 feet. (The daytime range was considerably less because of the adverse effect of sunlight on the light-sensitive transistor or phototransistor that served as the receiver's infrared sensor.) After completing the tests I wrote the project article, and we shipped it and the prototype Opticom units to *Popular Electronics*. Within a few months the magazine paid $400 for the completed project article, which we quickly deposited in the nearly exhausted MITS checking account.

Meanwhile, Ed arranged to finance the 200 kits we hoped to sell by borrowing a few thousand dollars from a friend. We also decided to move the planned Opticom kit production line out of Ed's crowded garage. Since I worked nights, and Ed and Stan worked days, I drew the assignment of finding a suitable building. Eventually, for $100 a month we rented a tiny brick structure that had been called "The Enchanted Sandwich Shop." We set up a row of wood tables, and when the parts arrived, we poured them into trays and boxes stretched out neatly along the tables where they formed a rainbow of colors. The clear, epoxy-encapsulated phototransistors sparkled in the light like siliconnected diamonds. We were quite proud of our primitive but very high-tech production line.

MITS Splits

My feature about light-emitting diodes and the Opticom article were both featured on the cover of the November 1970 issue of *Popular Electronics*. As soon as the magazine appeared in late October, we began to receive as many as a dozen orders a day. But within a few weeks the initial surge slowed to a trickle. We ended up shipping a little over a hundred Opticoms, only half the minimum number of orders we had expected. That the F.B.I. sent in an order intrigued but didn't cheer us.

Following the precedent set with the model rocketry telemetry gear, we had covered all the bases: the product was well engineered and worked fine, the magazine article looked great, the instruction manual was thorough, and our kit production line was efficient. But apparently too few people shared our enthusiasm for sending their voices a thousand feet or more over invisible infrared beams with state-of-the-art technology. In terms of cash flow we weren't even back where we started; we now owed Ed's friend for the unsold Opticom parts.

While waiting for the Opticom article to appear, Ed and Stan had begun preliminary work on a much more innovative project with potentially wider appeal, a desktop digital calculator. After the Opticom disappointment, Ed wanted to finalize a calculator kit before the big electronics companies became involved. Stan and I held back. Stan wanted to use up the leftover Opticom parts on a nearly complete infrared intrusion alarm kit. I remembered the competition that arose after we entered the model rocketry instrumentation business and worried about the inherent risk and high cost of a calculator venture.

But Ed was mesmerized by the prospect of a do-it-yourself calculator kit, and the disagreement over which path to take split the partnership. One night Stan came by the parking lot and suggested that he and I offer to buy Ed's stock, but as things developed, Ed offered to buy ours. Realizing Ed would proceed with the calculator project with or without us, we agreed to sell our stock. The three of us held our final meeting as MITS partners on November 10, 1970, in the Sunport parking attendant's booth. With help from his Air Force friend, Ed bought our stock for $300 cash now, $300 the following March, and $350 in equipment. When I asked Ed if unsold model rocketry gear qualified as equipment, he was happy to oblige. At the time, none of us had an inkling that six years later the value of those shares would grow to an equivalent of $15,000 each.

The decision to leave MITS was harder than trading a career as an Air Force research and development engineer for what was beginning to appear a lifelong job as a professional parking lot attendant. On the other hand, there was the excitement of seeing the light-emitting diode feature and the Opticom article in *Popular Electronics*.

Since Ed and I remained good friends after the split, I hoped to pick up extra money working for MITS on the side. For starters, a few days later Ed brought the prototype intrusion alarm by the Sunport one evening, and I spent a frigid night testing it along the long exit road that led to the attendant's booth. Unfortunately, its maximum detection range was only 210 feet, not enough for its intended purpose. Ed said he would revise the receiver's design, but he never got around to it. The intrusion alarm was forever shelved in favor of the calculator project.

•4•

The Altair Story

The Silicon Abacus

STAN CAGLE AND I had always been amazed by Ed Roberts's ability to find engineers, technicians, and financial backers. Before MITS split, for instance, we reached an impasse trying to locate a source of economical lenses for the *Popular Electronics* Opticom kits. Ed called Bill Saling, an old friend in Florida who was an experienced plastics engineer, and explained our plight. Bill asked us to send him one of the glass lenses that we were using, and within 6 weeks he shipped us a box full of plastic replicas, each equipped with a mounting shoulder, and tinted red to filter out the visible light that would interfere with the Opticom receiver's infrared sensor.

By the time Stan and I signed the papers transferring our stock, Ed had already recruited Bill Yates, a young lieutenant who had been assigned to the Laser Division before I left the Air Force. Bill was a bright mechanical engineer who relished tough and demanding assignments. Ed soon had him designing maddeningly complicated double-sided printed circuit boards for the calculator project. Bill bought some MITS stock about this time. In exchange for additional stock, Ed also secured financial backing from Major Ed Laughlin, a likable Weapons Lab officer with good business sense.

After moving the MITS assembly line from "The Enchanted Sandwich Shop" back to Ed's garage, Ed and Bill began assembling a prototype version of the calculator using a set of six special integrated circuits purchased from a California company called Electronic Arrays. Unfortunately, a costly catastrophe intervened, and the first primitive machine failed to work. The expensive integrated circuits had been installed backward.

Meanwhile, in August 1971 I resigned from the job at the parking lot to devote full time to writing. I would like to report that the income from selling magazine articles about science and electronics had reached a level adequate to support my family. In fact, I quit after an elderly security guard, who had spent a decade guarding nuclear bombs for the Air Force, went berserk one night and chased me around the attendant's booth with a loaded .45. Shortly before the crazed guard very nearly cut short my budding writing career, with Les Solomon's backing I sold *Popular Electronics* a pair of articles about semiconductor lasers. The articles explained the operation of and applications for them, and described how to build a semiconductor laser and receiver. Ed designed the receiver circuit, I designed the circuitry for the laser, and a MITS technician made the necessary circuit boards. Along with the shelved infrared intrusion alarm, the laser project had been on the agenda before MITS split, and Ed decided to proceed in hopes of using up surplus Opticom parts and Bill Saling's pretty plastic lenses.

In return for a royalty from MITS, I agreed to write assembly manuals for the laser and receiver, plus a manual of kit assembly tips. Consequently, I spent many evenings at MITS during the final development of what was to become a breakthrough project in *Popular Electronics*, the MITS 816 calculator kit. A few months earlier Ed and Bill had moved MITS from the silicon garage to a house. Ed Laughlin and Captain M. J. Soileau, a scholarly Laser Division physicist, signed on to work alongside Ed, Bill, and a few others to complete the calculator project.

Clear, complete, well-illustrated instructions are crucial to the success of any kit. Ed and I admired the manuals supplied with electronic kits made by the Heath Company, and I half-seriously promised that the manuals for the laser kit would be just as good. When the manuals were complete, Ed pronounced them as good as Heath's, and asked if I'd prepare the assembly manual for the 816 calculator in return for one of the machines.

Though the 816 calculator could only add, subtract, multiply, and divide, it was developed long before low-cost digital calculators were readily available. For its time, it was very much a leading-edge, high-tech product. Indeed, in some respects the design of the 816 was more complex than that of the computer that was later to secure Ed a place in personal computer history. As Ed might say, the 816 project was nontrivial.

As if the design of the machine's three printed circuit boards and 8-digit display weren't enough, there was the major hurdle of coming up with an attractive cabinet. Since Ed intended to publish the 816 as a project in *Popular Electronics*, he could have gotten away with housing the system in a painted aluminum box with a sloping front panel for the keyboard. Instead, with the help of plastic whiz Bill Saling, who moved to Albuquerque to work for MITS, Ed went first class and installed the 816 in a custom molded plastic housing. With its row of green digits softly glowing from behind a polarizing filter framed by a black bezel, the sleek, tan-colored 816 was as attractive as any electronic office calculator. The kit sold for $179.

The 816 was featured on the cover of the November 1971 issue of *Popular Electronics*. An accompanying editor's note described the machine as "an exciting new breakthrough construction project—a modern, high-speed, 16-digit calculator."

In the final few days before the magazine appeared on the newsstands, the Weapons Lab contingent at MITS headquarters was working furiously in preparation for the hoped-for onslaught of orders. I spent two incredibly busy weeks building the first production model 816 while simultaneously writing the assembly manual. (The laser project had been published in *Popular Electronics* the previous month, but only a hundred or so orders came in.) The response to the calculator was enormous—thousands of orders flooded into MITS. Ed hired me to develop a brochure to help promote the calculator.

In the black for the first time since MITS was formed, Ed didn't stop with the 816. Soon he developed the 1440 calculator, which included square root and memory keys. In addition, he continued work on an advanced programming unit that could be connected to special terminals inside the two calculators. The programmer enabled a user to enter a complicated formula or equation, and then it automatically solved the formula each time the operator punched in a new set of values. Today programmable calculators are available for $50. But before the MITS programmer their advanced capabilities were available only with expensive scientific calculators and computers. Imagine, in 1972, when the space shuttle was still a dream, tiny MITS offered an advanced programmable calculator for under $500. What would Ed think of next?

Growing Pains

It was time to move. MITS had grown so big that people, desks, workbenches, and equipment were stuffed into every available hallway and corner. Thanks to the 816 calculator, Ed's company had become far more than the pre-MITS split garage operation of the year before.

Ed moved MITS to a series of adjoining storefronts with 9,500 square feet of floor space only a few blocks from my mobile home. There he continued to introduce new calculators, low-cost digital clocks, and various kinds of electronic test instruments, some of which he described in project articles for *Popular Electronics* and the rival magazine, *Radio-Electronics*. Calculators remained his chief interest, and in a plan to sell not kits but factory-assembled number machines to businesses and the general public, he eventually set up a complete production line. At one end of the line of wooden tables, women known in the trade as board-stuffers inserted black integrated circuits, color-striped resistors, and red displays into brown circuit boards. Trays of stuffed boards were placed on a moving rack that carried them first over a dark-brown spray of sweet-smelling, frothy rosin and then over a gleaming, silvery wave of molten lead and tin in an operation that automatically soldered each and every pin and lead to the metal foil outline that interconnected the various components. It was an impressive operation.

For a time MITS was a major manufacturer of compact, hand-held calculators. Ed granted distributorships to businessmen around the world, and by June 1972 sales to overseas customers reached $150,000. By November 1973 MITS had 51 employees, 25 of whom worked full time. That month the company went public; it offered 500,000 shares of stock for a dollar each. Bold letters at the top of the prospectus warned: "These securities involve a high degree of risk."

In 1974 the warning became a reality when such big companies as Texas Instruments began to introduce low-cost calculators. For MITS the unrelenting competition became an economic disaster, a bloodbath of red ink. Though MITS was still selling calculators, it had been forced to reduce prices and lost money on every sale. Ed didn't understand how a competing calculator could sell for $19 when it cost $39 to assemble the MITS equivalent. What he didn't know was that his competitors sere selling calculators below cost to capture a share of the market; they too were about to lose their shirts.

Once 110 employees had worked two shifts at MITS. By the summer of 1974 70 employees worked a single shift, and creditors were owed $350,000. But Ed had a bold, brave plan to rescue MITS with another new siliconnected product, one even more revolutionary than the 816 calculator.

The Altair 8800

During the calculator years Ed and I collaborated on half a dozen magazine articles and the first book about digital calculators. Since MITS was headquartered across the street from the post office, I often stopped by to say hello and visit when I bicycled over to drop off mail. During the calculator calamity it was obvious there were big problems, but Ed never brought them up nor did he mention the magnitude of MITS's enormous debt. Instead, he talked enthusiastically about the new project that would, Ed claimed, outclass everything MITS had already accomplished. Burned by his defeat in the battle with big business-calculator companies, he planned to return to the marketing strategy that had served MITS best, direct sales to electronics experimenters.

During one of my visits, Bill Yates was helping a technician lay out the huge pattern for a printed circuit board with narrow strips of red and blue plastic tape. Ed showed me a metal box with a front panel covered by rows of red lights and toggle switches. This was the prototype version of a fully functional digital computer. I didn't know at the time that the future of MITS depended entirely on the success of that siliconcocted box. When Ed asked what I thought, instead of offering encouragement, I was unimpressed. "Unless you add a keyboard," I said, "you'll sell a few hundred at most." As it turned out, I was wrong.

Despite its complicated printed circuit boards, in some ways the computer was less complex than the old 816 calculator. It didn't even have a molded plastic cabinet. Nevertheless, being a fully programmable computer, it was infinitely more versatile than any calculator. That's why Ed was convinced that electronics experimenters, if no one else, would jump at the chance to buy one. At the time neither of us knew that since early 1974 Arthur Salsberg, then the editorial director of *Popular Electronics*, had been looking for a computer project for his magazine. Art was familiar with Intel's new microprocessors, and was sure that their 8080 would provide the means to design an affordable yet advanced computer for hobbyists. He finally came across a microcomputer trainer project designed by Jerry Ogdin, a noted microprocessor expert. Though the trainer was more an educational project than the full-scale computer Art had in mind, he scheduled it for the December 1974 issue.

Art's plans for Ogdin's trainer were placed in doubt when in July arch-rival *Radio-Electronics* published a computer project designed by Jonathan Titus. Titus's computer used Intel's 8008 micropro-cessor, a successor to the original 4004 but not as powerful as the newer 8080. Nevertheless, "I felt as if the rug was pulled out from under me," Art recalled a decade later.

Wanting to beat, not merely meet, his competition, Art asked Les Solomon if he knew of anyone developing a more advanced hobbyist computer, preferably one using Intel's powerful new 8080 microprocessor. Les told Art about Ed's new computer project. Could Ed get an article out in time for a winter issue? "Tell him that he's got to have an attractive cabinet in order for it to be a cover story," Art recalls telling Les. Les phoned Ed, and rushed back to Art's office to report that Ed's computer could indeed be ready for the January issue. The computer would use the state-of-the-art 8080 microprocessor, thereby outclassing *Radio-Electronics*'s 8008 machine.

The two editors were ecstatic. MITS had always been a reliable supplier of kits. Moreover, January was the magazine's best selling newsstand issue. Plans to run Jerry Ogdin's trainer in December were shelved; Art decided to hold it as a backup article should Ed fail to deliver his computer.

Intel's 8080 microprocessor cost $360. It was neatly packaged in a flat, white ceramic package the size of a row of three postage stamps, and bordered along either side by twenty golden pins. Ed had already designed the various circuits required to transform this high-tech chip, the collective term engineers apply to all integrated circuits, into a working 8-bit microcomputer. The most important aspect of the design proved to be Ed's decision to make it easy to add additional memory and other circuits to the computer. This was accomplished by means of a *bus*, a series of electrical terminals emerging from the main circuit board, which provided a direct connection to the all-important 8080, the computer's electronic nerve center. The concept of the bus was not new; virtually every digital computer includes one. Often, however, the bus is not readily accessible to the user. Ed elected to use an open bus. This would enable MITS to sell many kinds of additional circuit boards, particularly ones containing additional memory chips, which could be inserted into a row of bus-connected sockets inside the cabinet. No one could then know about the rash of companies that would later spring up to take a free ride on Ed Roberts's bus.

When trusty Bill Yates finished assembling the prototype computer, they shipped it to *Popular Electronics*, and Ed made plans to follow it to New York a few days later. But the magical machine that was going to save MITS never arrived. All Ed had to prove it actually existed was the sheaf of circuit diagrams he spread before Art Salsberg and Les Solomon. Though Ed had managed to borrow another $65,000 from an Albuquerque bank to float the computer project, he left New York with no written assurance from the magazine that they would actually publish the computer article. "What really bothered me," he later remembered, "was that Les Solomon said 'I think we're casting our pearls before swine on this one.'" Les was just being Les, but what he said bothered Ed all the way back to Albuquerque.

The magazine's art department needed a computer for the cover photograph, so Bill Yates hurriedly assembled a nonfunctional mockup. This package arrived in New York, as did a second package containing a fully working version of the machine. Les set up the machine in his office, and began trying to figure out how it worked.

Everyone but Ed was worried about the computer's name. David Bunnell, MITS's advertising manager and vice-president of marketing, developed a three-page list of possibilities. Little Brother, apparently a spoof of IBM's big brother image, was among his favorites. Ed wasn't attracted to any of the names on Bunnell's list. He decided to call the machine the PE-8, a reference to *Popular Electronics* and the computer's 8-bit capability. But Les thought

PE-8 was an unimaginative name for such a breakthrough project. Like Bunnell, he began casting about for a catchier name.

Alexander Burawa, then *Popular Electronics*'s associate editor, technical illustrator Andre Duzant, and assistant technical editor John McVeigh, now a patent attorney with the Federal Communications Commission, recently reminisced about what happened next. Les asked Al and John if they had any ideas for a name. Al recalled saying, "It's a stellar event, so let's name it after a star." Beginning with the letter *A*, analytical Al suggested Aldeberan. John thought this was too clumsy. Next, Al mentioned Althar, the planet in Edmund Hamilton's science-fiction novel *The Star of Life*. John immediately responded with Altair, the star Althar orbited. Altair was perfect. Les called Ed Roberts.

Ed was worried about unfinished circuit boards, undelivered parts, and unprepared assembly and instruction manuals. What to name the computer was among the least of his priorities. Ed told Les he didn't care what *Popular Electronics* called the machine so long as MITS could break even by selling 200 of them.

Bill Yates's dummy computer was featured on the cover of the January 1975 issue of *Popular Electronics*, its PE-8 label replaced by ALTAIR 8800. Though the machine's microprocessor was an 8080, the guys at the magazine thought Altair 8800 sounded better than Altair 8080.

"Project Breakthrough! World's First Minicomputer Kit to Rival Commercial Models," the cover copy proclaimed. Inside, Art Salsberg's editorial announced "The Home Computer is Here!" "For many years," Art wrote, "we've been reading and hearing about how computers will one day be a household item. Therefore, we're especially proud to present in this issue the first *commercial type* of minicomputer project ever published [a pointed poke at rival *Radio-Electronics*'s earlier, comparatively primitive 8008 machine] that's priced within reach of many households. . . . There'll be more coverage on the subject in future issues," Art promised. "Meanwhile, the home computer age is here—finally."

The reaction to Ed and Bill's Altair article was greater than they or anyone at *Popular Electronics* had anticipated. Savvy experimenters who knew about Intel's advanced 8080 microprocessor realized it would make an ideal nerve center for a powerful computer. But at $360 each when purchased in onesies and twosies, the trade's mocking reference to small-quantity purchases, who could afford the chip, much less the hundreds of additional components and circuit boards that would be required? Since Intel gave MITS a substantial discount on a bulk order of the sleek and shiny 8080's, Ed was able to pass the savings along and price a complete Altair kit at an incredibly low $397. Orders poured into MITS; Ed wanted 200, he received thousands.

The orders solved MITS's cash-flow crisis overnight. But they created delays while MITS waited for additional parts to arrive. In the midst of this chaos Ed remembered he didn't have an operator's manual for the machine. In early January a jovial Ed called and said, "I'm going to make you an offer you can't refuse."

I bicycled over to MITS and rolled my ten-speed Peugeot over to its usual parking space down the hall from Ed's office. Ed briefed me about the status of the Altair project, and asked if, in exchange for an assembled computer, I would write the operator's manual on a priority basis, preferably by yesterday. Ed was right; I couldn't refuse. After pausing a few milliseconds so as not to seem overly anxious, I accepted the job. He gave me a stack of Intel manuals, and I went to work.

Meanwhile, the editorial staff at *Popular Electronics* began receiving ecstatic letters about the Altair article. Several were published in the March 1975 issue under the heading "Minicomputer Makes Maxisplash." Little did the subscribers know that not everyone at the magazine shared Art Salsberg and his editorial staff's enthusiasm.

One of Art's superiors at Ziff-Davis, the company that published *Popular Electronics*, sent him a congratulatory note about the Altair scoop, but another questioned the wisdom of running a project article that wouldn't attract advertisers. He even demanded that Les Solomon remove from his office the clattering Teletype terminal Ed had sent him for use with the magazine's Altair. Though MITS bought a full-page ad in the February issue, Art's boss wasn't impressed. Nevertheless, Art continued to publish computer projects despite opposition. At the time, Art had no idea that publishing the Altair article had sparked a revolution that within eight years would transform Ziff-Davis into a major publisher of

computer publications, and *Popular Electronics* into *Computers &
Electronics*, a new magazine devoted almost exclusively to computers.

While working on the Altair manual, I made several visits to
MITS. Ed had always been very accessible, but now the place was
a beehive of activity. Salesmen, prospective employees, consultants, delivery people and even an occasional customer from out of
state were waiting to get past the receptionist, who frowned when I
rolled the yellow Peugeot by her desk. Getting in to see Ed required an appointment! When the manual was ready, Ed said to
bring it right over. Unable to penetrate the traffic jam in the reception area, I gave it to a secretary and left. MITS wasn't fun anymore.

By the end of 1975 the electronics company with the funny name
down in Albuquerque was well known to computer hobbyists all
over the United States. An important contributing factor was the
MITS-MOBILE, a motor home equipped with a full complement
of Altair equipment. After a trial tour through Texas, the MITS-
MOBILE team traveled across the country giving Altair demonstrations, seminars, and slide shows, and distributing literature,
posters, catalogs, and door prizes.

In June Dave Bunnell had begun editing a monthly tabloid called
Computer Notes, A Publication of the Altair Users Group. Each month
Computer Notes carried the MITS-MOBILE schedule, letters from
customers, computer programs for the Altair, news about new
products, programming tips and advice, and an editorial by Bunnell. Ed wrote a column for each issue.

The November/December issue was significant for it announced
in a banner headline: ALTAIR CONVENTION. Officially called the
"MITS 1st World ALTAIR Computer Convention" (WACC), it
was David Bunnell's project. WACC took place over a sunny weekend in March 1976 at the Airport Marina Hotel, only a few hundred yards from the parking attendant's booth where nearly five
years earlier Ed, Stan and I held our final midnight meeting as
MITS partners. An instant rerun of model rockets, the silicon
garage, telemetry modules, cigar-puffing Les Solomon, the Opticom, the crazy guard with the loaded .45, and the 816 calculator
flashed through my mind while I drove past the parking lot. MITS

had come a long way in those six busy years. Had I come as far on my own as I would have at MITS?

Though WACC will be remembered as the first of the hundreds of personal computer fairs, shows, and conventions held since, to many who attended its real significance was the tantalizing glimpse it provided of things to come. In the lobby of the hotel several people were buzzing excitedly about a major development, the presence in an upstairs suite of some fellows from a new California electronics company called Processor Technology. Since the model rocketry days MITS had attracted competitors as fast as it added new products. What were these upstart interlopers selling, I wondered? With a feeling of déjà vu I took the elevator up to the Processor Technology invaders' suite. I peered over and around the people jammed in the doorway and saw the future: computer memory boards designed specifically for the Altair bus but priced lower than those made by MITS.

The open bus Ed Roberts designed for the Altair, to be filled with circuit boards developed by MITS, proved irresistible. Soon dozens of silicon garages would sprout up to make circuit boards to fill the empty space inside those big blue and gray Optima cabinets, and a personal computer industry would be born.

The Legacy of the Altair

Six months before WACC, Ed Roberts took a friend for a ride in his new, dual-engine airplane equipped with a full complement of siliconized avionics gear. They took off at dusk and flew due east over the busy stretch of Route 66 that bisects the city. The mosaic of dark streets outlined by porch and street lights resembled a magnified view of an integrated circuit, the twinkling headlights of traffic mimicking moving electrons, and the traffic signals the transistors that controlled their flow. Albuquerque at night resembled an enormous microprocessor.

Owning an airplane and learning to fly it were two of Ed's goals back at the Weapons Lab when MITS was still a dream, and he would soon achieve those that remained. Though he didn't let on at the time, he was tiring of his management responsibilities at

MITS, what he later called the "soap opera" side of running a company. He had little patience with office politics, petty rivalries, and the flaps that developed when someone learned a coworker was making a few more cents per hour.

Shortly before the National Computer Conference in Dallas in the spring of 1977, Ed cashed in his chips and sold MITS to Pertec Computer Corporation for six million dollars. Happier and more relaxed than he'd seemed in a long time, Ed Roberts seemed bigger than life at the giant conference. David Bunnell was also there, manning a booth for *Personal Computing*, the new magazine he had just begun.

Realizing that personal computing was fast becoming a major industry, the NCC people had reserved a separate hall for the few dozen personal computer companies to exhibit their wares. The place was packed with exhibitors and people, many of whom said they were more impressed by what they saw there than by the expensive equipment displayed by the big computer companies in the cavernous main exhibition hall.

Ed and Bill Yates stayed with MITS for a while, and worked on special projects. But they both missed the heady spirit of earlier times. Ed later remembered Bill telling him, "It's no fun around here anymore." When Commodore, Apple, and Radio Shack were still new names in personal computing, Ed left MITS and Pertec. He moved Joan and their four boys to a 900-acre farm in Georgia, started medical school, and began several business ventures, among them Georgia Medical Electronics.

Today only a handful of pioneer computer users remember MITS and the Altair 8800, much less H. Edward Roberts. Weary of "sure you are" responses and disbelieving stares, Ed long ago stopped mentioning to salespeople in computer stores his former role in their industry.

The Altair wasn't a perfect machine, nor was Ed the ideal manager. But MITS pioneered virtually every area of today's personal computer industry: users' groups, software products and exchanges, seminars, newsletters, shows, quality documentation, hardware products, and inexpensive computers. Ed and his Altair paved the way for a plethora of small computer companies and established the Ed Roberts bus as an industry standard. Furthermore, Ed helped make BASIC the most popular computer language when he selected for the Altair a version of BASIC developed by Bill Gates and Paul Allen, two brilliant computer hackers from Bellevue, Washington, who moved to Albuquerque soon thereafter. While at MITS Gates and Allen formed Microsoft, the giant software firm, and their original Altair BASIC evolved into the versions of BASIC used by some of the largest-selling personal computers, including those made by Radio Shack and IBM. MITS and its Altair are gone, but the legacy lives on.

·5·

After Altair: The First Decade

Altair Connections

ON FRIDAY, July 27, 1984, I received a call from Dr. Uta C. Merzbach, curator of the Division of Mathematics at the Smithsonian Institution. Could she visit me in south central Texas the following Monday to inspect my collection of documents relating to the early history of MITS?

While visiting Washington, D.C., a few weeks earlier I had called Dr. Merzbach to ask if the Smithsonian had plans to develop an exhibit commemorating the tenth anniversary of the personal computer. Though they didn't have plans for an exhibit, she expressed a keen interest in MITS and the Altair, and asked if I would send her an inventory of my material. If the MITS material seemed to have historical value, she would make a personal inspection.

Several years earlier I had been retained by the National Geographic Society to help organize an exhibit commemorating the centennial of Alexander Graham Bell's invention of lightwave communications in 1880. While planning that exhibit, Elliot Sivowitch, a curator at the Smithsonian, had taken me into one of the storerooms where hundreds of early telephones, telegraphs, and other venerable electrical devices were stored. It was thrilling to see up close and actually touch electrical machines identical to those displayed behind glassy barriers out in the crowded exhibit cases. Now a curator from the Smithsonian wanted to visit my office to share that same experience. Had the ten-year-old Altair Ed Roberts gave me for writing the machine's operating manual earned a berth in the Smithsonian's National Museum of American History, the supernal destiny of all great inventions?

Even before receiving Dr. Merzbach's call, I had begun retrieving and organizing MITS gadgetry, photographs, and documents. I had often considered giving away the suitcase-sized Altair to make more room in the crowded office and electronics shop built into my silicon garage. Did the machine still work? I dusted it off and flicked on the power switch. The twin rows of red lights on the gray display panel glowed. After pressing the switch marked UN-PROTECT, I entered several nonsense instructions on the row of toggle switches, hitting the switch labeled DEPOSIT NEXT to load each instruction into the machine's paltry 256-byte memory. When the STOP/RUN switch was flipped to RUN, the two rows of data and address lights began flickering. The Altair was cycling through its memory looking for something to do. It worked.

Next I retrieved the MITS 816 calculator I had built back in 1971 while writing its assembly manual. I gingerly placed the ancient machine on top of the Altair, plugged its power cord into a socket, and pressed the power switch. Nothing happened. Returning to my electronics shop, I flipped the 816 onto its back, removed the six screws that held the machine together, and lifted Bill Saling's tan plastic cabinet away from the chassis. Everything inside appeared dust-free, and the connections on the circuit boards seemed just as shiny as when I soldered them in place years before. The mechanical design of the machine, particularly the stacked circuit boards and the tilted row of display tubes, was so impressive I almost forgot that the old calculator didn't work. A fragment of wire, a dislodged solder ball, or even a gossamer film of dust can shut down the most complicated digital electronics device. Though a careful inspection revealed none of these troublemakers, I took a deep breath, blew a few quarts of warm air through the circuit boards, and switched the machine back on. An invisible layer of dust must have been the culprit, for this time the display tubes formed a softly glowing row of green zeros.

The Altair 8800 and the 816 calculator were sitting atop a file cabinet next to my desk when Dr. Merzbach, accompanied by a briefcase, cassette recorder, and camera, arrived. She spent a hot July afternoon inspecting the Altair and the calculator, carefully reviewing every document, manual, and photograph in my files and asking probing questions about MITS, Ed Roberts, and other early personal computer workers. An expert on the history of the development of the first generation of digital computers back in the

1940s and 1950s, she was particularly well informed about the similarity of the sequence of developments in the evolution of the first-generation machines and personal computers.

Would I be willing to donate to the Smithsonian the Altair, the 816, the unsold model rocket telemetry modules, the folders stuffed with MITS documents, and perhaps even my homemade language translator computer, Dr. Merzbach wondered, showing me a sample donor's form plucked from her attache case? Imagine, one day Ed's Altair might be placed behind glass only a few feet from the historic Mark 1 and the panels from the ENIAC, two of the earliest pioneering computers on display in the National Museum of American History. My collection of MITS documents, "primary source material" Dr. Merzbach called them, would be filed safely away to be made available to scholars and journalists studying the history of personal computers. For sentimental reasons I was at first reluctant about donating the material. But after thinking it over for a few days, I called Dr. Merzbach to say she could have everything she wanted.

Even during the hundreds of fits of blue-sky speculation Ed and I had during our many discussion sessions, neither of us had suspected that anything from MITS might end up in a museum, much less the Smithsonian Institution. Our interest had always centered on the futuristic products and gadgets that would spring from the ongoing silicon revolution, and the avalanche of new integrated circuits and technologies emerging from Texas Instruments in Dallas, Motorola in Phoenix, and the clusters of electronics firms along Route 128 in Boston and in the Santa Clara Valley South of San Francisco.

Certainly none of the post-Altair personal computer companies that began springing up in 1975 had museum shelves in mind when they challenged MITS for a share of its business. Like MITS, most of these early companies have long since vanished, but their collective contribution to the foundation of personal computing was invaluable. While IBM, Digital Equipment Corporation (DEC), and the other established computer firms were ignoring the revolution that promised to transform the computer industry, little companies in Texas, Connecticut, Illinois, Utah, and California introduced more than a dozen low-cost computers during 1975 and 1976. Unlike establishment computer firms, the entrepreneurs who started these companies, many of them in garages, were tuned in to the microprocessor era and were probably not surprised to learn that a survey of 2,000 Californians revealed that tiny MITS was recognized as a computer company more often than giants like DEC and Data General. They knew that experimenters and hobbyists would pay cash for a real computer, even one they had to assemble from a kit, for they were themselves experimenters and hobbyists.

The Silicon Time Machine

As Dr. Merzbach pored over my MITS files, I thought about some of those early companies, and which of their computers might, like the Altair 8800, be destined for the Smithsonian. Which of the early computers had earned this place of ultimate honor?

Nat Wadsworth of Milford, Connecticut, was possibly the first entrepreneur to sell a hobby computer designed around a microprocessor, Intel's 8008. Though his SCELBI-8H and 8B machines were primitive by Altair standards, they were advanced for their time, and Wadsworth advertised them in amateur radio magazines long before *Radio-Electronics* published Jonathan Titus's Mark 8 in 1974. The Altair's advanced 8080 microprocessor proved too much for the comparatively primitive SCELBI machine, and Wadsworth eventually turned his energies toward developing microcomputer books and software. Yes, a SCELBI, if one could be found, belonged in my imaginary Smithsonian exhibit. So did, of course, Jonathan Titus's Mark-8.

While the SCELBI-8B was being driven from the market by the Altair, the Sphere Corporation, a startup company in Bountiful, Utah, tried to leapfrog MITS with a line of desktop personal computers complete with typewriter-style keyboards and video displays. Sphere's machines, along with the Altair 8800 and the SCELBI-8B, were among a handful of microcomputers advertised in the first issue of *Byte* magazine in September 1975. But features like a standard keyboard, the ability to save programs with a cassette recorder, the BASIC computer language, and reasonable prices—all remarkably advanced for their time—made Sphere stand out. Moreover, by November 1975 Sphere's ads pictured a console computer with a built-in monitor that bore an uncanny resemblance to today's desktop machines. Sphere's concept was years ahead of its time; but the company wasn't successful. The February 1977 issue of *Byte* was the last to carry a Sphere ad. In spite of its flaws, Sphere had earned a place in my imaginary Smithsonian exhibit if for no other reason than the modern appearance of the Sphere might influence Apple's advertising people to stop claiming that Apple invented personal computing.

In November 1975, just ten months after the Altair article appeared in *Popular Electronics,* Dan Meyer's Southwest Technical Products in San Antonio placed an ad in the third issue of *Byte* to announce his company's first microcomputer kit. Though Sphere's machine was prettier, and included a keyboard, Meyer's computer was backed by his firm's excellent reputation for supplying first-class audio kits. Indeed, it was Meyer's project articles in *Popular Electronics* that convinced me back in 1970 that MITS could do likewise and successfully sell kits through the same magazine.

Dan Meyer had an important advantage over Ed Roberts: Don Lancaster's TV typewriter, a typewriterlike keyboard complete with the complicated circuits necessary to display text and numbers on the screen of any television set. In fact, Southwest Tech had purchased the inside cover of *Byte*'s second issue to advertise the latest version, the CT-1024 Terminal System kit. The CT-1024, which sold for $175, featured a typewriter keyboard, and could place up to sixteen lines of text on a TV screen. By the summer of 1976 more than twenty computer stores sold the Southwest Tech computer. Certainly Southwest Tech's machine belonged in my fanciful Smithsonian exhibit, along with Don Lancaster's pioneering TV typewriter.

Though Dan Meyer's computer was reasonably priced, it had several major shortcomings. First, it used a different microprocessor than the Altair 8800, Motorola's 6800. The 6800 had a powerful set of instructions, but they were incompatible with those of the 8080 chip used in the Altair. Software developed for the Altair would not run on a 6800 machine; circuit boards designed for the Altair, which had begun to flood the market, would not work in a 6800 computer either. Moreover, Dan Meyer's computer lacked a good name: he called it the SWTPC 6800, hardly a catchy appellation for a machine having a personality of its own. Even Ed

Roberts's original name for the Altair, the PE-8, was better than that. Of course, none of this would have mattered if Dan Meyer's computer had arrived before the Altair. But it didn't, and the Texas company that unknowingly helped inspire the original MITS partners to establish a *Popular Electronics* link never gave MITS as much competition as a new firm in San Leandro, California, called IMS Associates.

The January 1976 issue of *Byte* carried an ad for a new computer called the IMSAI that looked surprisingly similar to the Altair 8800. Indeed, the ad claimed in a special note to Altair 8800 owners, ". . . you will be pleased to know that your ALTAIR 8800 boards are 'plug-in' usable—without modification—in the IMSAI 8080 cabinet." Of course Altair boards were "plug-in usable" in the IMSAI. The fellows at IMS Associates had disassembled a couple of Altairs and literally copied the MITS machine. No wonder the IMSAI looked like an Altair.

The IMSAI included a heftier power supply than the Altair so more boards could be added to the machine. Though the Altair was installed in a better-made Optima cabinet, IMSAI's cabinet was at least as attractive, and the row of red and blue paddle switches on its front panel was prettier than the bare metal, bat-handled toggle switches on the Altair.

IMS Associates soon changed its name to IMSAI Manufacturing Corporation, and eventually sold more of its computers than MITS did Altairs. Though IMSAI outlived MITS, the company filed for bankruptcy in the spring of 1979, a victim of mismanagement and serious reliability problems with a new computer. Unlike nearly all the early personal computer companies, IMSAI lacked the hobby electronics connection Ed Roberts, Dan Meyer, and all the others understood so well. The entrepreneurs who headed IMSAI seemed to be driven more by the amplitude of the bottom line than by the feeling of pride in having designed a successful new product. Why, their machine wasn't even new. In the parlance used to describe today's plethora of IBM PC–compatible computers, the IMSAI was an Altair lookalike, an electronic clone of another company's machine. Even though IMSAI did have a major impact on the market, I couldn't find a place for it alongside the upstanding, honorable computers in my fanciful Smithsonian exhibit. Anyway, the IMSAI has already received its fair share of attention. It was the machine used by the teenaged computer hacker in the movie "War Games."

In 1975 MOS Technology, a manufacturer of integrated circuits in Norristown, Pennsylvania, introduced the KIM-1, a complete computer assembled on a single circuit board about the size of a sheet of typing paper. KIM was a far cry from a personal computer, and didn't even include the power supply circuits necessary for her to work. Nevertheless, she was relatively inexpensive and was supplied with three thick manuals of well-written and beautifully organized documentation. Hobbyists, including me, snapped them up by the hundreds. The first thing most of us did when our KIM arrived was rush over to a nearby Radio Shack store and buy a transformer, a handful of capacitors, and an integrated circuit called a voltage regulator. These parts were then soldered to a small circuit board, and an attached power cord was plugged into a wall socket. The resultant power supply circuit provided the proper voltages to start KIM purring.

KIM introduced many low-budget experimenters to the 6502 microprocessor, the easily programmed chip used in the Apple and other post-1977 computers. But her real significance came later when a businessman named Jack Tramiel bought MOS Technology. Tramiel headed Commodore International. In the early and mid 1970s Commodore sold a line of sophisticated handheld business and scientific calculators. MOS Technology manufactured some of the chips used in Commodore's calculators, and Tramiel's purchase of the firm provided a degree of vertical integration almost unmatched in the burgeoning calculator industry. With the acquisition of MOS Technology, Commodore became much more competitive than companies like MITS that built calculators by stuffing printed circuit boards with integrated circuits and displays purchased from outside vendors. The expanded company designed and manufactured its own microprocessor and calculator chips and both the light-emitting diode and liquid crystal displays used in its machines. Smaller calculator companies like MITS were affected by the increasing competition from Commodore.

The logical offspring of the marriage of Commodore's calculators and MOS Technology's KIM-1 was the *P*ersonal *E*lectronic *T*ransactor 2001, or PET, a sleekly styled desktop computer reminiscent of the by-then extinct Sphere. I remember well both the excitement and the questions that surrounded PET's announcement. Dave Bunnell, who had left MITS in 1977 to found *Personal Computing* illustrated the cover of the September/October 1977 issue of his magazine with a painting showing a gauze-masked doctor delivering the PET from under a rumpled sheet. The cover caption read "BIRTH OF THE PET COMPUTER. Is it the first of a new generation?" Inside Bunnell devoted ten pages to interviews with Chuck Peddle, the machine's creator, and several well-known computer enthusiasts about the impact of the PET.

"Quite portable, very affordable and unbelievably versatile, the PET computer may very well be a lifetime investment," gushed a Commodore brochure handed out at the National Computer Conference in Dallas in June 1977. Those of us who saw Chuck Peddle demonstrate the PET at the Dallas show almost believed Commodore's hype; the machine was truly impressive. For only $595 one could purchase an 8-bit microcomputer with a built-in display, cassette recorder, 4K (4,096 characters) of user-accessible memory, and excellent graphics capabilities. Moreover, thanks to a built-in memory chip called a ROM (read-only memory), PET's keyboard was ready to receive BASIC instructions the moment the computer was switched on. Other machines could be programmed in BASIC only after part of their user-accessible memory (or RAM) was loaded with a special sequence of computer instructions. This usually required pulling a perforated paper tape through a special readout device connected by wires to the computer.

In spite of its impressive features, PET had the flattest, ugliest, and poorest excuse for a computer keyboard we had ever seen. Presumably to keep the PET's price down, Commodore had borrowed the flat keyboard technology used in cheap calculators. Worse, the labels on the keys soon rubbed off by finger friction. In spite of Commodore's hyperbolic predictions, the PET didn't prove to be a "lifetime investment." Commodore itself contributed to the product's eventual obsolescence by developing such wildly successful home computers as the VIC-20 and the Commodore 64. Nevertheless, its miserly keyboard notwithstanding, the PET provided a surprisingly accurate harbinger of things to come. It ushered in a new era in personal computing, one in which computer users didn't have to know which end of a soldering iron becomes hot or the differences between a 6502 and an 8080 microprocessor. It marked the beginning of the end of the necessity to possess do-it-yourself hardware hacking skills.

Alongside the PET in my Smithsonian exhibit wish list belong two other 1977-era computers, the Apple I and Apple II. How Stephen Wozniak and Steve Jobs founded Apple Computer Company has been widely portrayed in books and magazines. Even more so than MITS, Apple is the quintessential silicon-garage success story of two very young, almost counterculture friends whose eventual linkage with Mike Markulla, a retired Intel engineer with remarkable business sense, led to the formation of what is today a Fortune 500 company.

Wozniak's Apple I was among the very first microcomputers that included on a single circuit board a complete computer plus all the circuits necessary for connecting a keyboard and a television monitor. Remarkably, not only did Wozniak design the entire computer, he also developed the binary-encoded machine language instructions that allowed it to understand his version of the popular BASIC computer language. Even though the Apple I didn't come with a case, keyboard, monitor, or power supply, Jobs and Wozniak sold a few hundred of them. This success motivated them to design the finished ready-to-run computer that became the legendary Apple II.

Despite the wishful thinking of some enthusiastic Apple owners, copywriters, and journalists, and notwithstanding Wozniak's advanced single-board design, neither Apple was a technological breakthrough on the order of the Altair or the Sphere, machines that appeared more than two years before the first Apple II press release arrived in my mailbox. Indeed, Wozniak is reported to have developed the Apple I when as a member of San Francisco's Homebrew Computer Club he couldn't afford an Altair 8800. But the Apple I and Apple II didn't have to be firsts to earn the well-deserved Smithsonian slots I envisioned for them; Apple Computer Corporation is today one of the biggest and most successful personal computer companies.

Apple didn't have an exhibit at the NCC in Dallas in June 1977, but everyone who read *Byte* knew about the company because Wozniak, one of its co-founders, had written an eight-page technical article for the May 1977 issue describing the inner workings of the Apple II. Something about that article smelled like success: its author was one of those rare types who are adept at describing both the hardware aspects of programmable digital circuitry and the software necessary to make the circuits do useful work. Even before Apple's first press release, I had discussed the new machine with *Popular Electronics* editor Art Salsberg on a visit to Radio Shack's headquarters in Fort Worth. Though Radio Shack had just given Art a full tour of its impressive TRS-80 computer manufacturing facilities, he seemed more enthusiastic about Apple II's future prospects. When Art asked what I thought about the emerging competition between giant Radio Shack and upstart Apple, I remembered how the calculator wars almost buried MITS, and replied that Apple could never match Radio Shack's nationwide network of stores. Art thought Apple would emerge a winner.

In time both Apple and Radio Shack became giants in the personal computer field. Certainly Radio Shack's first machine, the TRS-80, belongs in the Smithsonian alongside the Apple I and Apple II. The origins of the huge electronics retailer's computer business can be traced directly to one man, Donald H. French. I met Don in 1973 when he was a buyer, one of the dozen or so men who shared the responsibility of buying at the lowest prices items within several dozen categories of products. Don's chief responsibility was electronic parts. Like most buyers, Don had once managed a branch store, and was very much in tune with the collective interests and eccentricities that seem to characterize electronic experimenters and tinkerers. An adept experimenter, he sometimes suggested electronic circuits to be included in the 96-page project books I was then writing for Leon Lutz, Radio Shack's book buyer.

Don was always excited about hobby electronics, but after the Altair arrived he became crazy about computers. A couple of times a year Radio Shack would fly me in from Albuquerque to discuss the book assignments that provided much of my income in those days, and an excited Don, knowing about my MITS connections, and himself an Altair owner, would share his plans for a Radio Shack computer to be sold as a kit. His biggest frustration was his failure to interest Radio Shack's management in the idea. After spending considerable time studying the various microprocessors that were available in 1975, Don selected National Semiconductor's advanced 16-bit PACE, and began building a computer on his kitchen table in his spare time.

Don's plan was to add the computer to the small line of kits in his product line, but his do-it-yourself 16-bit machine never got off the ground. Instead, near the end of 1975 Radio Shack hired away from National Semiconductor in Santa Clara, California, a bright electrical engineer named Steven Leininger. Leininger's first assignment was to evaluate Don French's plans for a computer kit. Eventually the company decided to allow Leininger to design a completely new machine using a recently developed microprocessor called the Z-80. The Z-80 was a faster, more sophisticated version of the older 8080 used in the Altair, and would lend considerable prestige to Radio Shack's new product.

A few weeks before the TRS-80 was officially announced in August 1977, David S. Gunzel, Radio Shack's technical editor, led me to a small building near the company's old warehouse headquarters in Fort Worth. On the way he emphasized that everything I was about to see was still secret and not to be divulged to anyone. We entered a room full of brand new gray and black TRS-80's. Several men emerged from an adjoining electronics laboratory, and Dave introduced me to Steve Leininger and a couple of engineers. After telling them I was one of the founders of MITS and had written the Altair's operating manual, Dave motioned me over for a closer look at a TRS-80 displaying an American flag on its monitor. "Go ahead and give it a try," someone said. Totally petrified by a severe case of computer phobia, I begged off, mumbling something about not wanting to erase the impressive flag graphic. After Dave's generous introduction, I simply didn't have the courage to admit that my Altair, since it lacked an expensive keyboard terminal, could be programmed only in machine language code entered via the front panel switches, and that I had never tried my rudimentary knowledge of BASIC on a computer that understood the language. In that moment of electronic mortification, I decided to get a TRS-80 as soon as possible, and learn to program it using BASIC.

Meanwhile, Dave Gunzel hired me to write a 26-page promotional booklet about the TRS-80, and Don French, who had been named merchandising manager of the newly created Tandy Computers, hired me to write some of the technical copy for his first computer catalog. Though I periodically begged Don for the loan of a computer, he never came through. Eventually, however, Dave provided a machine, and I soon learned that BASIC is such a popular computer language because it's ridiculously easy to learn. No wonder professional programmers were becoming so concerned over the proliferation of cheap, personal computers.

Hundreds of thousands of TRS-80's were sold before Radio Shack introduced the TRS-80 Model 2 business computer, and changed the name of the original machine from TRS-80 to TRS-80 Model 1. Even though the Apple II arrived a few months earlier, the Model 1 was cheaper, and available from thousands of Radio Shack stores across the country. It also used Bill Gates and Paul Allen's Microsoft BASIC, a version of the language many users prefer to Apple's BASIC. The Model 1 was also a much more compact machine than its two chief competitors, the console-style PET and the Apple II. The entire computer was on a circuit board installed behind a typewriter-style keyboard in a case connected by a wire cable to a televisionlike video monitor. Many of today's most popular desktop personal computers use the same detached keyboard concept so widely popularized by the Model 1.

Elliot Sivowitch, the curator who helped with the *National Geographic*'s Photophone Centennial exhibit in 1980, recently told me that personal computer technology has moved so fast that in the decade since the Altair the Smithsonian simply hasn't had time to catch up. Nevertheless, I'm convinced the Smithsonian will eventually recognize in a major exhibit the personal computing revolution. After all, the keyboards under the fingers of millions of people, particularly those which are linked to one another by telephone lines, are intellectual tools as powerful as the printing presses on display in the National Museum of American History. It's important to remember that Ed Roberts, Dan Meyer, Chuck Peddle, Steve Wozniak, Steve Leininger, and the other early microcomputer pioneers didn't invent the microprocessor. But their vision for the mind-expanding potential of microprocessors coupled to the human brain through typewriter keyboards sparked within a brief decade an intellectual revolution with consequences more far-reaching than anyone can imagine.

·6·

The Air Force Weapons Laboratory

Flights of Fancy

IT WAS A NEARLY perfect morning for a rocket launch. Hot, muggy, and not enough breeze to wave the swatches of broken grass stuck in the red sand. The slender test rocket waited on its metal launcher like a shiny yellow dart while the launch and recovery crews received their final briefing from the launch officer.

After the recovery team took its position downrange, the launch crew began the final countdown as an observation helicopter, a Bell UH-1 Iroquois, landed several hundred yards away.

"T minus sixty."

The camera operator made a last-minute check of lens setting and focus.

"T minus forty-five."

The launch officer ordered the launch area secured.

"T minus thirty."

The launch officer closed a switch that activated the rocket's siliconnection, a new kind of heat-seeking guidance and control system designed to steer the rocket to a target emitting infrared radiation. A *whrrrrrrrrr* emerged from the rocket as the infrared-seeking mechanism spun into action.

"T minus ten."

Click. The launch officer closed the launch system's arming switch.

"T minus five."

Everyone stared at the rocket as the clatter of the chopper drowned out the humming sound of its guidance mechanism.

"Four . . . three . . . two . . . one . . . fire!"

A surge of current flowed through the ignition squib inserted in the nozzle of the solid-fuel motor, coloring a nichrome coil cherry red and urging its flammable coating to burst into flame. Within milliseconds the blazing ignitor heated the rocket fuel to its flash point, causing it to explode into incandescent gasses that were jetted through the motor's ceramic nozzle.

Rockets that burn liquid fuel, the kind used for most manned space flights, rise slowly and majestically from their pads. Solid-fuel rockets like this one are frisky by comparison. Within a hundred milliseconds the bright yellow missile bolted from its launcher, emitting a steady *whooooosh* rather than the expected roar as it rode a dense trail of puffy white smoke.

Soon the yellow bird was invisible, but that didn't matter to the tracking officer who was busily photographing the trail of smoke as it twisted and screwed its way directly toward the rocket's infrared target: the sun. For this preliminary flight the objective was simply the midday sun, and the smoke trail indicated that the missile was indeed homing on the target. The siliconnected guidance system was working!

Its fuel exhausted, the rocket continued coasting upward, then gracefully arced over until its nose cone pointed at the horizon.

"*Pow!*"

An explosive charge clearly audible on the ground blew off the rocket's instrumented nose section and ejected a tightly wrapped parachute into the slipstream. The nose section rushed downward, the parachute unravelling behind, until the red and white checked canopy inflated and slowed its descent. Meanwhile, the main body of the rocket tumbled end over end as it fell earthward.

By now the recovery team had a good fix on where the freefalling rocket body would impact, and several members were dispatched to recover it. The remainder of the team raced toward a rendezvous with the siliconnected prize slowly descending under the checkered parachute. Suddenly the observation helicopter rose from a cloud of dust, and darted directly toward the launch site, its clatter becoming a deafening roar that roused me from daydreaming. I remembered that the launch crew was five Vietnamese boys, we were on the infield of Saigon's Phu Tho race track, and it was my day off as an Air Force intelligence officer in Vietnam.

That morning I had packed two test rockets, a camera, and some electronic gear into a bright red wooden box strapped onto the rack of a rundown 50 cc motorbike, and had ridden the three miles of Plantation Road that linked my apartment near Tan Son Nhut Airport with the race track. Sometimes quite a crowd of Vietnamese gathered to watch and help retrieve the rockets. One savvy teenager—he might have studied aeronautical engineering had he been born in another place at another time—usually pressed the fire switch so I could photograph the smoke trails left by the rockets.

Suffocating, skin-stinging red sand swirled everywhere. Looking up to wave the chopper away, I found myself staring into the barrel of an M-60 machine gun. A helmeted and goggled gunner peered over the barrel, ready to take the "Viet Cong" rocket crew out of action.

It later developed that the race track had previously been used by the Viet Cong as a launch site for rocket attacks against the runways at Tan Son Nhut. But I didn't know that during these terrifying moments when the green helicopter bobbed about erratically, all the while its black stinger pointed directly toward us on the ground. Desperately I shouted for the boys on the launch team to wave, but they couldn't hear over the sound of the gunship. When I began waving my shirt and taking pictures of the helicopter, the boys got the message and began jumping and waving. The gunship made two close passes before suddenly lifting its tail and pivoting toward the direction from which it had come. Then it rose off toward Tan Son Nhut on a billowing pillar of orange dust.

The Vietnamese boys chattered excitedly and pointed at the departing gunship. They spoke no English, but their shaking bodies and nervous laughter meant fear in any language. Earlier we had watched the helicopter land near the center of the race track after a previous rocket launch. Thinking its crew merely wanted to watch, I decided to continue with the main launch of the morning. As the gunship droned off toward its base, I thought how fortunate we were that the boys were so young. How would the gunner have reacted if the older teenagers who usually watched the launches been there that morning?

Such was a hazard of spare-time experiments with instrumented rockets in a country at war. I launched many more rockets from the race track, but not before notifying the air operations officer at Tan

Son Nhut. Needless to say, no rockets were launched when gunships were close enough to hear. Three weeks later, however, I made the mistake of temporarily changing the launch site from the race track to the roof of my apartment house. There was good reason for this change. Photography of the smoke trails, which was necessary to determine if the guidance system was working, was very difficult since the slightest breeze quickly distorted their appearance. Moreover, the ever-present clouds and haze reduced the contrast between the smoke and the sky, making it difficult to obtain clearly defined photographs. I constructed a new rocket, equipping its nose section with a small, battery-powered lamp. The plan was to launch a series of such rockets at night and photographically record, as time exposures, their flight paths. Deviations in the flight path would be clearly inscribed on the film. Since the launches were to take place at night, the only safe place to conduct them was from my roof. Surely the flights wouldn't attract that much attention. Hadn't the residents of Saigon celebrated Tet, the Lunar New Year, with swarms of blazing fireworks only a few months earlier? Convinced of the wisdom of the plan, I confidently lugged several rockets, the launcher, a tripod, and the camera up the outside stairs, set the equipment up, and waited for nightfall.

I used to spend many hours on the roof watching the lights of Saigon and, especially, the 1,000,000-candle-power parachute flares dropped every night around Tan Son Nhut by orbiting Douglas AC-47D's armed with 7.62mm multibarrel Miniguns or Lockheed AC-130A's equipped with four Miniguns plus four 20mm multibarrel cannons. The power of those weapons, which could fire some 18,000 rounds per minute, was awesome. Sometimes the enemy, or at least something moving on the ground in the no-man's land near the end of the runway, would be spotted, and streams of tracer bullets would fall from the planes in a red and yellow shower, followed by a fearsome *burrrrrrrrrr*.

After it became dark I decided to fly a disposable test rocket, one without a light, to observe the effect of the light wind on its flight path, and to determine where to point the camera for the main launch. I made expendable rockets like this from rolled lengths of aerial reconnaissance film. The flight went well, the flame trail from the rocket's motor being clearly visible. After pointing the camera in the direction taken by the test bird, I prepared the larger experimental rocket for flight. After twisting together the two wires that switched on the lamp, I opened the camera shutter and pressed the firing switch. The rocket whooooooshed away into the darkness atop a fiery trail of brilliant yellow flame and orange sparks. When the motor burned out, the tiny tracking light was clearly visible as a stream of flashing dots caused by the rocket's spinning trajectory.

As I fiddled with the camera and reflected on the success of the launch, the surrounding rooftops were suddenly swept by criss-crossing beams of brilliant light. Searchlights. Fearing the worst, I grabbed everything together, rushed down the stairs, and stashed the gear in a closet. Since I had a good fix on where the rocket appeared to have landed several blocks away, I hopped on my motorbike and put-putted over to nearby Troung-Minh Ky Street. That I was wearing only swimming trunks and shower shoes and that it was past curfew didn't enter my mind until a helmeted soldier in a jeep full of heavily armed military policemen waved me down.

"The base is under rocket attack!" the driver shouted. "Get off the street!" I tried to explain about my rocket experiments, but they roared off to find the enemy. As for the rocket, even though it was wrapped with a map and a reward offer, it never turned up. Though many more test rockets were flown from the race track, the validity of my guidance and control ideas wasn't fully established until two years later when dozens of test rockets were launched, some with Ed Roberts's help, from a field in Albuquerque. Many of those test rockets were launched during marathon all-night sessions, and their flame trails recorded on film. A tiny transistorized light flasher I'd designed, which later evolved into the first product sold by MITS, was carried by each night-launched rocket to assist in its recovery. Though rockets launched during the day were sometimes lost, *none* of the night-launched birds equipped with a tracking light was ever lost.

In Vietnam some of my friends in the Air Force intelligence squadron wondered aloud why a guy with a degree in government would spend days off and evenings stuffing miniature electric motors and transistors soldered to postage-stamp-sized circuit boards in toy rockets made from paper and balsa. None of us suspected that those flyweight guided rockets would become the ticket for an assignment to the Air Force Weapons Laboratory at Kirtland Air Force Base in New Mexico.

Blue Suits

The three major branches of the United States armed forces each operate a system of research and development laboratories. Among these the Air Force Weapons Laboratory (AFWL) is unique, for only there do scientists and engineers wearing Air Force uniforms outnumber the civil service scientists. That's why the Weapons Lab is known as the "blue suit lab."

The Weapons Lab is a coveted assignment for serious Air Force scientists and engineers. Research funds are generally ample, and there are opportunities to work with state-of-the-art apparatus and instrumentation. Moreover, the informal environment more closely resembles that of a university than a military installation. Newly arrived young officers are not arbitrarily assigned to a particular program. Instead, they spend their first several weeks interviewing at each division and their respective branches. This allows the division and branch chiefs to meet every new arrival. And even if the newcomer's specialty or background makes the eventual assignment obvious from the start, the interviewing procedure provides a valuable overall picture of how the lab is organized and functions.

Depending on the eventual assignment, the newcomer's perspective of the lab can be blurred somewhat by security considerations. Though all incoming officers are cleared to be briefed on matters classified as secret in the military's multitiered security classification system, comparatively few have a top-secret security clearance or even what is known as "need to know." The security factor didn't limit my introduction to the Weapons Lab for I was assigned to the Laser Group of the Effects Branch, an organization that worked on the lab's most highly classified projects. Strange as it might seem, many of the research projects carried out by the Laser Group, which later evolved into the biggest and most heavily funded division of the Weapons Lab, were unclassified.

The scholarly atmosphere of the Weapons Lab, and the top-secret nature of some of the work carried out there, sometimes clashed. The results ranged from sheer frustration to major security breaches. Moreover, the Weapons Lab contributed its share to military waste, and a few of the senior officers seemed more bent on empire building than admitting that the results of their own research sometimes justified cancelling an expensive program. Nevertheless, the lab provided a fertile environment for those with initiative and ideas who wished to devise elaborate experiments, manage major contracts, and pursue research on the fringe of technology.

The man in charge of all this when I arrived in March 1968 was Colonel David R. Jones. A career officer and a pilot, Jones was a booster of the then-radical concept that the Air Force, with the help of a handful of civilian scientists, could do its own research. On his many trips to the Pentagon, Air Force installations, contractors, and universities, the enthusiastic Colonel Jones spread the word about the Weapons Lab and its cadre of blue-suited scientists and engineers. He also recruited new officers. How he arranged my Weapons Lab assignment provides insight into his uncanny ability to get things done.

My rocket experiments and the tests of my homemade infrared travel aid at a school for blind boys in Saigon had come to Jones's attention while he was on temporary duty in Vietnam. A meeting was arranged at which he reviewed my laboratory notebooks, rocket guidance mechanisms, and a box of siliconnected electronic circuits I'd built. After asking some pointed technical questions, Jones asked if I would like to be assigned to the Weapons Laboratory. Of course I would. Since reading about Army rocket research in the same 1954 issue of *National Geographic* that introduced me to the transistor, my ambition had been to work at White Sands Missile Range in New Mexico. The Weapons Lab was a few hundred miles north, but that was close enough.

Unfortunately there was a catch to Jones's job offer; my lack of an engineering degree would be a major obstacle. Skeptical about the chances for the new assignment, and excited by an offer to join the staff of General Westmoreland's science advisor, several weeks after the meeting with Jones I applied for and received an extension to the requisite one-year stint in Vietnam. Learning of this, Colonel Jones wrote, "I believe that your motives for wanting to stay over in Vietnam for another year are thoroughly admirable." In fact, Saigon was more like an exotic adventure than a combat zone, and so long as one exercised care when launching homemade rockets the city was comparatively safe. "However," Colonel Jones's letter continued, "I think it is about time you realized you have a much larger role to play, one that can only be satisfied in an R&D environment. Accordingly, I have asked the Air Force Personnel Center to set up procedures whereby you can be rotated back to the United States immediately. . . . What I have in mind for you is an assignment to the Air Force Weapons Laboratory."

Though Jones allowed me to complete the standard one-year tour in Vietnam, he cut through the convoluted layers of military bureaucracy and cancelled the extension. He also managed to bypass the clause in the Weapons Lab charter that required all officers to possess at least a Bachelor of Science degree. When the personnel office notified my division chief that an officer with a Bachelor of Arts degree was not supposed to be assigned to the Weapons Lab, Colonel Jones arranged for a special assignment classification that fooled their computer. Because of tricks like this, his contagious enthusiasm over even the most obscure research projects and his genuine interest in the personal lives of his people, Jones was well respected by those assigned to the Weapons Lab.

Black Boxes

Considering the tendency to make pronounceable words out of the alphabet soup designations the military gives its organizations, programs and projects, the temptation to verbalize as *awful* the acronym formed by the initials of the Air Force Weapons Laboratory, AFWL, was ever present. But rumor had it that Colonel Jones would explode at anyone who called the lab *awful*. Those rumors were unfounded, however, for at my initial meeting in his office he had several times referred to the mission of *awful* and even the *awful* mission.

In fact there really was an awful side to AFWL. Though some people genuinely enjoy designing weapons of destruction, a few of the officers at the Weapons Lab battled their conscience over the issue. In my case, the objective of an important top secret project to which I was assigned was particularly malevolent. This so bothered one new officer that he requested a different assignment. It didn't bother me in the least, for early on I had deduced the scheme was wildly impractical. Eventually I designed an experiment that proved my point. Later, having spent several million dollars on the program, the Weapons Lab reached the same conclusion and cancelled the project.

Fortunately, most of the projects upon which I worked were comparatively harmless and completely unclassified. Many of them involved the design and construction of so-called *black boxes*, electronic circuits housed in a compact enclosure usually painted black. Sometimes black boxes were separated from their builders and paperwork when borrowed by an engineer in another lab. For whatever reason, an assortment of orphaned black boxes was scattered throughout the storage cabinets of the Weapons Lab. Sometimes when we were searching through the cabinets for a spare xenon lamp or a box of o-rings, the black boxes stored there proved quite distracting. The urge to stop work long enough to open them up and explore their contents was identical to the temptation to become sidetracked reading about carniverous plants or the invention of the bicycle when looking up an obscure entry in an encyclopedia.

Homely looking black boxes and electronic circuits not enclosed in cabinets were referred to as *kludges*, especially by everyone other than their builder.

Often we cannibalized old kludges and black boxes for parts to build new kludges and black boxes, a strategy which allowed us to build the instrumentation for unbudgeted projects and experiments. Using new components from the Weapons Lab stockroom would have been prohibitively expensive, a lesson I learned after once selecting a handful of parts to build a monostable multivibrator, a fancy word for a simple digital electronic circuit. The stockroom was like the ultimate electronics store and an electronics buff's dreamland. Its aisles were lined with hundreds of bins containing thousands of silvery transistors, shiny diodes, colorful resistors, coin-like capacitors and a vast array of screws, bolts, connectors, wire, circuit boards, enclosures, paint, decals and all the other hardware necessary to transform a clumsy kludge into an elegant black box. I simply wanted to kludge up the monostable multivibrator, not glorify it with all the cosmetics that were available. Therefore, with circuit diagram and parts list in hand, I strolled through the aisles picking out the required parts: three transistors, half a dozen resistors, a couple of capacitors and a perforated board upon which to mount everything.

A sergeant at the checkout table totalled their value, which would later be subtracted from the budget alloted the project in which they would be used. After the sergeant announced the ten or fifteen dollars' worth of parts I selected were valued at nearly $120, I asked if he had made a mistake. No, he explained, the transistors, which sold for a dollar at any Radio Shack store, cost $30 *each*. They and every other part in the stockroom were high quality, *mil-spec* (military specification) devices designed to take wider extremes of temperature, humidity, vibration and shock than ordinary components. Though I understood the need for mil-spec parts in operational systems like supersonic aircraft and missiles, most of the kludges and black boxes built in the Weapons Lab performed their tasks while perched on immobile lab benches in dust-free, air-conditioned comfort. Every time I soldered a transistor in place I thought how much money could be saved and how many more circuits we could afford to build if the Weapons Lab would simply allow Radio Shack to set up a franchise next to the stockroom.

Sometimes I wonder what became of the black boxes I built at the Weapons Lab. Periodically those responsible for disposing of surplus property would roam through the labs, collecting unclaimed gadgetry and black boxes which would then be donated to a university, sold for a quarter a pound at a government surplus sale or stolen somewhere along the way to their ultimate disposal. I'd like to think my black boxes were too good for this fate and that they're still being used or were cannibalized by an eager beaver lieutenant hustling parts for an unbudgeted kludge needed for an unauthorized experiment.

The AFWL Monkey Experiment

Meet Dr. Roger G. Mark, a bonafide genius with the credentials to prove it. Born in Boston in 1939, Roger has a Ph.D. in electrical engineering from the Massachusetts Institute of Technology and a doctorate from Harvard Medical School. With all that education packed between the ears, and his energetic work habits, Roger

Mark was a real catch for the Air Force Weapons Laboratory, essentially a two-for-one deal. Roger was my immediate supervisor, an unforeseen bonus to my Weapons Lab assignment—working with Roger was like serving an apprenticeship with a master experimentalist. When I first met him he was introduced simply as Captain Mark; I wasn't aware of his reputation inside and outside the Weapons Lab.

On my arrival in March 1968 Roger was completing preparations for an elaborate experiment. Because the military was developing laser distance measuring devices and laser guided "smart" bombs, the Air Force was concerned about its pilots being inadvertently struck by the beam from a friendly laser. Could a partially blinded pilot still fly a high-performance aircraft? Just as monkeys preceded the astronauts into space, animals would be substituted for pilots in Roger's complicated experiment.

My first assignment was to help Roger and a civilian technician finish building a large plywood test chamber. After a few days of sawing, drilling, and hammering a major in our branch told me about Roger's background. In Saigon Colonel Jones had explained that I would be working with exceptional talent at the Weapons Lab, but it was difficult to believe that the hard working, good natured guy with a screwdriver in his pocket and sawdust in his brown hair was as close to being a genius as anyone I'd ever known. Roger Mark was certainly not the aloof, ivory-tower type one might have expected.

In addition to me, Roger had somehow managed to inherit an antique civil-service lab technician named Ollie Westfall. Those concerned about the rapid pace of technology had little to fear from Ollie, for years of work at the Bureau of Standards had instilled in him a deep respect for the principle of inertia in Newton's second law of motion: the rate of change in the velocity of a body is directly proportional to the force exerted on it. Though Ollie seemed to work, talk, and think in slow motion, no one could criticize his skills as a machinist, model maker, glass blower, scrounger of hard-to-find parts, and general-purpose lab technician. So long as time wasn't of the essence, Ollie could single-handedly construct from scratch virtually anything mechanical Roger or I asked him to make. Though Ollie's manner was maddeningly methodical, he wasn't lazy. Shrouded in his soiled lab coat, gray hair sprouting from his head like springs from an old sofa, Ollie could almost always be found muttering under his breath as he melted solder onto the end of a copper tube, blew molten glass into a glistening sphere, or bent over a whining metal lathe.

Roger was cheerfully indulgent of Ollie's slow as molasses work habits even though he had to spend much of his time building hardware and performing other chores normally handled by lab technicians. For reasons that can probably be attributed as much to the state of equilibrium predicted by the laws of thermodynamics as to the compatibility of our personalities, somehow I managed to fit right in and, in spite of my lack of a formal technical education, I felt very comfortable working with Roger and Ollie as we completed work on the instrumentation for the monkey experiment. If Roger needed something that couldn't be found at the Weapons Lab, he went to his desk and designed it, and the three of us then built it.

Since the laser used in the experiment incorporated a potentially lethal high-voltage power supply, and since accidental reflections of its invisible beam could easily blind an onlooker, Roger's monkey experiment eventually came under the scrutiny of a well-intentioned civil servant whose job as a health physicist was to protect the scientists at the Weapons Lab from injuring themselves and one another. Enthusiasm for the project had altered our perceptions, and although in retrospect the health physicist was a nice guy we then considered him a meddlesome safety inspector, a busybody intent on halting progress by placing obstacles in our path. He was horrified to find us happily at work amid fat cables snaking across the floor, and a spiderweb of smaller cables suspended overhead. After a brief discussion, we acquiesced to his demands that the cables be placed under rubber mats or in overhead trays. But we balked at wearing protective goggles every time the laser was charged and ready to be fired rather than for the few seconds just before a test shot. Not that we didn't have a healthy respect for the power within the laser beam. We simply had a healthier respect for the very high voltages associated with the laser. The goggles blocked our peripheral vision, making it difficult to see the high-voltage cables and exposed electrical terminals on the laser. Nevertheless, we put the green rubber goggles on whenever the safety inspector was watching, sometimes posting a guard to warn us when he was stealing his way to the door of our lab.

Though we kept the ever vigilant safety inspector fairly busy, we more than once managed to save him from certain apoplexy. For instance, I never told him about the two technicians in one of our labs who used to light cigarettes with the spectacularly beautiful but highly intense blue-green beam from a powerful argon laser. Once their laser ignited a black cloth draped over a light sensing apparatus I had built. While I put out the fire, they laughed and told me about the time they set fire to the lab coat of an absent-minded scientist who happened to wander through their part of the lab.

The safety inspector's jurisdiction didn't extend to protecting the monkeys from the consequences of Roger's experiment; he was concerned only about protecting us from the monkeys. The animals were trained to respond to visual symbols under the supervision of Dr. Donald N. Farrer, a civilian research psychologist at the Aeromedical Research Laboratory at Holloman Air Force Base a few hundred miles south of Albuquerque. Even though the first batch of rhesus monkeys was trained without resorting to the electrical shocks so often used in animal research, those animals were an ornery lot. Given the chance they would have gladly bitten off our fingers or scratched out our eyes. We had to hold them with special bite-proof gloves when transferring them between their cages and the steel-and-plastic restraint chair they were strapped into for the experiment.

When seated in the test-chamber chair, the monkeys immediately stopped their chattering and went to work. If a triangle was projected on a miniature viewing screen, they were to pull a lever on the right side of the chair; if a square appeared they were to pull a lever on the left side. A clever arrangement of prisms and beam splitters permitted Roger to flash the symbols to either the animal's left or right eye. After each correct response the monkey received a food pellet. The monkeys became adept at this task, and would pull the correct lever and snatch the pellet as fast as we could flash the symbols on the screen.

We gave the monkeys a week to become accustomed to their new handlers and the darkened test chamber. Then we ran the first experiment. While Roger checked the instrumentation and watched the monkey on a television monitor, I made sure the laser was properly aligned and working. After the monkey was performing properly one of its eyes was automatically exposed to a one-megawatt pulse of near-infrared radiation lasting only about ten-billionths of a second. The laser beam was aligned by means of mirrors so that it emerged directly through the center of the projected image at which the monkeys stared. Therefore the laser pulse blasted away a tiny part of the retina in or near the macula, the area of central vision. If the lesion was hemorrhagic, blood would ooze into the ocular media, blocking part of the monkey's field of view.

Our months of careful preparation paid off, for all the hardware in the experiment—laser, cameras, monitoring instruments, optics, and black boxes—worked flawlessly. But the object of the experiment—how the monkey's vision was affected by the destruction of part of its retina, and the intervening blob of blood—was unknown, since the animals refused to perform after being zapped by the laser. For this reason Roger and Dr. Farrer decided on a major revision in the experiment—the positive reinforcement of the food pellet was replaced by the negative reinforcement of a potent electrical shock. This had the desired effect, for in a subsequent run with a new batch of monkeys seated on an electrically conductive pad installed in the restraint chair, now dubbed the hot seat, the animals continued working even after being zapped by the laser. Roger was able to measure the visual acuity of the animals before and after the laser exposure by substituting a new set of symbols.

The Silicon Zoo

Although I understood the need for the monkey experiment, and enjoyed the technical challenges it provided, having spent several years designing travel aids for the blind and testing them with dozens of blind children and adults, I didn't enjoy what we were doing to those monkeys. On the other hand, in Vietnam I had developed a keen respect for bravery of Air Force and Navy pilots. Particularly memorable were the men who at great personal risk flew unarmed and unescorted reconnaissance missions over North

Vietnam and Laos. If the Air Force wanted to explore what might happen if the beam from a laser target designator struck a pilot in the eye, that was fine with me. My conscience was eventually relieved somewhat by the fact that the blood in the ocular media of the zapped monkeys was gradually reabsorbed. Since only a tiny spot on the animal's retina was destroyed by the laser, the monkeys lost only a small part of their central vision.

For most of the first year the monkey experiment was conducted at Holloman. Although the Aeromedical Research Laboratory had excellent primate facilities, and Dr. Farrer was a likable and thoroughly professional scientist, it was difficult to develop an affection for the place. The vacant New Mexico desert, as unlikely a site for a major colony of monkeys and chimpanzees as one could imagine, seemed better suited for the aircraft and missile tests that were conducted there. Inside the lab were electronics shops, operating facilities, testing chambers, and room after room filled with neat rows of cages of screeching monkeys kept immaculate by an industrious staff of custodians.

Primate restraint chairs were scattered about the laboratory, some of them occupied by busy monkeys or chimps who pressed buttons or pulled levers in response to colored lights or sets of symbols. Next to each chair stood an electronics rack containing as many as two dozen transistorized modules that controlled when the stimulus was presented to the animal, tallied correct responses, and activated the solenoid that kicked a food pellet into a feeding cup in response to a correct response. The busy monkeys, working to a staccato tune of clicking relays and clacking solenoids, presented quite a contrast to the bored, green-smocked technicians and animal handlers who slouched sleepily in chairs while waiting for a test to be completed or for something to go wrong with the apparatus.

The Aeromedical Research Lab's claim to fame was the chimpanzees it trained for rocket flights in the early 1960s. By the time Roger and his experiment arrived, the space chimps had long since been replaced by spaced-out monkeys, trained animals who were administered carefully controlled doses of hallucinogenic drugs to determine their effects. The electrical sockets on the heads of some of those high-flying primates were connected to oscilloscopes, chart recorders, and black boxes. I sometimes wondered if the brains of the wired animals who looked like furry little robots were being not monitored but controlled by the siliconnected instrumentation.

Many of the experiments were planned and supervised by talented teams of researchers and graduate students from major universities. After the laser experiment was working well, there were plenty of opportunities to visit with some of these people while we waited for our respective animals to go through their daily practice sessions. They understood my qualms about animal research, but listed the advances in medical science that would not have occurred without animals' help. As for their ongoing projects, none seemed trivial or frivolous.

Laser Reflections

After nearly a year of frequent trips between our headquarters at the Weapons Lab and the monkey experiments at Holloman, we moved everything back to the Weapons Lab. A young airman named Rod Chambers who had been assigned to the project was responsible for the six trained monkeys who were kept inside a cage-equipped trailer parked outside our lab while they become accustomed to their new home. Considering the idiosyncratic nature of some of the humans who worked with Roger, Rod and his troupe of monkeys fit right in. Though moving the experiment to the Weapons Lab allowed us to add important improvements to the apparatus, it also led to disaster when one batch of monkeys baked to death over a hot weekend after a technician forgot to turn on the air conditioner in their trailer. That setback cost the experiment several months, the time required to train a group of replacement animals.

For the first few months the monkey experiment had required a good deal of time. The twelve-hour days I had often worked in Vietnam provided excellent training for working with a man as tireless as Roger Mark. Simply learning to align, operate, calibrate, and maintain the laser became a full-time job. The pump that circulated chilled water over the powerful flash lamp coiled around the purple glass laser rod had to be disassembled and cleaned. The 20,000-volt pulse that triggered the laser's flashlamp had to be measured and its timing accurately coordinated with Roger's apparatus by means of a black box we had built. And the delicate mirrors at either end of the laser had to be painstakingly adjusted until they were precisely parallel with one another in order to provide the most uniform laser beam possible. After all this, dozens of test shots had to be made to measure the power in the laser's beam.

We studied many different kinds of lasers, and a few were even invented by Weapons Lab personnel. Though all these lasers emitted beams of visible light or invisible infrared, some had less power than a penlight while others could cut a gaping hole through an aircraft wing. Some, like the monkey laser, produced only ultra-brief pulses of light. Others emitted light continuously. There were lasers made from semiconductor pellets smaller than grains of sand; there were liquid lasers and gas lasers. There was even an enormous gas-dynamic laser that resembled and sounded like a jet engine, and required its own building and test facility.

I was especially fascinated by the laser used with the monkeys because its operation was in many ways identical to that of the original ruby laser invented by Theodore Maiman at Hughes Aircraft in 1960. Though considerably more powerful, the silicon-nected circuitry that powers such lasers is in principle not unlike that inside a photographer's electronic flash unit. The laser is prepared for firing by closing a switch that allows a bank of brick-sized capacitors to be charged to about 600 volts. As a rough illustration of the power that can be stored in a single such capacitor, consider that when a screwdriver blade is shorted across its two terminals, the energy released creates an explosion as loud as a gunshot, and vaporizes the entire tip of the screwdriver.

When the capacitor bank is fully charged, the laser is ready to be fired, but only after a warning countdown has been given: "Firing! 3 . . . 2 . . . 1!" At the conclusion of the count the fire button is pressed, and a brief 20,000-volt pulse is applied to a fine wire wrapped around the length of the flashlamp. This pulse causes the xenon gas in the flashtube to become ionized, allowing the xenon to conduct electricity. Since the metal electrodes at each end of the flashlamp are connected directly across the capacitor bank, when the xenon becomes conductive the energy stored in the capacitors is suddenly dumped through the flashlamp, producing a brilliant burst of white light. The glass laser rods we used contained a trace of neodymium, the element that gives laser glass its characteristic purplish tint. Some of the light from the flashlamp is absorbed by the neodymium atoms, and after a few millionths of a second is spontaneously reemitted from some of the atoms as photons of invisible infrared radiation. These photons, in turn, cause neodymium atoms that have yet to release their light to do so. Some of these photons emerge through the ends of the rod where they are reflected back inside by one of the mirrors. There, in a sort of chain reaction, the reflected photons cause the release of even more photons. Since one of the mirrors is partially transparent, some of the light bouncing back and forth through the rod soon emerges in a brief but powerful beam of infrared.

One time I cranked the voltage level of our laser so high its glass rod was destroyed by the intense concentration of energy pumped into it by the flashlamp. When I pressed the fire button, there was a loud pop and the end of the laser rod flew across the room and struck a wall. It wasn't unusual to fracture a laser rod in this fashion. In fact, those in our branch who were being transferred were presented a plaque upon which was mounted a fractured synthetic ruby laser rod. Even now when I look at my plaque, I remember the long days required to get the monkey laser back in operation after it blew its top.

After the first six months the monkey experiment became fairly routine and less time-consuming. While awaiting new batches of animals to be trained we pursued other projects and monitored the various contracts for which we were responsible. During one of these lulls I attended a laser safety conference in another state and was invited along with other attendees to observe an experimental laser surgical procedure at a nearby hospital. As we stood behind a transparent, green safety shield in the futuristic operating laboratory, the goggled surgeon pointed a tapered quartz rod which dangled from an overhead ruby laser at a patch of skin cancer on the shoulder of an elderly patient. The familiar countdown followed. The brilliant flash from the laser's xenon lamps made the room look momentarily like a photograph negative. A curl of white smoke formed a question mark over the patient and the stench of burnt flesh polluted the room. "Damn!" the surgeon exclaimed, "I missed. Let's try again." This rather ludicrous event, which caused a great deal of murmuring in the crowd of onlookers, reinforced my disdain for laser safety goggles.

Between sessions with the monkeys we also designed and conducted experiments, among the most interesting being a complex outdoor test Roger designed to make some important measurements for a top-secret laser target designator project. It required a fair number of late-night sessions in the foothills east of Albuquerque near Manzano Air Force Base, the super-secret installation encircled by multilayered fences, guard dogs, and TV cameras for the sole purpose (it is rumored) of safeguarding nuclear bombs stored in tunnels dug into Manzanita Mountain. Though the hours were long, the experiment was fascinating, particularly when we switched on a helium-neon gas laser that projected a brilliant, shimmering red beam across thousands of feet of desert mesa. The safety inspector back at the lab would have been frantic if he'd seen the hundreds of feet of cable that connected our various instruments and black boxes. The test van looked like the inside of a spaghetti factory.

Roger remained at the Weapons Lab for about sixteen months after my arrival before he left in July 1968 to return to Boston and the electrical engineering faculty of M.I.T. I learned more about real science and engineering during my brief association with Dr. Roger Mark than in all my previous years of independent experimentation. He patiently explained how to use state-of-the-art siliconnected test and measurement equipment. He taught me how to manage my first contract, the procurement of a high-powered semiconductor laser system. Finally, thanks to his careful preparation, after Roger's departure I was able to supervise additional runs of his complicated monkey experiment and even design experiments of my own.

·7·

Confessions of a High-Tech Spy

Wishful Thinking

FEBRUARY 4, 1976. Though it was a dark, moonless night, the building 208 feet away was clearly outlined in eerie hues of yellowish-green in the eyepiece of the infrared viewing scope. The invisible infrared beam projected from a miniature semiconductor laser was made visible through the scope as a bright green spot on the side of the structure. Between nervous glances over my shoulder to see if anyone was watching, I carefully adjusted the tripod on which the laser was mounted until the invisible beam struck a window. I then moved a light-sensitive siliconnected receiver perched on a second tripod until it was centered in the beam reflected from the window. After switching on the power, and making a few slight adjustments in the position of the receiver, every word of the serious discussion between two men in the room emerged perfectly audible from the receiver's speaker. The sound waves from their voices were causing minute vibrations in the glass pane, thereby impressing on the reflected laser beam their conversation. I pressed a button on a recorder and began taping the purloined discussion, occasionally tweaking the receiver's controls when the breeze buffeted the window and caused vibrations of the pane that masked some of the transmission with bumps, thumps, and undulating roars.

What red-blooded American male wouldn't accept his country's call to become a spy? As a child I spent hours devising secret codes and concocting invisible inks. Being an Air Force intelligence officer was the closest I came to being a real spy. But James Bond never spent six or seven nights a week supervising a team of glassy-eyed photo-interpreters who stared at countless frames on endless rolls of aerial reconnaissance film. While I was a student at Texas A&M University, a C.I.A. representative visiting the campus on a recruiting tour learned of my miniature radios, lightwave communicators, and other gadgets, and invited me to apply for a position with the agency—after completing my four-year Air Force obligation. A year later a senior intelligence officer at the Armed Force's Air Intelligence Training Center at Lowry Air Force Base near Denver learned about my gadgets, and suggested I apply for a position with what was called the Air Force's Human Source Intelligence Program—after completing a year in Vietnam. After being in Vietnam a few months, I received a letter from a Pentagon intelligence officer who urgently asked that I consider applying for a position "within the collection area." He wrote, "There are a number of positions within the intelligence community that often go begging for people with both interests, i.e. intelligence and a scientific discipline." I replied to the letter, even filling out the enclosed biographical form, but the assignment to the Weapons Lab arranged by Colonel Jones sidetracked my ambition to become a professional spy.

Actually, I didn't want to be a spy in the traditional sense; I merely wanted to design their electronic gadgetry. My hero wasn't James Bond; it was Q, the master designer who dreamed up all those incredible gizmos that made James Bond's feats possible. My eavesdropping on that cold February night was the culmination of five months of circuit design, experimentation, and cryptic telephone conversations and correspondence with a mysterious contact man with a British accent who insisted that the laser bugging equipment I'd designed be kept totally secret. Though the conversation in the room was being recorded without the knowledge of the participants, no law was broken for the building was the remodeled storage shed that served as my office and electronics shop, and the two men were participants on a local talk show being received by a radio on my desk. Successfully intercepting and recording their conversation demonstrated that the laser bugging apparatus worked. At 9:30 the next morning I called the anonymous contact man to report the night's successful results. He instructed me to fly to Florida, with the equipment, on Monday,

February 9, 1976, and to take a taxi to the Howard Johnson's in West Palm Beach where I was to rent a room. A few days later a round-trip airline ticket to West Palm Beach arrived in the mail. Curious about how long the trip would take, I glanced at the ticket. The space for the return flight was marked "Open."

An hour after I checked into the motel there was a knock at the door. Two men wearing suits and ties walked in and introduced themselves. One, Bernard D. A. Scott, was the face behind the familiar voice. His partner was introduced as Tony Brenna. After half an hour inspecting the laser apparatus they drove me to a pair of spacious, single-story buildings hidden from a nearby avenue by a beautifully manicured botannical garden. This, they explained, would be the site of a demonstration of the laser bugging gear before I was flown to the Bahamas for the actual mission. As we drove down a side street looking over the facilities and selecting a few possible sites for the demonstration, one of them pointed toward a pale Rolls Royce slipping out a back entrance, and said, "That's our boss." Later we drove to a nearby restaurant where they asked lots of questions about my background. The one topic we didn't discuss was the laser gear back at the motel. They repeatedly emphasized the necessity of not discussing with anyone the purpose of the equipment.

I wish I could report that Messrs. Scott and Brenna were secret agents of the C.I.A., Secret Service, or F.B.I. Actually Bernard Scott and Tony Brenna were journalists. I also wish I could report that they were preparing for *The New York Times, Washington Post,* or *The Wall Street Journal* a breaking story about state-of-the-art surveillance methods. Actually Scott was an associate editor and Brenna was a reporter for the largest-selling tabloid in the United States, the one whose banner headlines each week titillate millions of shoppers standing in supermarket checkout lines. Scott and Brenna worked for the *National Enquirer.* The pair of modern buildings in the botannical garden was the headquarters of the *National Enquirer* in Lantana, Florida. The man in the Rolls Royce was Generoso Pope, the *Enquirer's* publisher. And their urgent, top-secret objective and the reason for my presence was a plan to surreptitiously intercept the conversations of Howard Hughes. Hughes was living somewhere on the top floor of the Xanadu

Princess Hotel on Grand Bahama Island. If the laser eavesdropping apparatus worked to their satisfaction, they fully intended to fly me and the laser gear to the Bahamas that very week.

Silicon Tools for Inquiring Minds

My short-lived career as a high-tech spy was sparked by a telephone conversation with Bernard Scott on August 21, 1975. The *National Enquirer* was planning a major feature about lasers, and one of the technical publishers he consulted suggested me as a possible author for the piece. During that initial discussion with Scott, he casually asked if I knew anything about recent press reports concerning the development of a method of intercepting conversations in closed rooms by means of a laser beam reflected from a window. When I told him it would be possible to assemble an apparatus for that purpose from supplies in my shop, Scott seemed flabbergasted and asked me to elaborate. The laser article suddenly took a back seat as he then revealed the *National Enquirer*'s interest in investigating the private life of Howard Hughes in an effort to uncover what can be described only as suspicious business practices. Would I participate in their investigation by contributing the necessary technical know-how? After I reminded Scott about the proposed laser feature, he closed the conversation by asking me to submit a proposal for the piece. He also asked, with much more emphasis, that I keep our discussion secret and that I prepare a proposal on the assembly of a laser bugging device. Within a day I had prepared a 3,000-word proposal for the laser feature, and 600 words on "Listening in on a Personality."

The latter proposal began: "It has been proposed that the conversations of a famous personality be intercepted for public release. Conventional interception methods are out since this personality is almost totally inaccessible. It is proposed that a laser be used to intercept conversations by bouncing the beam from a window. If a conversation is taking place near the window, subtle vibrations in the air will be transmitted to the glass pane and subsequently superimposed on the laser beam striking the window. The reflected laser beam, now amplitude modulated with the conversation, is detected and demodulated and the conversation tape recorded." I then listed three phases of the project:

"1. Feasibility Study—An experimental apparatus will be designed and assembled. The apparatus will be tested against a 'typical' window and a tape recording produced of any sounds present. . . . The tape will be forwarded to the *National Enquirer* for evaluation.

"2. Demonstration Experiment—The experimental apparatus will be demonstrated before representatives of the *National Enquirer*. If the demonstration is approved, a final apparatus will be assembled for the actual intercept.

"3. Actual Experiment—The final apparatus will be taken to an on-site location and used in an attempt to intercept conversations."

The proposal continued with additional information and a list of questions regarding the location and nature of the target windows for both the demonstration and the actual mission. Apparently it was received with considerably more interest than the proposal for the laser feature. In a telephone conversation on September 5 Scott discussed at some length the second phase of the project, that the apparatus be demonstrated against a window at the offices of the *National Enquirer*. He particularly wanted to impress his publisher with the feasibility of the concept by making his office window the subject of the demonstration. He described in great detail the furnishing and dimensions of the office, the size and locations of its two windows, and the location of Pope's desk. According to my notes, Scott said the office measured 20 by 25 feet, had wood-paneled walls, and was carpeted. The head of a person seated at the desk in one corner of the room would be approximately 3 to 4 feet from each of two corner windows, the upper portions of which measured 3 feet square and were 8 feet above the ground outside. During the conversation Scott reminded me several times about the "top secret" nature of the project and the urgent need for the *National Enquirer* to have "this capability" in order to back up some of its stories. As for the laser feature, my proposal had been approved but first I was to build the laser bugging apparatus.

During a discussion four days later, I told Scott about successful results of some preliminary night tests in which the sound from a radio in my office was intercepted more than 100 feet away by detecting with a simple receiving system the pencil-thin, window-reflected red beam from a Hughes Aircraft Company Model 3193H helium-neon gas laser. I also told him that similar results had been obtained in broad daylight by detecting sunlight reflected from the same window. He seemed elated, and explained how "the device," as he called it, should be reliable and easy to use so the inquiring Enquirers could make use of it "when it's needed." At this point reality hit home: Scott was serious about bugging Howard Hughes and other notables.

On September 15, in a letter accompanying a test tape, I informed Scott that I would not pursue the project if it necessitated "involvement with illegal operations." I reminded him of my earlier suggestion that we use the laser apparatus in an *Enquirer*-sponsored demonstration of the vulnerability of sensitive government offices to laser eavesdropping by foreign governments. Scott responded positively, even suggesting that his newspaper had contacts who knew Senator Barry Goldwater, and that perhaps we could request Goldwater's permission to surreptitiously bug his offices in the Senate Office Building.

Meanwhile, I continued working on and testing the laser eavesdropping system. Intrigued by the possibility that reflected sunlight might replace the laser, in a vacant lot across the street from my office I set up a cardboard box fitted with a glass "window" and equipped with a radio that served as a sound source. This arrangement proved moderately successful, but it very nearly ended my budding career as a high-tech spy. Staring all afternoon at the glaring sunlight reflected from the glass window while making receiver adjustments produced a distinct afterimage in both my eyes even though I'd worn sunglasses. The effect was identical to that produced by a flashbulb in one's eyes, except the afterimages didn't fade away after a few minutes or even a few hours. Indeed, the next day as I stared at a blank piece of paper on my desk, I saw a distinct black hole where one didn't exist. Hurriedly I placed a card first over one eye and then over the other while looking at an X marked on the paper. Both times the X was hidden from view behind a solid black disk. Though my peripheral vision was unaffected, the central vision of each eye was severely impaired by a scotoma or blind spot. I thought I had done to myself what Roger Mark and I had earlier done to those rhesus monkeys at the Weapons Lab. The *National Enquirer* project was the last thing on my mind.

After an anxious week, during which an examination by an opthalmologist revealed no obvious signs of retinal damage in either eye, the scotomas began fading. Eventually, both blind spots disappeared and my central vision was restored. Alas, so was my interest in the unfinished *Enquirer* project. Without telling Scott about the accident, I resumed our exchange of cryptic telephone conversations and continued sending progress reports. In early November I realized that Scott had yet to send a single letter in response to my four, much less the $150 check he had promised for the proposal about the laser feature. Therefore, on November 11 I wrote to advise him I would no longer be able to continue the project ". . . until I have some word about the use of the apparatus and my fee for developing it." Piqued about the let's-put-it-on-the-back-burner status of the laser feature, I concluded, "I believe the laser article and the interception apparatus should be treated as two entirely separate projects, and I would prefer not to have the former conditional upon success of the latter. So where do we stand?" Scott received the letter the next day, and called to allay my concerns. He reaffirmed the *Enquirer*'s continued interest in the laser feature but stressed the need first to complete the laser eavesdropping project, which we then discussed in detail.

I summarized the project: The red helium-neon laser worked fine, but the beam was so brilliant that it would compromise the covert nature of the project if used at night. It would therefore be necessary to assemble an illuminator using a state-of-the-art infrared laser diode. I had three such lasers on hand, each of which emitted an invisible beam having about the same intensity as that of the gas laser. I also suggested exploring an alternative laser eavesdropping method with which I'd toyed. In the first method sound waves striking a window cause the pane to become slightly convex and concave, thereby changing the intensity of the light reflected to a distant detector. The sound waves, in other words, modulate the intensity or amplitude of the light beam. The new method would exploit the pure nature of laser light, the coherent or lockstep organization of its wavelengths. The laser beam would be transmitted through a half-silvered mirror whose surface is parallel to the target window. If the laser is placed so its beam strikes the window at a

90° angle, the reflected beam will return directly to the laser along the same path it took on its way to the window.

This forms what physicists call a Fabry-Perot interferometer, a simple arrangement of two parallel mirrors that transforms a coherent light beam reflected between them into concentric rings of light surrounding a central light or dark disk. The central disk changes from light to dark if one of the mirrors (the window in the eavesdropping application) moves as little as a single wavelength of light, less than one-tenth the diameter of a human hair. The concentric rings can be reflected toward the receiver by inserting a second half-silvered mirror called a beam splitter in front of the laser. The beam splitter and receiver are then manipulated until the central disk falls directly on the receiver's detector. This scheme provides much more sensitivity than the amplitude modulated method, which merely detects gross changes in the intensity of the reflected light.

Though he didn't seem to grasp all the principles involved, Scott asked how much additional equipment I would need to complete the coherent-detection apparatus, and sent a letter obligating the *Enquirer* to pay up to $350 for parts. Though Scott's letter stated "We have also agreed to pay you on a weekly rate basis for the time you will spend trying to perfect this equipment . . . ," he failed to mention the agreed-on fee, $500 per week, in my estimation a bargain rate for a high-tech spy at a time when television's ace private investigator, James Rockford, made $200 a day plus expenses.

I ordered the optical supplies from the Oriel Corporation in December, and by January 8, 1976, the optical apparatus was assembled and ready for testing. I then began designing and installing in a blue metal box an improved light receiver that incorporated a very high degree of amplification plus electronic circuitry to remove much of the noisy, voice-masking interference superimposed on the beam of the gas laser. The new receiver, which included sensitivity and volume controls, incorporated a built-in, adjustable lens for its light-sensitive detector, and a phone jack for connecting several kinds of additional detectors.

The blue-box receiver was ready by the end of January. It worked well in successful tests with the red laser of both the amplitude-modulation and coherent-detection methods. In these tests the laser and receiver were 208 feet away from my office. Though the coherent method proved phenomenally sensitive, the requirement that the distant window and the half-silvered mirror be parallel made it excruciatingly difficult to align. On February 3 I called Scott to inform him about the success of the experiments, and he responded that he wanted me and the equipment in Florida the next week. I immediately began assembling a battery-powered, miniature infrared laser illuminator. It was ready that afternoon, and with the help of an infrared image converter the successful demonstration I described earlier was accomplished late the following night. I sent a detailed report to Scott, asking him to have ready a pair of sturdy tripods and a grounded extension cord to power the Hughes gas laser, the only part of the system that wasn't battery-powered.

The Secret Mission

The morning after the initial rendezvous with Bernard Scott and Tony Brenna at the Howard Johnson's in West Palm Beach on February 9, I was taken to *National Enquirer* headquarters. In view of the paper's controversial, sometimes sleazy image, I was surprised to find that the facilities inside the *Enquirer*'s editorial building were as neat and organized as the gardens outside. The editors were particularly proud of a computerized file that stored information about every story published in the *Enquirer*. Tony Brenna explained how new story ideas were matched against topics in the file and usually rejected if the subject had been covered. (Of course stories about UFO's, famous personalities, cancer cures, and other high-interest items were exceptions to this rule.) They also explained that their poor image was undeserved. In their opinion they exercised more care in verifying facts and quotations than did most major newspapers. Indeed, Scott and Brenna reminded me, that's precisely why they were so interested in the laser eavesdropping equipment. They planned to use it to verify quotes, not invade privacy.

Before setting up the laser gear, I spent a fast hour or so visiting with Bernard Scott. I wanted to pursue the idea of securing permission to use the laser eavesdropping system to stage a demonstration of the vulnerability of an important government office in Washington, but he had Howard Hughes on his mind. Showing me several photographs of the 13-story Xanadu Princess Hotel, he pointed to Hughes's sleeping quarters on the right side of the top floor, the parapet that protected the top floor from the one below, and the pyramidlike structure on the roof that prevented helicopters from landing.

Scott mentioned the major news value of an authentic photograph of Howard Hughes. When I asked how much the *Enquirer* would pay for such a photo, he responded $100,000 for a full-face picture, but it was highly unlikely anyone would ever be able to get one. I jokingly proposed that the *Enquirer* station a quiet, radio-controlled, camera-equipped miniature blimp near the hotel's top floor. Scott perked up, and asked if I knew of anyone with such a blimp. I had read about radio-controlled blimps years before in *American Modeler*, so I suggested he contact the magazine's editor. Much to my surprise, Scott called an editorial assistant to his desk, and instructed him to call *American Modeler*. Within fifteen minutes they had located a radio-controlled blimp and had spoken to its owner on the telephone.

Later that morning, using some tripods and a power cord borrowed from the photography division, I set up the laser apparatus on the putting green–like lawn and performed tests against a window in a conference room in which we had placed a radio. Aside from Scott, Brenna, Pope, and another man with a British accent who was introduced as the editorial director, no one else on the staff knew who I was or why I was there. My strange apparatus attracted considerable attention, particularly at lunch when a fair-sized crowd gathered to watch. A quick test of the system was to pass my hand through the laser beam several times while listening for clicks from the receiver. One time when I did this a woman watching nearby assumed I was waving at her. She waved back, then walked over for a closer look at the apparatus. While the woman probed me for information about the system, I spotted a man wearing a sports coat peering at us from under a tree about fifty feet away. Earlier I had noticed him lurking behind a nearby hedge, and now he was taking photographs of us with a 35-millimeter camera equipped with a telephoto lens.

More curious than concerned, I looked right at him, and he slowly wandered over, smiling and pausing to take additional photographs. He introduced himself as the one-man show behind the *National Enquirer*'s in-house newspaper. He was the paper's editor, writer, and photographer, and he wanted to scoop the *Enquirer* with a piece about the mysterious experiment that had the place buzzing. He had been waiting for a chance like this, and if only I'd give him a few clues he'd finally have his scoop. Every *Enquirer* employee had seen me at work, he persisted, and he would sure like to satisfy their curiosity about the top-secret project going on outside their office windows.

While I would have liked to help him get his scoop, periodic glances from a tall, distinguished-looking man served as a pointed reminder of Scott's penchant for secrecy. The man was Generoso Pope, publisher of the *National Enquirer*. I could see him clearly through a window whenever he stood up. During the two days of tests, I often saw him staring my way, but he never once approached for a closer look at the apparatus, much less introduced himself or uttered a single word that I could hear.

The eavesdropping system worked well when the small window back at my office served as the target. But the *Enquirer* demonstration fizzled. The window panes in their buildings were extra-thick hurricane-proof glass, which refused to vibrate when struck by a puny barrage of soundwaves. I had anticipated such a problem, and had brought along a small aluminum tube to which was cemented a very thin, ultraflexible mirror. A conventional radio-transmitting bug is referred to as an active device since it emits electromagnetic waves. The thin-mirror device is a passive bug since it emits nothing. When the device was secreted in the corner of a window with tape or a bit of clay, any nearby sound could be easily intercepted by illuminating the mirror with either the bright red beam from the gas laser or the invisible beam from the infrared laser. In a demonstration for Scott and Brenna, I concealed the mirror assembly in the *Enquirer*'s conference room, and asked them to search the room for bugs. While they searched, unsuccessfully, for the mirror, I recorded every word, cough, and sound they made. Though they were impressed, Scott said the system had to work against windows.

Since the receiver worked somewhat better at night, we retested the system after supper. The equipment again failed to work when the hurricane-proof windows served as the target. However, excellent results were obtained over a distance of 112 feet with the passive thin-mirror bug we planted in an office, and some success was had by pointing the laser at the glass pane along the top edge of a cubicle.

The next morning we again monitored the conference room with both the visible red beam from the gas laser and the invisible infrared beam from the battery-powered semiconductor laser. I also spent a good deal of time with Brenna and Scott. They were particularly interested in ways to expose Soviet intelligence-gathering operations. Scott had learned that Soviet agents had planted sophisticated monitoring devices near key military installations in the United States. These devices transmitted signals when Soviet spy satellites passed overhead. Was I interested in designing radio direction-finding equipment to locate one of these devices? We also discussed efforts by the Soviet Union to bug the United States embassy in Moscow with microwave beams transmitted from nearby buildings. I suggested the *Enquirer* identify and publish the names of Soviet spies in the United States. The inspiration for this was the recent publication in several European newspapers of the names of alleged C.I.A. agents.

And of course we talked about Howard Hughes. The *Enquirer* man stationed at the Xanadu Princess had informed Scott about suspicious activities indicating that the nomadic recluse might be planning another move. Before the hurricane-proof windows foiled the eavesdropping demonstration, Scott had asked seriously if I was prepared to fly to the Bahamas that very week with the equipment. I was fascinated by the spell Hughes had unwittingly cast over them. They apparently hoped to use the eavesdropping system to confirm rumors about Hughes's poor health and some unspecified shady business dealings.

During a final round of discussions following still more tests of the system, Scott received an urgent call from his man on Grand Bahama Island. Hughes had just flown off the island. Even though their primary objective had once again eluded them, the *Enquirer* people were still interested in my apparatus. Scott insisted that the *Enquirer* needed the capability to back up quotations in their controversial stories. He also reaffirmed his interest in staging a demonstration of the apparatus in Washington, D.C., if he could secure his publisher's permission. He would follow up with me later. I departed West Palm Beach the next day with my system.

Reflections and Feedback

Though I would never have agreed to fly to the Bahamas with the laser eavesdropping equipment, I remained concerned that conversations in government offices could be intercepted by means of an apparatus similar to the one I assembled. Shortly after the demonstration at the *Enquirer*, the bombardment of the U.S. embassy in Moscow received extensive press coverage. Though many articles speculated that the Soviets were attempting to impair the health of our diplomats, I suspected that they were probing the structure for metal surfaces that might move in response to sound waves so that they might be able to monitor conversations inside.

On February 18, 1976, Bernard Scott called to explore this topic. He asked me to send him a proposal for an optical and electronic search of the area around the United Nations building in New York City, thinking it a likely site for extensive high-tech eavesdropping. I prepared the proposal the same day, suggesting in it the use of various kinds of infrared sensors to detect laser beams, plus a special receiver to check for microwave emissions. Nothing came of the proposal. Nor did the *Enquirer* follow up on the laser feature that initiated my first conversation with Bernard Scott.

In late March, however, Scott called to report that Howard Hughes had been traced to the Princess Hotel in Acapulco. How soon could I locate a multi-band shortwave scanning receiver, and fly to Mexico to attempt to monitor radio transmissions from the hotel? I refused. On April 5, about a week after Scott's call, Hughes became seriously ill and was flown by private jet from Acapulco to Houston. He died en route over south Texas.

The *National Enquirer* hasn't called since Hughes's death. To my knowledge, the only outcome of my visit to the paper was an Associated Press item dated March 15, 1976, reporting that the *Enquirer* had published a list of 23 Soviet espionage agents operating openly in the United States. Several of the purported agents were said to be diplomats who frequented the White House, Congress, the Pentagon, and other federal agencies. From time to time popular science and trade magazines speculate about laser interception of conversations in closed rooms. Under very special conditions, and with a good deal of patience, it can be done. But, as the next chapter reveals, there are far simpler ways to obtain classified information.

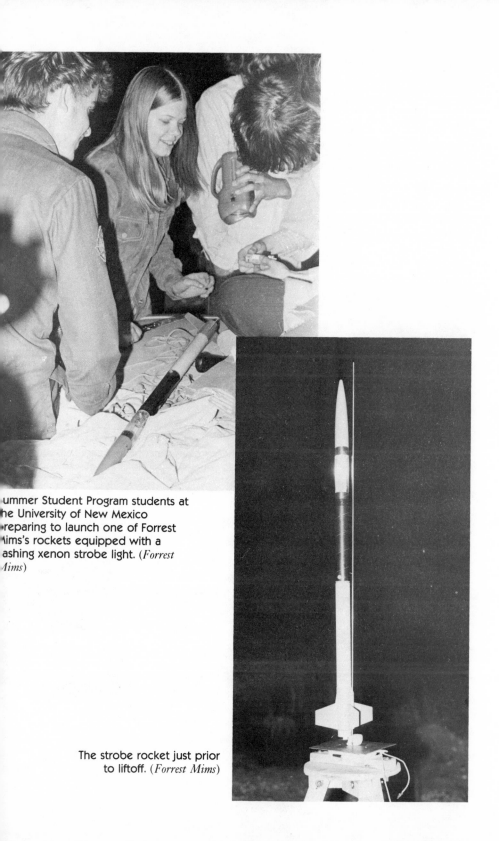

ummer Student Program students at
he University of New Mexico
reparing to launch one of Forrest
Mims's rockets equipped with a
ashing xenon strobe light. (*Forrest Mims*)

The strobe rocket just prior
to liftoff. (*Forrest Mims*)

H. Edward Roberts (left) and Dr. Roger G. Mark
helping Mims launch his rockets in 1969 shortly
before MITS was formed. (*Forrest Mims*)

The Silicon Garage at Ed Roberts's former residence in Albuquerque.
(*Richard Pipes*)

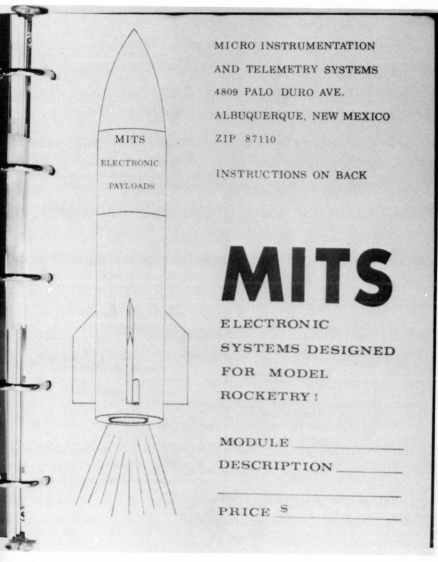

MICRO INSTRUMENTATION
AND TELEMETRY SYSTEMS
4809 PALO DURO AVE.
ALBUQUERQUE, NEW MEXICO
ZIP 87110

INSTRUCTIONS ON BACK

MITS

ELECTRONIC
SYSTEMS DESIGNED
FOR MODEL
ROCKETRY!

MODULE _____
DESCRIPTION _____
_____
PRICE $ _____

MITS
ELECTRONIC
PAYLOADS

Instruction brochure for MITS model rocket instruments.
(*Forrest Mims*)

Ed Roberts at work at MITS in
early 1974. (*Forrest Mims*)

The cover of the now-historic
January 1975 issue of
Popular Electronics.

Dr. Uta Merzbach of the
Smithsonian Institution
reviewing Forrest Mims's
collection of MITS
memorabilia. (*Minnie Mims*)

Forrest Mims preparing to launch a radio-controlled rocket
at the Saigon race track in 1967.
(*United States Air Force photo*)

A Vietnamese returning the
guidance section of one of
Mims's test rockets.
(*Forrest Mims*)

Some of the boys who helped Mims recover rockets launched in Saigon. (*Forrest Mims*)

Launch of the test rocket from Mims's roof. Time exposure shows exhaust from rocket motor and series of dots from light aboard rocket. (*Forrest Mims*)

In the background is one of the world's largest lasers, a gas dynamic laser operated by the Air Force Weapons Laboratory. In the foreground, Forrest Mims holds a compact MITS semiconductor laser (black box) and a helium-neon laser. (*Forrest Mims*)

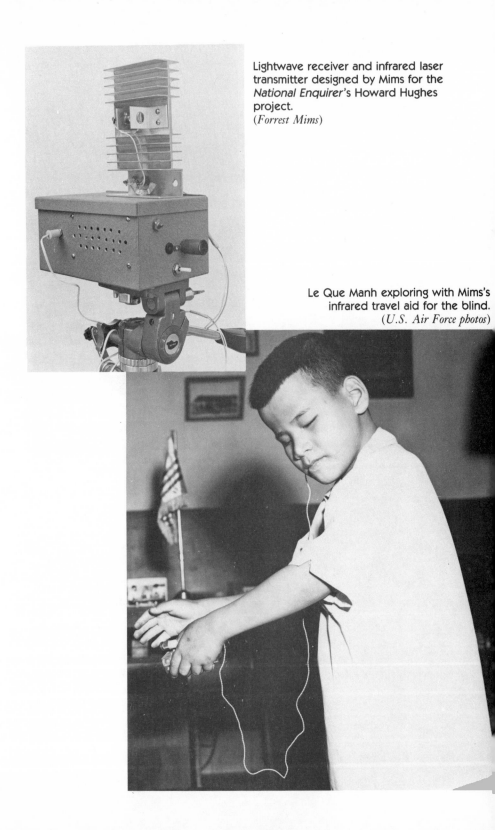

Lightwave receiver and infrared laser transmitter designed by Mims for the *National Enquirer*'s Howard Hughes project.
(*Forrest Mims*)

Le Que Manh exploring with Mims's infrared travel aid for the blind.
(*U.S. Air Force photos*)

Representatives from Bell Labs, the *National Geographic* and the Smithsonian Institution with Mims at the Washington, D.C., site of the first transmission of voice over a beam of light 100 years before. (*Photo by Otis Imboden*, National Geographic)

Jim Lowell of Bell Labs examines Alexander Graham Bell's original photophone. (*Bell Labs photo*)

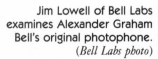

Western Electric attorney Patrick
Leach removing box of documents
from Mims's attic. (*Forrest Mims*)

William F. Keefauver, Vice
President and General Counsel
of Bell Labs. (*Bell Labs photo*)

Les Solomon (left), former technical editor of *Popular Electronics,* and Mims in Solomon's New York office shortly before Solomon retired. (*Eric Mims*)

These pages are from one of Mims's best-selling hand-lettered Radio Shack books.
(*Forrest Mims*)

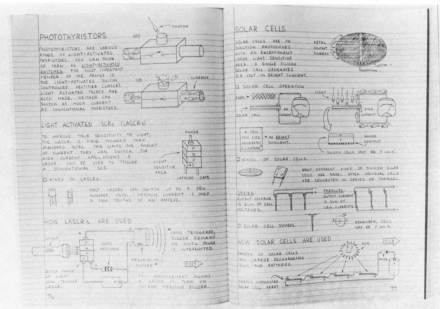

Arthur P. Salsberg, former editor of
Popular Electronics and now editor
of *Modern Electronics.*

David S. Gunzel, director of
technical publications for Radio
Shack, at Mims's office in Texas.
(*Forrest Mims*)

Mims and Eniac at the Smithsonian Institution. (*Eric Mims*)

·8·

High-Tech Security

Hot Air and Chromatic Nylon

THE SOLID-STATE ERA has made many of us preoccupied with secrecy. This concern extends from the solitary inventor to national governments. The problem is that the maintenance of security is a never-ending battle against the ultimate high-tech computer, the gelatinous mass of ten billion neurons inside the skulls of thieves, employees, industrial spies, foreign agents, and teenage computer hobbyists. For some of these people acquiring forbidden fruit is a profession while for others it's a form of intellectual recreation. In either case the task is often simplified by the carelessness of those entrusted to safeguard today's high-tech secrets.

The need to protect high-tech secrets has given rise to an arsenal of innovative countermeasures and a host of companies that offer security-related products and services. Yet breaches of high-tech security continue to occur at all levels of industry and government. Before addressing this problem, it's important to put to rest any notion that siliconnected countermeasures will eliminate theft or penetration of secured areas. There is a prime example to support this conclusion: the bizarre aerial invasion of one of our most secure and highly classified laser weaponry test ranges and a major nuclear-weapons storage facility by a seventeen-nation armada of primitive airships descended from technology pioneered two centuries ago.

Flying in a basket suspended from a hot-air balloon is an entrancing experience. The busy preflight preparations are a contrast to the tranquility of the flight itself. First the basket is laid on its side upwind from where the 500-pound canopy of polyurethane-coated, calendered nylon will be spread. People hustle about as the huge, brightly colored sack is stretched over the ground. A droning,

gasoline engine–powered fan forces air into the limp bag and transforms it into a pulsating tent the size of a small house. The helmeted pilot bravely ignites the twin propane burners and points the
roaring tongues of orange and yellow flame into the open throat of
the envelope. For a few tempestuous minutes the balloon bulges
and quivers, then suddenly it lurches into the air above the basket,
jerking it upright. Some of the ground crew members hold onto the
basket while the pilot tops off the seventy-foot-high balloon with
occasional blasts from the burners and checks the cluster of instruments that reveal canopy temperature, ambient temperature, and
altitude. Finally, the passengers, at most two or three, climb into
the basket and prepare for the flight.

After a long blast from the burners the basket rises into the air. It
ascends firmly and steadily and doesn't accelerate or lurch. Indeed,
there is no feeling of motion; the ground appears to slip away while
the basket remains where it always was. There is no breeze, for
now the ballon follows the currents of the atmosphere. The seren-
ity of balloon flight becomes forever imprinted in that special part
of one's consciousness reserved for ultimate experiences.

Because of its agreeable climatic conditions, Albuquerque is a
major center of hot-air ballooning. The First World Hot Air Balloon Championships were held there in February 1973. That historic competition, which attracted 60 percent of the world's hot-air
balloonists, was headquartered at the New Mexico State Fairgrounds only a block from where MITS was then manufacturing
digital calculators. The main event each morning was a spectacular
mass ascension of more than one hundred colorful balloons. For
several days, however, the prevailing northerly breeze created a
string of major security breaches by blowing the balloons over
highly classified military installations directly downwind from the
fairgrounds.

For the security police at Kirtland and Manzano Air Force Bases,
the championships became The Great Balloon Invasion of 1973.
My bird's eye view of the Keystone Kops spectacle that accompanied the first wave of the balloon invasion was provided by Bob
Kinsinger, a businessman who had transported his multi-colored
Piccard balloon, "Aerotiva," from Michigan. After lifting off from
the race track, we joined a swarm of colorful bubbles lazily floating

over Albuquerque. Soon we were drifting toward Manzano Air Force Base, a super-secret installation where nuclear weapons are supposedly stored in tunnels carved in a small mountain. The entire mountain is surrounded by multiple layers of barbed wire, monitored by television cameras, and patrolled by guard dogs and heavily armed security patrols. To avoid the mountain, the balloons began descending on the restricted zones of Kirtland Air Force Base. Security police vehicles, sirens sounding and lights flashing, scurried across the mesas below chasing after descending balloons. After we nearly collided with a high-voltage power line when Aerotiva ran out of fuel, Bob bounced the basket off the ground a time or two before settling down a few thousand feet from the Manzano Base fence. So many balloons were landing around us the outnumbered security police were too busy to confiscate the film in my camera.

The next day the balloons followed precisely the same course. Seeing a good opportunity to photograph foreign balloonists flying over one of this country's most restricted military zones, I drove to Kirtland Air Force Base and set up my camera equipment near the Weapons Lab's classified high-power laser range. While I was photographing five balloons that had overflown Manzano Base and the laser range, two military vehicles ground to a halt in front of my car. Several security guards armed with M-16's sprang from the vehicles, ordered me to turn over my film, and tried to decide if I should be arrested. Meanwhile, balloons began descending on the classified laser test range. Seeing a way out of my predicament, I informed the officer in charge that he was wasting his time with a United States citizen while balloons manned by foreign nationals were landing on the test range. This strategy worked. The men piled back in their vehicles and raced back toward the test range in a cloud of brown dust while I sped back to the outside world.

A few weeks later two Air Force officers knocked on my front door and gave me a yellow box of slides. It was my confiscated film. Apparently they didn't seriously believe any secrets had been compromised—they had sent the film to Kodak for processing. The legacy of this tale is that, in spite of an inpenetrable security system, an antique technology outclassed the most advanced spy satellites. Fortunately, to my knowledge, no spies were numbered among the foreign balloonists. Though the Air Force lost a little pride and a lot of gasoline during The Great Balloon Invasion of 1973, it lost no secrets.

Burn Bags and Wire Taps

Ironically, the protection of classified high-tech secrets by insiders at Kirtland was not as effective as the efforts of the security police to keep out intruders. At least not at the Laser Division of the Weapons Laboratory where I was assigned. While there I had the misfortune of tracking down numerous security infractions because, in addition to my regular research work, I was Top Secret control officer for the Laser Division's Solid State Laser Branch. This dreaded job required accepting responsibility for hundreds of top-secret papers, documents, photographs, and visual aids stored in two four-drawer, fireproof cabinets equipped with combination locks and steel security bars. The Top Secret control officer was also responsible for periodically incinerating sacks of top-secret refuse (used carbon paper and typewriter ribbons, notes, papers, and the like) stored in burn bags kept in each top-secret safe.

Only the most sensitive information qualified for the TOP SECRET stamp. According to Executive Order 10501, "The use of the classification TOP SECRET shall be authorized . . . only for defense information or material which requires the highest degree of protection. The TOP SECRET classification shall be applied only to that information or material the defense of which is paramount, and the unauthorized disclosure of which could result in exceptionally grave damage to the Nation . . . or the compromise of . . . scientific or technological developments vital to the national defense."

At the Weapons Lab there was a strangely ambivalent attitude toward the spirit of Executive Order 10501 that made being Top Secret control officer a particularly thankless duty. The Solid State Laser Branch was responsible for so much top-secret research that highly classified matters were often handled almost casually. Janitors with no security clearance had access to all areas of the laboratory. Armed with brooms and mops, they walked into offices whose desks and tables were strewn with top-secret plans, diagrams, photographs, and papers. Once two uncleared civilian contractors had to be quickly escorted out of an office while two civil service scientists loudly disputed a super-secret topic. New secretaries waiting for their security clearances to be approved were sometimes given classified material to file or type.

We had constant reminders about maintaining security. For example, much of the classified research and development of new kinds of solid-state lasers was conducted inside windowless, room-size vaults that were protected by huge steel doors with combination locks. Yet the lab resembled a university campus more than an operational Air Force base. While most of the scientists and engineers were reasonably security conscious, the laid back, scholarly atmosphere set the stage for the security infractions that occurred with alarming frequency.

Each spring at least one hapless young scientist fell victim to the gusty winds when a sheaf or two of carelessly handled papers stamped CONFIDENTIAL or SECRET was blown across the desert and along the flight line. The worst of these disasters occurred when a captain spilled a briefcase full of classified papers on a blustery March day. He and a friend managed to retrieve all but three of the documents, leaving the commanders only one recourse: a complete search of the base. Within half an hour several hundred officers, white lab coats flapping in the wind, were formed into a line stretching from the north perimeter fence to the flightline. The highly educated scientists and engineers then joined the rolling tumbleweeds and blowing litter in a quest for the missing secrets. After three hours of searching, two of the documents were recovered during a house-to-house canvass of a base residential area. A woman had deposited the pages in a trash can when they blew into her yard.

By quitting time the third document had not been found. An emergency conference of lab officials expediently concluded that the missing page had been improperly classified secret in the first place. The search was called off, but not before the searchers found several classified papers that hadn't even been in the captain's briefcase. They were mixed in with piles of windblown newspapers and refuse trapped against the barbed wire-topped, perimeter fences.

Outdoor document searches cost hundreds of man-hours and wasted entire afternoons. But they provided a tangible demonstration of how seriously the Air Force took security. But somehow that message wasn't fully absorbed by some of the researchers. Highly classified meetings were often conducted in rooms that had not been checked for electronic surveillance devices and that offered little or no acoustic shielding. During one memorable briefing, uncleared workers in nearby offices and hallways were treated to details about several of the lab's most important top-secret projects. The briefing officer's resonant voice wafted through the thin walls and the two doors topped by red flashing lamps that informed everyone in the area that the information they could clearly hear was indeed classified.

Sometimes the security of the high-tech programs at the lab was jeapordized by visiting scientists, engineers, or technicians who did not have the proper clearance. Though these people were never briefed about the lab's classified work, sometimes they managed surprisingly accurate guesses about secret projects. How do you respond to such a situation, particularly when national security is genuinely at stake? Lie and deny the facts? Reply with a polite "No comment," and thereby confirm the visitor's suspicions? Admit the truth and swear him to secrecy?

Some people didn't even have to guess the nature of the lab's top-secret projects; they simply listened in on our telephone conversations. Everyone knew that a communications security group working with the Air Force Office of Special Investigations (OSI) was authorized to monitor our phone calls without giving prior notice. Only a few lab personnel discussed classified information on the phone. But those who didn't still revealed enough unclassified details to enable a wily eavesdropper in the security group to figure out what we were developing.

Several captains and majors in the Solid State Laser Branch had the annoying habit of leaving top-secret documents in their desk drawers during lunch or overnight. The two top-secret safes were located far from the lab where I usually worked, and sometimes officers left them open and unsupervised for hours at a time. The Top Secret control officer was responsible for correcting security problems like these, an awkward task for a first lieutenant. I politely reminded them about what could happen to all of us if they didn't properly safeguard their materials. My complaints went largely unheeded until an Air Force inspector general, breathing hints about violations of Air Force Regulation 205-1 and "court-martial offenses," made an unannounced inspection and reported ". . . an unsatisfactory condition in Top Secret control." Since AFR 205-1 spelled out the fines of up to $10,000, and terms of imprisonment of not more than ten years that could be assessed for the improper handling of classified material, suddenly my position of Top Secret control officer was viewed with respect. The commander of the Solid State Laser Branch issued a directive that all top-secret documents were to be stored in a single safe, which was moved to my lab. "The access to this safe," the directive read, "will be only the Top Secret control officer and his alternates." From then on it was possible to concentrate on the work at hand without being sidetracked by security hassles.

"Loose Lips Sink Chips"

This slogan can be found on posters at semiconductor manufacturers and computer companies. It characterizes the silicon industry's almost militant concern about security. The rapid pace of technological development is a key reason for the need for security. Manufacturers of integrated circuits, for instance, don't disclose details about new chips they are developing for fear their competitors will begin work on more advanced versions of the same devices. For the same reason, major computer manufacturers like IBM, Hewlett-Packard, Data General, and Tandy usually don't talk about plans for new machines. Tight security can give a good product many months of valuable lead time over the competition, while unintentional leaks can cost market share and even lead to disaster.

In private industry, security gaffes often occur despite stringent in-house security practices. Besides Weapons Lab–style carelessness, two major contributors are the contagious enthusiasm that accompanies high-tech research and development and the high turnover rate at many semiconductor companies. After all, it's only natural that an engineer will want to tell a former co-worker about the exciting, state-of-the-art project to which he's been assigned. Sometimes secrets spill out during overanxious efforts to recruit new workers. Leaks also occur when scientists and engineers discuss sensitive topics within hearing range of others. This is a major problem, for business discussions are often held in restaurants and at technical conferences and conventions. A front-page article in *The Wall Street Journal*, for instance, described how an overheard conversation in a Silicon Valley seafood restaurant provided Alan Lefkof, the marketing vice-president of GRiD Systems Corporation, with valuable intelligence. Mr. Lefkof's company manufactures a notebook-size portable business computer. The conversation he overheard revealed important technical details about a then unannounced competing computer Hewlett-Packard didn't introduce until two months later.

The steady stream of information leaking from high-tech companies fuels an incessant barrage of rumors in computer magazines and the financial and semiconductor trade press. Some of the rumors are merely embarrassing; like the report in *PC Week* that most of IBM's incredibly popular personal computer, the PC, is assembled by Texas Instruments, one of IBM's competitors. According to an unnamed TI employee, the PC's are manufactured by the same manufacturing facility in Tennessee that produced TI's discontinued home computer.

Other rumors have more ominous implications. More than one computer company has seen sales of a current product plummet following rumors of the possible announcement of a newer and better product. Rumors like this can have an immediate and significant impact on the price of a company's stock.

Experienced watchers of the semiconductor industry have learned there is often an element of truth behind leak-stimulated rumors. Indeed, a cynic might conclude that the level of accuracy is directly proportional to the number of denials issued by the company in question. For example, when the president of AT&T denied a widely circulated rumor that his company was planning to introduce a personal computer, I received an excited call from Harry Helms, a savvy author and editor of high-tech books. Harry had long suspected that AT&T planned to introduce a PC, and the high-level denial provided all the proof he needed. Several months later AT&T announced a personal computer.

Then there was the spate of speculation early in 1984 about a sensitive high-tech agreement between Texas Instruments and National Semiconductor. For months both companies vigorously denied persistent rumors in the trade press that the two semiconductor giants were planning a joint venture to manufacture an important new 32-bit microprocessor. Later, of course, the deal was confirmed in a press release.

Like most high-tech silicon foundries, National Semiconductor jealously guards its trade secrets. Yet their security was accidentally penetrated from within by a law firm that represented the company in a particularly bitter lawsuit against Linear Technology, Inc., a competing firm formed by several former National executives. The lawyers had inadvertently supplemented their complaint with twelve pages describing the confidential trade secrets on which the suit was based. The proprietary information was first discovered and then published by Don C. Hoefler, editor of the trade newspaper *Microelectronics News*. Hoefler even suggested that readers could obtain copies of the complete document by sending $6 to the clerk of Silicon Valley's Santa Clara County Superior Court. The elated attorney for Linear Technology immediately claimed that publication of the information meant it could no longer be considered "trade secrets."

The success of new computers is tied directly to good publicity and the availability of compatible software, the programs that tell a computer how to process words, calculate spread sheets, and play games. An essential ingredient of successful computer marketing is making information available to the computer press and software development companies prior to the product's formal announcement. This provides publishers the lead time necessary to schedule a feature to appear when the product is announced. Likewise, both software companies and the manufacturer of the new computer will benefit immensely if programs for the new machine are ready at or soon after the official announcement. Often, especially in the case of software companies, actual preproduction models of the new computer are provided as well.

Companies that provide advance information and product samples generally require recipients to sign nondisclosure agreements in which the recipient acknowledges receipt of confidential information and promises not to divulge or make use of the information without permission. Some agreements even prohibit the recipient from discussing the information or product with employees of the company other than those listed in the agreement. Though nondisclosure agreements are taken seriously by some, others freely share information supposedly protected by the legally binding agreements. Indeed, the silicon industry, particularly the computer segment, is awash with rumors and leaks that can be traced to people who have signed nondisclosure agreements.

According to *Office World News*, the manufacture of document shredders has blossomed into a $60-million-dollar-a-year business. Given enough time and patience, even documents that have been transformed into a tangled bundle of slivers can be reconstructed by a team of dedicated laborers. The U.S. Government learned this lesson after the takeover of its embassy in Iran. For total security it's necessary to chop documents into bits of confetti or to incinerate or dissolve them. Data Destruction Services, Inc., offers the driveup services of the DataGrater, a noisy, $20,000 shredder on wheels that transforms reams of confidential documents into particles no larger than 3/32 of an inch.

As for the highly publicized invasion of computer systems and networks by clever hobbyists and wily industrial spies, a combination of ordinary common sense and sophisticated protective measures makes such intrusions considerably more difficult. Many such intrusions can be prevented simply by frequently changing the password required to access the system from the outside, and by limiting the number of persons with knowledge of the password.

Even a perfect internal security program cannot keep a competitor from analyzing a product to determine how it works. Commercial computer programs can be "disassembled" to learn how they operate. The protective cover on an integrated circuit can be removed to expose the silicon chip inside. By photographing the tiny chip before and after applying chemicals to remove one or more of its layers, a set of photomasks can be produced that permit an exact copy of the chip to be manufactured by a rival firm. This practice is known in the trade as "reverse engineering."

Commercial competitors aren't the only ones who sometimes reverse-engineer siliconnected high-tech products. A 1984 Pentagon survey of the military strength of the Soviet Union observed that, "No areas of Western technology are given higher priority than computers and electronics." According to the report, "Virtually all major Soviet computer systems, such as the entire RYAD-series and the Soviet SM-series of minicomputers, are based on and reverse-engineered from Western computers acquired both legally and illegally." As for the silicon chips used in such computers and in military hardware, the report concluded that, "More than one-third of all known Soviet integrated circuits have been copied from U.S. designs." The Pentagon's conclusions are nothing new to regular readers of electronics trade publications and computer magazines. For instance, the April 1984 issue of *Byte* carried an article by Ruth Heuertz of United Telephone Company about two Soviet microprocessors that were reverse-engineered from U.S. devices made by Intel and Digital Equipment Corporation.

Other countries can glean much about high-tech developments in the United States simply by sending representatives to technical conferences and trade shows, and by keeping up with the outpouring of high-tech developments reported in unclassified trade publications, technical journals, and patent reports.

Many U.S. firms, sometimes supported by strident editorials in trade magazines, aren't enthusiastic about restrictions on sales to Russia and its allies. Nevertheless, in October 1981 the United States Customs Service began "Operation Exodus," a program to keep actual hardware from the Soviet Union and its allies. Within two and one-half years "Operation Exodus" intercepted 2,851 shipments of high-tech goods valued at $177 million. Of 298 arrests made in connection with the illegal shipments, there were 199 convictions. These impressive statistics must be viewed in light of the magnitude of the massive effort by the Soviet Union to acquire state-of-the-art hardware by means of so-called third-party transactions through Canada, South Africa, West Germany, and other countries. A front-page article in *The Wall Street Journal* on July 24, 1984, quoted retired C.I.A. official Harry Rositzke as saying, "The avenues for transfer open to Russia are so broad that they are almost impossible to control."

Several years ago I observed two Russian seekers of U.S. high-tech in action at an optoelectronics convention and trade show in San Francisco. They had stopped by the booth of a struggling California electronics company for which I was then doing some technical writing. One of the Russians was outgoing, tall, and ruggedly handsome; the other, who only grunted when we were introduced, was short, plump, and balding.

The tall man seemed to have a technical background for he was keenly interested in a state-of-the-art semiconductor laser communications system. As he fondled one of the communicators in his big hands, he asked the company's president if he had made any progress in obtaining an exemption from the export restrictions that prevented the communicator from being sold to a Communist country. The company's president, desperate for an order to keep his floundering firm alive, reluctantly responded that he had not. Then he pleaded with the Russians to join him in a formal appeal to his congressman for an exemption.

After the Russians had moved on, I joked that the short man was probably there to keep his more astute companion from defecting. Actually, it's likely both men were with the KGB's "Service T" group based at the Russian consulate in San Francisco. In any event, it was evident that their meeting at the convention with the laser company president was not their first. The company president assured me he didn't really want to sell his sophisticated gadget to the Russians, but his circumstances left him no alternative. While I remembered Lenin's boast that "The capitalists will sell us the rope with which we shall hang them," he said that the U.S. Navy had expressed strong interest in the laser communicator for covert ship-to-ship communications. Unfortunately, however, the Navy couldn't afford to buy any of the units, and his only customer to date was the Iranian navy. Perhaps the Russians finally received one of the coveted communicators when the Shah was overthrown.

·9·

Tripping Through the Silicon Mart

Powerful Ideas

WHILE THE BLAST FURNACES of the rust bowl crumble into orange powder, the silicon extracted from molten sand is fueling a thousand Horatio Alger success stories. Intersil, Inc., the culmination of one of those success stories and an innovative maker of integrated circuits, sent its customers a large poster bearing a drawing of Victor Hugo and his observation that "There is nothing more powerful than an idea whose time has come." That poster hangs over my electronics workbench, a silicon transistor taped over the word "idea."

The transistor, the invention that ushered in the silicon era, was born at Bell Laboratories a few years after the end of World War II. The three scientists who developed the transistor, John Bardeen, Walter Brattain, and William Shockley, shared the 1956 Nobel Prize in physics for their invention. Only the names of Bardeen and Brattain appear on the patent for the transistor since Shockley, a brilliant theoretician, didn't personally participate in the actual invention. Shockley did, however, play a key role as the director of the transistor development team. Moreover, a few years later Shockley perfected a considerably improved and more easily manufactured kind of transistor.

Shockley's role went far beyond that of inventor. "I had come to the conclusion," he later told a Congressional subcommittee, "that the most creative people were not adequately rewarded as employees in industry." Accordingly, in 1955 Shockley left Bell Labs and returned to his hometown of Palo Alto, California, and established Shockley Semiconductor Laboratory in nearby Mountain View. In those days all transistors were made from germanium, an excellent semiconductor with the annoying habit of overheating and even self-destructing when too much electrical current is allowed to flow through it. In other words, though the transistor held great promise as a solid-state amplifier, existing devices had limited power-handling capability and were notoriously unreliable. Nevertheless, Shockley attracted to his infant venture some of the brightest semiconductor physicists in the United States. Soon, however, his unpopular management style and his preoccupation with the development of a nontransistor device called the four-layer diode discouraged Shockley's brilliant research team.

At Texas Instruments in Dallas in 1954, Gordon Teal, a Bell Labs protégé who had worked with Shockley, had learned how to produce transistors from silicon, a material that had much more promise than the fickle germanium but whose very high melting point made it extremely difficult to purify. Shockley's team wanted to join the transition from germanium to silicon. In 1957, the year the Soviet Union launched the first Sputnik, eight members of Shockley's team left their famous mentor to found Fairchild Semiconductor, the first company devoted exclusively to making silicon transistors. Shockley derisively referred to the defectors as "the traitorous eight"; others called them "the Shockley eight." Though their departure eventually proved fatal to Shockley Semiconductor, Fairchild Semiconductor became the catalyst that led to the establishment of what is now known as Silicon Valley. In 1958 Fairchild's success was secured when Jean Hoerni, a physicist with two doctorates who was one of the Shockley Eight, invented the planar process, a new and much more effective way of making transistors. Later that year Jack Kilby, an engineer at Texas Instruments, made the first crude "solid" or integrated circuit by forming a transistor and several other components on the surface of a germanium bar about the size of this printed *i*. Kilby's idea was inspired by his experience at Centralab, Inc., where he contributed to the engineering of miniature transistorized circuits used to make hearing aids. Six months later Robert Noyce, another member of Fairchild's Shockley Eight, combined Kilby's pioneering but primitive solid circuit with Hoerni's planar process to produce a much more practical kind of integrated circuit. By 1961 both Fairchild and

Texas Instruments were selling integrated circuits made by the planar process.

More than two dozen semiconductor companies were eventually spun off from Fairchild Semiconductor by defecting engineers and physicists turned entrepreneurs who emulated the Shockley Eight in their quest to turn silicon to gold. Among Fairchild's protégés, which today have a multi-billion-dollar cumulative worth, are such leaders as Intel, National Semiconductor, and Advanced Micro Devices. Fairchild Semiconductor, which hasn't fared as well as some of its offspring in recent years, is today owned by France's Schlumberger. Intersil, founded by Fairchild's Jean Hoerni, is now a subsidiary of General Electric.

The ambition that led Shockley to form his pioneering semiconductor company still flourishes within economic systems that nurture and cultivate entrepreneurship. There is no better example than the personal computer that sprang from Ed Roberts's silicon garage in late 1974. The Altair 8800 spawned a high-tech cottage industry of thousands of entrepreneurs operating from garages, attics, and basements. Some of these tiny firms developed electronic circuit boards designed to be inserted inside computers manufactured by bigger companies. Others developed computers of their own. Still others created innovative computer programs. Like some of the original Silicon Valley firms, many of these ventures were eventually bought out or driven out of business by larger, established companies. A few, like Apple Computer, ratified the ultimate promise of entrepreneurship and became spectacularly successful.

A siliconnected company that survives its entrepreneurial stage is not guaranteed continued success or immunity from setbacks. The skills required to start a company aren't the same as those necessary to effectively manage a stable business. This poses a serious dilemma because many entrepreneurs, who are by nature innovators and risk takers, grow restless and feel trapped when saddled with management responsibilities. Another problem is that the maturing entrepreneurship risks losing the talent that conceived and engineered the product that made the company possible in the first place. The key innovators are virtually always few in number, and often include the entrepreneur himself. Sometimes these people depart when competition forces their company to devote its entire research and development effort to the improvement of its single existing product. A one-of-a-kind high-tech product, and incentives like stock options and profit sharing, can together forge a dedicated, stick-it-out-to-the-bitter-end loyalty. Otherwise, creative design engineers are prone to look elsewhere for more exciting work or, perhaps, reenter the entrepreneurship cycle.

When Ed Roberts, Stan Cagle, Bob Zaller, and I formed MITS, we knew all about the romantic side of entrepreneurships. After MITS was formed we soon learned that a company doesn't run on a love of electronics and a good idea. Money had to be borrowed, a lawyer hired, incorporation papers drawn up, and tax returns filed. Countless hours were spent designing products, preparing advertising copy, ordering parts, writing manuals, and processing orders. When Ed Roberts designed the first MITS calculator, he quickly realized that for the machine to be successful its physical appearance would have to be given as much attention as its sophisticated circuits. Every entrepreneurship experiences a similar learning curve as it attempts to transform an exciting idea into a marketable product.

Siliconcoctions, Ltd.

If a young engineer were to seek my advice about forming an entrepreneurship, I wouldn't bore him with facts and figures or raise his hopes by repeating the Altair story. Instead I would warn him about the bewildering array of obstacles that lie along the path to high-tech success.

Consider the trials and tribulations of Siliconcoctions, Ltd., a mythical electronics firm founded by Mike Roe and Solis Tate, a pair of dropouts from MicroBrain, Inc. While still employed at MicroBrain, Mike Roe, affectionately known to his friends as "Micro," designed the key circuits for a microprocessor-controlled, motorized robot. Tate developed some preliminary computer programs that allowed the proposed robot, which featured a low light–level television system, to function as a roving security guard. When MicroBrain's management turned down their request to build a prototype robot, Roe and Tate left the company and founded Siliconcoctions. In exchange for 51 percent of their stock, Golden Chips, Inc., put up $5 million of venture capital to finance the new firm. Within two months Siliconcoctions had moved into the Silicon Valley community of Alto View.

Three months after startup Siliconcoctions had thirty employees on the payroll. In addition to Roe and Tate, they included a business manager, a purchasing agent, three electrical engineers, three mechanical engineers, four assembly language programmers, a plastics engineer, two machinists, six technicians, two board stuffers, a stockroom clerk, a receptionist, two secretaries, and a custodian and groundskeeper. Though the monthly payroll of $62,000 was processed by Alto View's lone bank, only a few thousand dollars stayed in town. The rest left with the employees, all of whom commuted to their jobs since they couldn't afford the $147,394 average price of Alto View's typical three-bedroom, two-bathroom house. The engineering staff commuted from their homes elsewhere in Silicon Valley. The nonprofessional workers arrived in van pools from their apartments and mobile homes in a nearby community.

Only six months after startup work on the robot's circuits was completed, and tests were begun using prototype hardware designed and built by the mechanical engineering team. Meanwhile, the programming team completed much of the software development for the three microcomputers in the system, and the electrical engineers finalized the design of the novel encoding circuits that transmitted totally secure pictures from the robot to a television set equipped with a special decoder. Finally, three complete robots were ready. At a company party to celebrate the occasion Roe and Tate christened their wonder product "Spybot." Reporters from the trade press were there, and the following week several technical magazines and the local newspaper carried glowing reports about Spybot. "An idea whose time has come," proclaimed *Robot World*. "Spybot sees in the dark and will never fall asleep on the job!" declared *Mil-Spec Weekly*. "They're so cute!" gushed Ella Troniks in the *Alto View Enquirer*. In two days of active trading, Siliconcoctions' stock tripled in value.

Ten days after the christening party General Ira Gadgetphreek was given a demonstration of Spybot technology. The demonstration went well, and the general promptly had the Army issue a sole-source procurement order for all three Spybots. Two days later Siliconcoctions received more good news when the Immigration and Naturalization Service ordered one hundred Spybots for border patrol duty. Roe, Tate, and the high rollers at Golden Chips were elated. Then bad news arrived. Since the first three Spybots were assigned the task of patrolling a top-secret nuclear weapons storage facility, the Army designated Spybot television transmission technology as secret. The Spybots could not be sold to the I.N.S. until the sophisticated television encoding circuits were eliminated. Moreover, all of Siliconcoctions' employees had to be issued security clearances and the company was ordered to hire two on-premise security guards.

While the electrical engineering staff hurriedly redesigned Spybot's video circuits, the company set up a production line to fill the big I.N.S. order. Then, only a day before the rollout of the first declassified Spybot, the Army abruptly returned the three original machines. It seems that a teenage computer hacker who lived thirteen miles from the secret nuclear munitions dump patrolled by the Spybots had inadvertently intercepted perfectly clear pictures of the highly classified facility. The pictures appeared on the screen of the portable television set he used as a computer monitor every time his do-it-yourself music synthesizer program played middle C. His father, a local antiwar activist who owned a hundred shares of Siliconcoctions' stock, contacted a TV station, which taped the secret pictures and featured them in an hour-long special about the perils of high-tech warfare. The program was later rebroadcast by the Public Broadcasting System.

Golden Chips was horrified by this development, more by the loss of sales than by the breach of military security. Fortunately, Roe and Tate were able to reassure both the venture capitalists and the stockholders by reminding them about the big I.N.S. order. Alas, the I.N.S. cancelled its order when the employee background checks ordered by the Army revealed that the company's brightest programmer, both board stuffers, and the custodian were in this country illegally.

Roe and Tate, who were engineers and not salesmen, spent weeks trying to drum up additional orders. Roe finally took a six-day business trip to Hawaii where he spent most of an hour convincing Admiral Gunther Gunboat that Spybots would be ideal for patrolling the decks of aircraft carriers looking for foreign objects that might be sucked into jet engines. Eventually the Navy agreed to buy the Army's three rejected Spybots, but the deal fell through when an alert civil service quality-control inspector peered inside one of the machines. There he found thirteen microchips made by Sili-Con, Inc., a major semiconductor company whose top management had been indicted for failing to adequately test "mil-spec" components, those designated for military applications.

After this setback the engineering teams initiated a contingency plan ordered by an emergency oversight team from Golden Chips. The Spybot program was placed on hold, and a cheap $575 toy version of the robot was hurriedly developed. Progress on the toy robot, however, was slowed by the absence of the company's best programmer. He vanished along with the board stuffers and the custodian after the I.N.S. debacle. So did several hundred expensive memory chips that were then in high demand and not readily available. The local sheriff eventually recovered the chips, but they were zapped and rendered useless by the static electricity generated when he poured the hoard into a plastic trash bag.

Meanwhile, Siliconcoctions was plagued by an assortment of in-house catastrophes. Though technical development of the Spybots had proceeded without a hitch, Alto View's public sanitation department had cited the company for illegally pouring corrosive solvents into the sewer system. Siliconcoctions was forced to install a large underground tank to store the used solvent along with some poisonous chemicals the sanitation department had not detected. Shortly before the Army returned its three Spybots, both secretaries took maternity leave. Two technicians were injured when one of them dropped a lithium battery into a pot of molten solder. The battery exploded, splashing solder over the custom safety helmet worn by an inspector from the Occupational Safety and Health Administration who was making a routine inspection at the time. Siliconcoctions was fined $1,000 for allowing a hazardous situation to occur. Finally, Mike Roe caught a pair of engineers from Rittal Lobots, a Japanese toy company, photographing a Spybot he had taken to a trade show in San Francisco.

Word of the problems leaked out, and Siliconcoctions' stock plunged to a fifth its original value. Golden Chips sent in a crisis management team to run the company, but it was too late. Eighteen months after startup Roe and Tate left Siliconcoctions. Within a month Golden Chips decided to salvage what it could, and sent in its liquidation administration team. Everything from the fixtures and desks to the test equipment and unused electronics were consigned to an auction company. The company almost sold the inventory of 5,000 Spybots to an electronics chain for twenty dollars each, a fraction of their value. But just before the deal was closed Japan's Rittle Lobots offered the chain an identical product for only ten dollars. Half the Spybots were eventually sold to a mail-order surplus electronics dealer for twelve cents a pound.

Although this yarn is admittedly apocryphal, regular watchers of the high-tech electronics industry will recognize every incident, mishap, and calamity as representative of actual events. If would-be entrepreneurs first reviewed the case histories of both successful and unsuccessful siliconnected companies, perhaps the success rate of startups would be increased. In any event, though multi-million-dollar giants dominate the high-tech electronics scene, there's still plenty of room for the entrepreneur with a good, marketable idea. Even the lone inventor without entrepreneurial instincts or ambitions can sometimes sell a new product idea to a startup company or an established firm. Not all good ideas are necessarily marketable, however, as I learned firsthand during several post-MITS attempts to interest established electronics companies in products that I believed had excellent potential for success. I remember one of those experiences well, for even though the product has yet to be fully developed, much less marketed, it profoundly influenced my career as a siliconnected person.

An Idea Whose Time Has Not Come

As you may recall I began developing and testing homemade electronic travel aids for blind people while a college student. These handheld devices, about the size of two packages of chewing gum, contained a solid-state, infrared-emitting diode like those found in modern infrared remote-control units for television sets. When the pulsating infrared beam from the diode struck an object up to ten or twelve feet away, some of the invisible infrared was reflected back to a sensitive detector also installed in the aid. A tone warned the blind user about the object. Though the travel aids worked, tests with nearly fifty people showed that having to hold the aids was a major nuisance. In 1971 I decided to design a travel aid that would fit entirely inside modified eyeglass frames.

At the Air Force Weapons Laboratory Dr. Roger Mark had taught me much about designing siliconnected experiments. One evening after a run of the monkey-blinding experiment he showed me how to derive mathematical equations that predicted the distance at which a hypothetical travel aid would detect various objects. Thanks to Roger's influence, from the outset I decided to undertake the development of the eyeglass travel aid as if it were a Weapons Lab project, even though I had little test equipment and even less money. First, I recruited Pat Miller, a fellow model-rocketry enthusiast who was studying mathematics at the University of New Mexico, to transform Roger's equations into a computer program. The university's computer then produced a stack of graphs showing the maximum distance at which the aid would detect materials that reflected from 1 to 100 percent of the infrared striking them.

In March I began a series of complicated experiments designed to test the accuracy of Roger's equations. Friends at General Electric, RCA, and EG&G provided the expensive calibrated infrared-emitting diodes and detectors necessary for the tests. In April I began designing the circuits, and by May a handheld test version was ready. During the summer and fall the test aid was modified a dozen times in an unsuccessful effort to increase its sensitivity so that it would function properly when installed on eyeglasses. On December 23 the required sensitivity was finally achieved with a new, more powerful kind of infrared-emitting diode sent by a General Electric engineer. I worked furiously all day Christmas Eve to assemble the components on a pair of exposed circuit boards that were then taped to the temples of a pair of old sunglasses.

I was eager for Noel Runyan, then an electrical engineering student at the University of New Mexico, to test the crude eyeglass-mounted device. Noel, who was blinded by an explosion when he was a teenager, was my favorite test subject. A skilled user of the long mobility cane, Noel was also a good friend who taught me a little about what being blind is all about. One night he blindfolded me, stuck one of his spare long canes in my right hand and led me on a walk around the University of New Mexico campus. After ten minutes of joking about the blind leading the blind and worrying about falling into open manholes and crossing streets, I quit peeking through the bottom of the blindfold and began to relax. For six years I had periodically tested homemade travel aids with dozens of blind people. Now, for the first time, I tuned into the surrealistic symphony of subtle but ever-present sounds and noises that give blind people special clues about their surroundings. The rasping cadence of our tapping canes bounced back clearly from curbs and walls, its tone providing hints about the surface texture of nearby objects. Smooth, hard surfaced objects returned abrupt, sharp-sounding echoes; soft echoes indicated leaves, grass or fabric. I experienced firsthand how my blind great-grandfather used to "hear" buildings, fences and trees. So long as a droning air conditioner, moving vehicle or other sound source was present somewhere beyond, utility poles and even curbside bus benches could be detected by their sound shadows.

Noel tested the crude eyeglass-mounted aid for the first time when my wife and I visited his apartment on New Year's Eve. The pulsating infrared beam easily detected walls, shelves, a refrigerator, and Minnie and me. It even detected, at an impressive range of fifty-five inches, a narrow chinning bar installed in a doorway. In later tests Noel found that the aid provided advance warning of overhanging signs, tree branches laden with new snow sagging over normally unobstructed sidewalks, and other obstacles above and beyond his probing cane. An unexpected finding was that the eyeglass aid provided a convenient means for staying in a line without the embarrassment of touching or tapping the person ahead to determine when the line has moved forward. Though the prototype aid was primitive, through Noel's experiences with it we both became convinced that it might provide an important supplement to the traditional mobility cane. First, however, the device needed much more work. The exposed circuits needed to be installed in protective housings; the earphone, which blocked some of the rich repertoire of environmental sounds on which Noel so heavily depended, had to be eliminated.

During January 1972 I worked full time improving on and miniaturizing the aid's circuits. The siliconnected components were mounted on dainty printed circuit boards installed inside a pair of small brass tubes. A glass lens was pressed onto a sticky bead of epoxy applied around one end of each tube. Both tubes were then baked in an oven until the gummy epoxy was transformed into a rock-hard seal. The circuits were powered by midget mercury batteries that slipped into a spring-loaded chamber in the end of each tube. The batteries were locked in place by a metal and plastic fixture that contained a small on-off switch. Inside one tube was a diode that emitted a few hundred pulses per second of invisible near-infrared radiation. The lens formed the pulsating infrared into a narrow cone that spread to the size of a saucer at a distance of two paces.

When the pulsating infrared beam struck an object up to ten or fifteen feet away, some of the infrared was reflected back toward the lens on the second tube and focused onto a sensitive silicon infrared detector. Much as a solar cell converts light into electricity, the detector then generated a tiny electrical signal. Miniature electronic circuits in the tube amplified the weak signal and sent it to a pea-sized hearing-aid speaker. A clear plastic tube then carried to the user's ear the amplified warning tone that indicated an object. A small tube was used to avoid blocking ambient sounds.

Finally, a full year after beginning work on the project, a prototype eyeglass-mounted travel aid was ready. The completed aid worked better than any of the handheld aids I'd built. The infrared-emitting diode was more powerful, and the combination of the silicon detector and amplifier in the receiver proved remarkably sensitive. The receiver could detect as little as twenty-billionths of a watt of infrared reflected from a target, only about a millionth of the power in the transmitted beam. Though the device was imperfect, it was the best I could do without outside funding. Unfortunately, from previous contacts with several major companies, I had begun to conclude there was insufficient profit motive for private industry to invest the funds necessary to design, test, and manufacture this kind of device. These experiences reminded me of the friendly but greedy hearing aid dealer for whom I used to repair miniature behind-the-ear aids for five dollars each when I was a college student. Sometimes he tried to sell an elderly client an expensive new aid during the few minutes it took me to fix their old aid by squirting some contact cleaner in the volume control or by cleaning dirty switch or battery contacts.

In spite of my prior discouraging experiences with private industry, the upbeat test sessions with Noel renewed my desire to interest a manufacturer since the time spent on the project was beginning to erode my meager earnings as a freelance writer. One way to inform hundreds of companies about the device made itself known a few months later when an issue of *Industrial Research* magazine included an invitation to enter the magazine's tenth annual IR 100 new products competition. The magazine claimed that the award had become known as "The Nobel Prize of industrial research." The 100 innovative technical products selected each year to receive the coveted award were judged by a panel that included "Nobel laureates, university presidents, research directors and the inventors of the laser, radar, communications satellites, radiocarbon dating and stroboscopic photography." Though the odds for winning an IR 100 award seemed slim at best, I submitted the entry form. The form asked for the name of the company that developed the product so I made up the name Sensory Aids Research. The form also asked for the name of the product, so I called it the Model E-2 Seeing Aid. The question about the product's development cost was more troubling. I had spent only about $200, hardly within range of the $419,000 average development cost for the previous year's winners. Therefore, figuring the lost income the project had cost, I claimed a $6,000 development budget.

After mailing the application, I began a study of how well the travel aid could detect hundreds of objects and materials. First I built a portable instrument called a reflectometer that measured the percentage of infrared reflected from various materials. For most of a month I walked, bicycled, and drove around Albuquerque looking for typical obstacles or "targets." I placed the sensing probe of the reflectometer against the surface of the target, read the reflectance percentage from a meter, and entered the value in a notebook.

The reflectance study raised a good deal of curiosity among passersby. This helped me to measure the infrared reflectance of the most unpredictable target of all: people. Most fabrics have a near-infrared reflectance of fifty percent or more; clothing, therefore, would be easily detected by the travel aid, a fact I had learned from previous experience. Would differences in skin color pose a problem? The near-infrared reflectance of white skin is only about five percent higher than that of black skin. When the target is human skin, in other words, infrared travel aids are color blind.

In July *Industrial Research* magazine sent word that Sensory Aids Research had won a 1972 IR 100 award. A few days later a letter arrived from Neil Ruzic, founder and president of Industrial Research, Inc. Mr. Ruzic wanted a model of the Seeing Aid "to wear on some TV shows" arranged to publicize the upcoming IR 100 conference and awards ceremony. When I wrote back that I didn't want to give false hopes to blind people by hyping an experimental travel aid that wasn't yet commercially available, he responded that only eight or ten of the IR 100 winners would be shown on television. "I wish you would change your mind and let me present the Seeing Aid," he pleaded. I agreed on one condition: the device could be shown to the press only if I was given the opportunity to explain its operational limitations and its early state of development.

Mr. Ruzic was also worried that I didn't plan to exhibit the Seeing Aid in a booth at the IR 100 exhibition. All IR 100 winners were expected either to rent or provide a booth to display their products. The products would then remain for several weeks at the Chicago Museum of Science and Industry where "300,000 persons are expected to view the exhibits." Renting a commercial booth or building and transporting one from Albuquerque to Chicago would far exceed the development cost of the Seeing Aid itself. I couldn't even afford to rent a tuxedo for the banquet and awards ceremony.

In the hope of attracting a corporate sponsor for my project, I took the cheapest possible night flight to Chicago to attend the awards ceremony. There I learned that the 1972 winners included General Electric, M.I.T., Hewlett-Packard, IBM, Bendix, Bausch & Lomb, and Texas Instruments. By a remarkable coincidence even the Air Force Weapons Laboratory was an IR 100 winner. Together we received New Mexico's first two IR 100 awards. Though my cheap plaid sports coat was rather conspicuous amidst the rows of 99 tuxedos lined up behind the banquet tables on the stage, the IR 100 ceremonies were certainly a memorable experience.

Alas, though I met a number of prominent industrialists and entrepreneurs, and consented to television and newspaper interviews, none of the corporate officials who seemed so fascinated by the travel aid and the diminutive size were in a position to manufacture the device. The only tangible results of the IR 100 award were an engraved steel-on-walnut plaque, a lapel pin, Thor Heyerdahl's autograph, and heart-rending letters from blind people and their relatives and friends. Instead of the hoped for letter from a manufacturer offering to produce the devices, the only company that responded, believe it or not, was Ripley International, Ltd., the company that operates several "Ripley's Believe It or Not!" museums. Mr. D.R. Copperthwaite, the firm's exhibits director, requested a Seeing Aid to exhibit along with such remarkable items as "Transistors through the Eye of a Needle" and "World's Smallest Watch Screws." I thanked Mr. Copperthwaite for his interest but declined his request.

Eventually I convinced the Veterans Administration to buy two aids at cost and test them with blind vets. The V.A. was intrigued by the concept but the aid never got past the prototype stage. Developing the device and its handheld predecessors taught me much about miniaturization, optoelectronics, optical radar, electronic circuit design, and computer simulation. I also learned the importance of packaging, the art of designing sturdy, human engineered enclosures. This new knowledge provided the background necessary to design several kinds of infrared sensing devices and lightwave communications systems that sent voice, tones, or digital signals through air or transparent fibers of plastic or glass. It also allowed me to develop a short course for an engineering society, and to write a dozen books, many magazine articles, and several professional papers. I've recently renewed work on the eyeglass-mounted travel aid project. Advances in solid-state electronics since I built the first three devices now permit development of a much more sophisticated aid. Someday, perhaps.

·10·

The Knowledge Business

Professor Bell's Encore

THE EMERGING AMALGAM of computers linked by a nationwide network of high-speed transmission paths will do for information what paved roads did for the automobile. Later I explore the silicon-connected knowledge business, giving particular scrutiny to some of its emerging trends, inherent problems, high-tech products, and big business battles. First, let's recall the contribution of Alexander Graham Bell, the master teacher of elocution for the deaf who first conceived the invention that more than a century later offers a promising method for the lightning-fast transmission of digital information. The invention is not the one for which Bell is best known; it is the photophone, a family of devices that permitted speech to be transmitted over beams of light.

Computer information can be easily transmitted over telephone lines. One way is to convert into distinctive audio tones individual digital bits, the binary 0's and 1's that when formed into patterns represent numbers and characters. Thus if the pitch or frequency of the bit 0 is low and that of 1 is high, then the binary equivalent of the number eleven, 1010, would be sent over a telephone line as the tone sequence high-low-high-low. This method is reliable, but by electronic standards it is incredibly slow. Faster methods can be used, but telephone lines were designed to carry the relatively slowly changing frequencies of voice, not the millions of bits of digital data a typical computer can process in one second. Coaxial cables like those used to carry cable television signals provide a much faster means for carrying digital information, but the wave of the future is light. Whether sent through air, the vacuum of space, or ultra-transparent plastic or glass filaments, light waves have thousands of times the information-carrying capacity of copper telephone wire.

Amid paneled walls prepared with maps, honorary degrees, photographs of sailing ships, and autographed pictures of explorers, presidents, and kings, I discussed this intriguing topic with Bell's grandson, Melville Bell Grosvenor, in May 1977. Dr. Grosvenor, who died in 1982, was then chairman emeritus of the National Geographic Society, a position he assumed after serving forty-three years in every editorial department and as editor of *National Geographic*. The purpose of my visit was to propose that the Society formally recognize the forthcoming centennial of Bell's invention of lightwave communication. The Bell connection sanctioned my visit for in 1899 Gilbert H. Grosvenor, Dr. Grosvenor's father, was commissioned to begin the magazine by the president of the National Geographic Society and his future father-in-law, Alexander Graham Bell himself.

I had brought to Dr. Grosvenor's office in Washington, D.C., a briefcase filled with the siliconnected gadgetry necessary to transmit voice and computer information over beams of light. Excited as a ten-year-old in a candy store, Dr. Grosvenor watched wide-eyed as I demonstrated the various devices. He was fascinated by the transceivers I'd built that allowed us to talk to one another via beams of invisible infrared projected across his office or through hair-thin fibers of glassy silica. He marveled over the image converter that made visible their invisible beams. But he was most intrigued by a small metal cylinder with a thin glass mirror cemented to one end. I explained that it was patterned after one of the many kinds of photophone transmitters invented by his grandfather in 1880–81, and he scrambled out onto the balcony with the device, captured some sunlight, and reflected it back toward a lightwave receiver I was holding. He then spoke excitedly into the tube, thereby flexing the mirror with the force of his breath and, in turn, modulating the shining beam with his happy voice. During those thrilling moments Dr. Grosvenor exhibited the contagious enthusiasm of his famous grandfather who, shortly after the first successful demonstration of the photophone on February 19, 1880, wrote: "I have heard articulate speech produced by sunlight! I have heard a ray of the sun laugh and cough and sing! . . . Can imagination picture what the future of this invention is to be! . . . We may talk by light to any visible distance without any conducting wire."

That memorable experience with Melville Bell Grosvenor was genuine Bell, a vicarious visit with the great inventor, medical researcher, and teacher of the deaf from whose fertile mind sprang powerful ideas. Among his favorite projects were man-lifting tetrahedral kites, speedy hydrofoil craft, wax cylinder and disk graphophones for recording sound, and sonar, a way to find objects via their sonic echoes. Though today Bell is best known for his invention of the first undulatory speech telephone, in 1921, shortly before his death, he told a reporter that he considered the photophone "in the importance of the principles involved . . . as the greatest invention I have ever made; greater than the telephone." Those principles are so easily grasped that I once made for an eleven-year-old boy in search of an idea for a science fair project a sketch of a photophone on the back of an envelope: a cardboard cylinder with aluminum foil stretched tightly over one end for a transmitter, and a silicon solar cell connected to a transistor amplifier for the receiver. After purchasing a solar cell at a Radio Shack store, within a few days the young man was sending his voice over a beam of reflected sunlight.

Though disarmingly simple by today's standards, the photophone was vintage high-tech and among the first electronic devices made possible by infant semiconductor technology. Consider the impact on the knowledge business of its progeny as we return to the genesis of the silicon era, a time when primeval solid-state detectors of light were concocted by high-tech pioneers who melted selenium in pots heated over gas flames.

While honeymooning with his deaf bride in England in 1877–78, Bell, already famous for his invention of the telephone, read reports about the newly discovered light-sensitive properties of the element selenium, the semiconducting metalloid appropriately named after the Greek word for moon. Purposing to "hear light" by connecting some selenium between a battery and a telephone receiver, Bell brought back to the United States some of the scarce element. His plan was interrupted, however, by a climactic patent infringement suit pressed by the telephone company against the powerful Western Union Company. Bell's historic telephone patent had stimulated scores of such suits, along with charges that the kindly professor had misappropriated the work of other inventors. This durable canard was again dredged up during the legal battle with Western Union. The pressure on Bell the inventor was intensified when his wife wrote him about comments by officials of the telephone company to the effect that "the discovery of the telephone was an accident, and you can do nothing further." She then encouraged him to "bring out something no matter what, so it proves that was not the end of you." Bell replied, "I can't bear to hear that even my friends should think that I stumbled upon an invention and that there is no more good in me."

As the battle with Western Union moved toward settlement in favor of the telephone company, Bell made plans to continue his research in the fall of 1879. Though he possessed inventive genius, Bell often lacked the manual skills necessary to reduce his ideas to practice. To fill this void while developing the first telephone, he had in 1876 employed Thomas Watson as technical assistant. In 1879, however, Watson was unavailable; he was then employed by the fledgling Bell Telephone Company as its superintendent of manufacturing. Instead Bell hired Charles Sumner Tainter, a young but experienced instrument maker, for fifteen dollars a week plus half interest in any inventions he made.

In December 1879 the Bell family moved from Cambridge to Washington, and Bell and Tainter established a laboratory. Bell and Tainter soon formed a working relationship much like the fruitful union enjoyed by Bell and Watson. Though at first they labored to complete a new telephone transmitter for which the telephone company had contracted, the two visionaries soon set their sights on a more exciting quarry. On January 22, 1880, they entered in the laboratory notebook this declaration: "We recognize that an Electric Photophone if perfected would probably be found of less practical utility than many of the other ideas we have discussed; but we are both so fascinated by the scientific prospects opened up, that we have determined to make the electric photophone our great object of search." They immersed themselves in making light detectors of selenium better than any yet developed. On the morning of February 19 they illuminated the latest in a long series of selenium detectors with periodic flashes of sunlight passed through perforations around the perimeter of a rotating disk. A musical tone was clearly heard from a telephone receiver connected in a circuit with the selenium and a battery. Realizing their goal was at hand, Bell and Tainter hurriedly fashioned a crude transmitter with the help of a piece of mirrored glass fashioned into a comblike grating by scribing into the silver coating a series of parallel lines. Tainter suggested that the grating be divided and one of its halves attached to the flexible diaphragm of an old box telephone transmitter; the other half was installed in a fixed position alongside. The selenium cell was mounted a few centimeters away. A beam of sunlight was then projected through the two gratings and onto the selenium detector. If the apparatus worked as expected, sound waves striking the diaphragm would move the attached grating with respect to the fixed grating, thus modulating the intensity of the sunlight reaching the detector. After Bell retreated to the basement of the laboratory with a pair of telephone receivers connected by wires to the selenium detector, he clearly heard Tainter say, "Hoy, hoy" and sing "Auld Lang Syne." After excitedly changing places, Tainter heard Bell's light-carried voice.

Bell was so elated that he proposed naming his second daughter, born four days earlier, Photophone. Fortunately for young Marian Bell, common sense prevailed. Meanwhile, the triumphant duo went to work improving their apparatus which, after all, had sent their voices only across the gap of a few centimeters between the gratings and the selenium detector. After several elaborate but unsuccessful efforts to transmit from the roof of the Franklin School to Bell's house, they placed the photophone transmitter in an alley and from it cast a beam of reflected sunlight to a selenium receiver in a back window of their laboratory 261 feet away. As in the original successful demonstration, Tainter uttered the first words and Bell recorded the results in his notebook: "I heard quite distinctly the words 'Halloo, Halloo, Halloo, come to the window' followed by quite a loud and distinct trilled R in a high pitched voice. Then came the first verse of Longfellow's 'Psalm of Life.' . . . We have thus at last succeeded in accomplishing the object for which we have been working and have produced the sounds of articulate speech at a distance by the action of light." Six days later Tainter deposited in the Archives of the Smithsonian Institution a sealed tin box containing the original photophone transmitter and selenium receiver.

On June 21 Tainter used a new transmitter made from a thin mirror attached to a mouthpiece to send his voice from the roof of the Franklin School to a window in the lab. Bell later recorded in his notebook, "I distinctly heard the sentence 'Mr. Bell—if you understand what I say come to the window and wave your hat.'" Years later he remembered the experiment in a speech at Cornell: "It is unnecessary to say that I waved with vigor, with enthusiasm which comes to a man not often in a lifetime."

On August 27, 1880, Bell publicly disclosed the results of the photophone experiments in an extraordinary paper read before the American Association for the Advancement of Science. This paper has no parallel in the annals of lightwave communications research. Though the eloquence of its style and its detailed survey of the prior art are themselves remarkable, the paper's principal attribute is its treasure trove of information on the fabrication of selenium detectors and many kinds of transmitter and receiver arrangements.

While the photophone paper was well received by the scientific community, not everyone was as impressed. For example, a mocking editorial in *The New York Times* on August 30 allowed that while scientists might understand the photophone's operation, "The ordinary man . . . may find a little difficulty in comprehending how sunbeams are to be used. Does Prof. Bell intend to connect Boston and Cambridge . . . with a line of sunbeams hung on telegraph posts, and, if so, what diameter are the sunbeams to be, and how is he to obtain them of the required size? What will become of the sunbeams after the sun goes down? Will they retain their power to communicate sound, or will it be necessary to insulate them, and protect them against the weather by a thick coating of gutta-percha? The public has a great deal of confidence in Scientific Persons, but until it actually sees a man going through the streets with a coil of No. 12 sunbeams on his shoulder, and suspending it from pole to pole, there will be a general feeling that there is something about Prof. Bell's photophone which places a tremendous strain on human credulity."

On February 19, 1980, precisely one century after Bell and

Tainter first spoke to one another over a light beam, the objective of my 1977 meeting with Dr. Melville Bell Grosvenor was fulfilled when the Photophone Centennial Exhibit was opened to the public in Explorer's Hall at the headquarters of the National Geographic Society. The star of the exhibit, which was jointly sponsored by the National Geographic Society and Bell Laboratories, was the original photophone, retrieved in perfect condition from the tin storage box deposited at the Smithsonian Institution a century earlier. Later I stood at the site of Bell and Tainter's laboratory, which is now a parking lot, and remembered the article in *The New York Times*. Accompanying my wife and me that chilly afternoon were representatives from the National Geographic Society, the Smithsonian Institution and Bell Laboratories. First we celebrated the photophone by exchanging nostalgic greetings over beams of sunlight reflected from vibrating mirror transmitters. Then, by means of infrared transmitted in both directions through a single, ultra-transparent fiber of silica, we welcomed the second century of lightwave communications with a pair of handheld transceivers I had built for the occasion.

Aside from experimenters and the military, interest in photophone technology faded after Bell and Tainter completed their historic experiments. The invention of the laser in 1960 and high-efficiency infrared emitting diodes in 1962 stimulated renewed interest in photophonic communications, but the fickle nature of the atmosphere limited practical lightwave links to a maximum distance of a few thousand feet. Then in 1966 Charles Kao at Standard Telecommunication Laboratories in England supplied the missing ingredient that reignited the communications revolution sparked by the photophone when he reported that, "Theoretical and experimental studies indicate that a fiber of glassy material . . . represents a possible practical optical waveguide with important potential as a new form of communication medium." In those days fibers made from the clearest glass almost completely absorbed a ray of light after only a few feet. Today tens of millions of infrared flashes per second can be carried through more than a hundred kilometers of hair-thin fiber drawn from the glassy oxide of silicon called silica. Thus the emerging high-speed information network that is beginning to link siliconnected computers is itself silicon-based.

Knowledge Tools

The battery-powered computer into which this book was typed is a genuinely personal and highly interactive knowledge tool. When not busy storing and organizing words typed into its typewriterlike keyboard, it can be programmed to perform thousands of tasks ranging from calculating income tax and alphabetizing names to drawing bargraphs and playing games. Though smaller than a three-ring notebook, it is equipped with a built-in circuit called a modem that can send text over a conventional telephone line at a rate of 37.5 characters per second. This feature of my high-tech knowledge tool is decidedly low-tech, for at that miserly speed it would take nearly four hours to send every word of this manuscript to the publisher's computer. Some modems can send information four times faster, the upper limit for ordinary telephone lines. Special telephone circuits having a transmission speed of 19,200 binary bits per second would permit this book to be transmitted in several minutes. Coaxial cables and strands of silica are even faster. At one standard transmission rate, which is nowhere near the maximum possible, this entire book could be flashed to a distant point in only a tenth of a second. Sending drawings and, especially, photographs digitally takes far longer than text. But as cable television so clearly demonstrates, ultra-fast data highways make practical the transmission of illustrated knowledge.

Imagine the impact on the information business as a whole and personal knowledge tools in particular of a nationwide and readily accessible network of ultra-fast data transmission highways. Even now that highway is being planned. Though coaxial cable technology is time-tested, silica fibers are cheaper, smaller, and carry more information. Moreover, pencil-thin cables of silica fibers can be slathered with grease and slipped through the narrow spaces between conventional cables in existing underground tunnels. Telephone companies in the United States, Japan, Italy, France, England, Brazil, and elsewhere are in the early phases of making the switch from coaxial cable to silica fibers. Eventually the spidery web of copper that links virtually every home and business in the United States will everywhere be supplemented and often replaced by silica.

In a later chapter I cover some of the societal implications of a high-speed silica-based network. Meanwhile, let's return to the knowledge tools themselves and examine the origins of an ongoing battle kindled by their popularization. It is an intellectual guerilla war waged against professionals and businesses who create the lists of instructions, known as programs, that tell computers what to do. In the trade the guerillas are called pirates. To one another they are simply teenage computer hobbyists, university students, business-men, engineers, and scientists who would never consider stealing a tangible piece of computer hardware. A computer program stored as microscopic magnetic domains within the brown oxide film on a plastic disk is different. The hundreds, often thousands, of hours required to create the program are as invisible as the magnetic patterns on the disk. In only a few seconds the programs encoded on a disk can be deposited in the memory of a computer or transfer-red to a second disk. The purloined software has become pirated freeware. When some companies inserted in their programs special protection codes that made copying impossible, other companies created programs to break the codes. Substantial profits have been lost, but more than money is at stake. Fearing widespread piracy, some people in the business of creating commercial computer pro-grams are now reluctant to develop new software. Others have become distracted filing legal actions against poachers.

Since the latest salvos and sorties in the ongoing battle of the programmers versus the pirates are reported in the computer press, there's no need to relate them here. More intriguing are the obscure origins of the conflict. The pioneering computer enthusiasts who bought thousands of Altairs in 1975 were forced to program their machines in binary machine language, coded patterns of 0's and 1's that tell the microprocessor in a computer what to do. This re-quired a ponderous and error-prone session of flipping front-panel toggle switches. The complex procedure required simply to add one number to another nicely illustrates the problem. First, the instructions necessary to add two numbers had to be entered into the computer's paltry memory. Not just anywhere, but in a specific block of memory addresses not reserved for other instructions or data. After advancing to the first memory location in the selected block, the machine language program was manually toggled into the Altair by following this excruciating sequence of steps (off is 0, on is 1):

| STEP | INSTRUCTION SWITCHES | | | | | | | | DEPOSIT |
	7	6	5	4	3	2	1	0	SWITCH
1	0	0	1	1	1	0	1	0	PRESS
2	1	0	0	0	0	0	0	0	PRESS
3	0	0	0	0	0	0	0	0	PRESS
4	0	1	0	0	0	1	1	1	PRESS
5	0	0	1	1	1	0	1	0	PRESS
6	1	0	0	0	0	0	0	1	PRESS
7	0	0	0	0	0	0	0	0	PRESS
8	1	0	0	0	0	0	0	0	PRESS
9	0	0	1	1	0	0	1	0	PRESS
10	1	0	0	0	0	0	1	0	PRESS
11	0	0	0	0	0	0	0	0	PRESS
12	1	1	0	0	0	0	1	1	PRESS
13	0	0	0	0	0	0	0	0	PRESS
14	0	0	0	0	0	0	0	0	PRESS

The program was then ready to run, but first the two numbers to be added had to be converted into their binary equivalents and loaded into the memory addresses specified in the program (10000000 and 10000001) by another round of switch toggling. The program was run by advancing the computer to the memory address where the first instruction was stored and pressing the RUN switch. The sum of the two numbers could then be learned by pressing the STOP switch, advancing the computer to the address (10000010) where the sum was automatically loaded, and pressing the EXAMINE switch. A pattern of red lights would glow indicating the binary equivalent of the sum, which then had to be converted back to arabic numbers.

As any Altair owner can attest, the novelty of this intricate procedure was short lived. Shortly after the Altair was featured on the January 1975 cover of *Popular Electronics*, Ed Roberts of MITS, Inc., contracted with Bill Gates and Paul Allen to develop a version of BASIC for his machine. When MITS announced BASIC, Altair owners cheered: now two numbers could be added simply by typing into the keyboard of a teletypewriter connected to the Altair "PRINT 2+2." The machine would immediately respond by printing a "4." The cheers turned to boos, however, when Altair owners learned it would cost from $60 to $150 for one of the three special programs that would enable their machine to understand BASIC. And those were discount prices that applied only when the necessary extra memory boards were purchased from MITS. Those who didn't buy their extra memory from MITS had to pay from $500 to $750 for BASIC.

In 1975 BASIC was not yet available on the preprogrammed memory chips or diskettes we now take for granted. Instead, it was encoded as patterns of holes punched in a long paper tape or as magnetic patterns on recording tape. Paying MITS all that money for a cassette tape or a fanfolded ribbon of perforated ticker tape irked some Altair owners, especially since the BASIC encoded on paper or cassette tape required additional, expensive hardware before it could be loaded into the extra memory. What's more, after the BASIC was loaded, it couldn't be used unless the Altair was connected to a terminal equipped with a typewriter-style keyboard and a printer or video monitor. Used and new teletypewriters were favorite choices, especially since these machines could be supplied with built-in paper tape readers that could also punch out copies of programs, including Altair BASIC, on blank tape.

Bill Gates's arrangement with Ed Roberts provided him a royalty on the sale of each BASIC tape. After he realized some Altair owners were using bootleg tapes, on February 3, 1976, a frustrated Gates sent "An Open Letter to Hobbyists" to various computer newsletters and *Computer Notes*, the monthly tabloid sent free to Altair owners. In his letter Gates came right to the point. "Most of you steal your software," he charged. "Hardware must be paid for but software is something to share. Who cares if the people who worked on it get paid?" Gates noted that the theft of computer programs would "prevent good software from being written," and he closed with a plea for "letters from anyone who wants to pay up. . . . Nothing would please me more than being able to hire ten programmers and deluge the hobby market with good software."

This letter ignited what came to be called "The Altair Software Flap." Because of MITS's purchasing requirements for BASIC, the letter chafed virtually all computer hobbyists, pirates, and straights alike, and galvanized a good deal of ill will toward Gates and MITS. Bill Precht, editor of the Denver Amateur Computer Society Newsletter, observed that only half the forty members of his group who owned Altairs had enough hardware to run BASIC, and only seven of these were running BASIC. All of them purchased their BASIC from MITS. He summarized the feelings of most by asking, "Would it not have been better from everyone's viewpoint to charge a reasonable price, and add it on to the price of an Altair?"

Dan Meyer, president of Southwest Technical Products Corporation, which introduced one of the first computers to compete with the Altair, watched from the sidelines. After SWTPC introduced its first computer programs, Meyer priced his versions of BASIC at only $4.95 and $9.95, and summarized his attitude on software in a bright yellow handout: "Unlike some of our competitors, we . . . have realized for some time that you can't profitably sell software to hobbyists. Of course, you can always sell a few copies, but before you know it there will be five to ten copies in existence for every one sold. . . . None of the programs available from SWTPC are proprietary. Where available, you may either purchase a tape and instruction manual from us or copy them from a friend. We don't care."

For entirely different reasons, the arrival of low-cost personal computers and high-level languages like BASIC engendered terror in the minds of some professional computer programmers and consultants who developed software for major corporations and universities. Both privately and in letters to computer periodicals they ridiculed the free thinking, independent style of the young, often teenaged, computer hackers who had invaded the fringes of their turf. They mocked their homemade and built-from-a-kit computers, calling them toys, and arrogantly denounced the programming style of hobbyists as inelegant, sloppy, and inefficient. Some even called for the licensing and regulation of programmers to preserve the reputation and professionalism of their profession. These professional programmers were themselves castigated as a "high priesthood" in computer club meetings and by magazines aimed at computer hobbyists.

Important lessons for the future of the knowledge business can be learned by reviewing the pre-1980 clashes. Bill Gates's concern that the threat of piracy would stifle the development of new software is as much a concern today as it was in 1976. Nevertheless, Gates, who is still at the helm of Microsoft, has become one of the most successful and wealthy programmers in history. His Altair BASIC was adopted by Radio Shack in 1977 for the original TRS-80. When IBM decided it was time to enter the personal computer business, it elected not to develop its own version of BASIC. Instead, it licensed from Microsoft an advanced version of Altair BASIC, and today Microsoft BASIC is an industry standard. Dan Meyer's decision to sell affordable BASIC and to let hobbyists copy his programs certainly cannot be faulted, for his company is one of the very few early personal computer firms still in the business of making computers.

On the other hand, Ed Roberts found that trying to lock out competition by tying discounts for BASIC to the purchase of memory boards stimulated the creation of the very things he wished to avoid. As for the elite, high priesthood of computer programmers, their worst fears have come to pass, and in the long run we'll all be better off.

The pirates, of course, are still plying the endless seas of the knowledge business. Many simply enjoy the intellectual challenge of defeating copy-protection schemes; for them pirating software is like solving crossword puzzles. Some have even become collectors who openly brag about the thousands of bootleg programs in their collections, none of which they would have bought otherwise, and only a few of which they use. Today's counterpart to Bill Gates's open letter is the development of antipiracy, copy-protection schemes that booby-trap the computers of those who use unauthorized software. Vault Corporation, developer of a leading copy-protection method that is sold to software publishing companies, has developed a program called "Killer Prolok." If an unauthorized copy of software protected by Killer Prolok is used, a destructive software bug called a "worm" is surreptitiously loaded into the user's computer. The worm wreaks havoc by causing unexplained, potentially serious malfunctions such as erasing the contents of the computer's memory. Booby-trap programs like Killer Prolok caused such a heated reaction among computer users that they'll probably never see widespread use. Besides, old-fashioned low-tech curses can help reduce illegal copying without any program modification whatsoever. For instance, Mother Jones' Sons' Software Corp. warns that should a customer make illegal copies of a program it sells, "ownership of your eternal soul passes to us, and we have the exclusive right to negotiate the sale of said soul to the first smoking, blood-drenched apparition with fangs that meets our price."

Battling Giants

The high-tech knowledge business is advancing toward more consolidation and an inevitable struggle for dominance between IBM and AT&T. All companies in the knowledge business, whether with hardware or software, are influenced to some degree by IBM and AT&T. Let's look at IBM first, the company most admired by 7,000 business executives and financial analysts surveyed by *Fortune* magazine in 1983. When demand for IBM's family of personal computers reached new highs in 1984, many of the electronic components used in the machines became virtually impossible for smaller companies to buy. IBM's PC has become the industry's standard, and many companies now make so-called IBM-compatible machines. A few of these firms have ridden IBM's coattails to spectacular success. Compaq Computer Corporation, for example, developed a thirty-pound transportable version of the deskbound PC and grossed $110 million in 1983, its first year of operation. IBM's domination is so entrenched that non–IBM compatible personal computers for business applications are often ridiculed in the computer press and avoided entirely by potential customers.

On the positive side, the IBM standard has stimulated the creation of abundant software that can be used with IBM-compatible machines made by different companies. On the other hand, the rush by competitors to build IBM-compatible clones has stifled innovation. The state-of-the-computer-art is determined by IBM. Many small companies have introduced highly advanced and creative computers, only to see them passed over by admiring buyers who for reasons of compatibility have been forced to stay with a more boring IBM product or one of its clones.

Innovation isn't the only victim of IBM's dominance. Though the company has an excellent reputation for service and reliability, its standards may be slipping. Elizabeth B. Staples, editor of *Creative Computing*, described a string of misadventures with an IBM PC wherein the keyboard died and the plastic door on a disk drive self-destructed, all within a few months after the expiration of the machine's warranty. Some users of IBM's most expensive personal computer, the PC AT, experienced potentially serious problems, such as the loss of valuable programs and irreplacable information presumably safely stored in memory. The PC AT reviewed by *InfoWorld* in 1985 exhibited enough problems to cause the reviewer to "strongly recommend you don't purchase it now. Wait until . . . the company works out the kinks in the system."

Whether IBM can maintain its white-shirted reputation for reliability and quality in the fast-paced world of personal computers remains to be seen. Meanwhile, in a bid to secure a prominant role in the emerging knowledge network, IBM has set its sights on the acquisition of computerized telephone technology. Its first major step was the purchase in November 1984 of Rolm Corporation, a major manufacturer of business telephone switching equipment.

IBM's move came after AT&T was divested of its regional operating companies and freed of federal constraints that prevented the communications giant from entering the commercial computer business. Several months before IBM announced its buyout of Rolm, AT&T invaded IBM territory by announcing its first personal computer. Now AT&T competes directly with IBM with a complete line of personal computers. A series of television commercials used the slogan "Watson, watch us now." Though Charles Marshall, chairman and chief executive officer of AT&T Information Systems, explained that the slogan referred to the first words Alexander Graham Bell spoke over his telephone, industry pundits had another explanation. They claimed the slogan was a sly reference to Thomas J. Watson, the former chairman of IBM who played a key role in leading his company to its position of dominance.

Its interest in personal computers has not sidetracked AT&T from upgrading the biggest computer of all, the siliconnected network of complex switching circuits that collectively manage traffic on 932 million miles of long-distance lines. By 1990 AT&T will have spent more than $2 billion adding the ability to carry computerized information to much of this long distance system. Professor Bell would have been delighted to know that the expanded network will include 21,000 miles of fiberoptic cables.

·11·

Silicon Law

High-Tech Silicontentions

BUSINESS IS BOOMING for siliconnected lawyers. Consider D. A. Pettifogger, Esq., who, in exchange for 10 percent of the stock and $125 per hour, presided over the paperwork when Silicontraptions, Inc., was incorporated. Pettifogger, a versatile barrister, later wrote one of the two claims in the patent application for the microprocessor-controlled mousetrap, the Mousezap 4000, that earned for Silicontraptions $10 million of venture capital and for Pettifogger a position on the board of directors. A news story about the high-tech Mousezap 4000 quadrupled the value of Pettifogger's stock, which he then sold.

Supported by a staff of four legal assistants, two law clerks, and three secretaries, Pettifogger singlehandedly steered Silicontraptions through the alphabet soup of governmental regulations, charting a course through every available loophole while keeping a wary eye on the latest edicts in the Federal Register and the newsletters of the House Mouse Defenders League. One month Pettifogger battled a team of fixed-fee attorneys representing Overkill, Ltd., in a lawsuit alleging the poaching of trade secrets and the pilfering of chips from Silicontraptions; the next he defended Silicontraptions against charges by civil service lawyers of false advertising and plagiarizing software. Pettifogger settled both actions out of court, and for this received a substantial bonus in shares of stock, which he again sold.

Software bugs and a shortage of test mice forced a delay in the introduction of the Mousezap 4000. This allowed Overkill to beat Silicontraptions to the market with its low-tech, spring-powered Model A Ratbuster. Two mysterious sales of big blocks of its shares had already driven Silicontraptions' stock to new lows. With its venture capital gone and its target market captured by the Rat-buster, Silicontraptions was stuck with an overdesigned product and no cash flow. Being experienced in such matters, Pettifogger presided over Silicontraptions' bankruptcy proceedings. For these farewell services he received a generous portion of the proceeds when Silicontraptions' assets were purchased by Overkill at a public auction. Pettifogger was then retained by Overkill, Ltd., as its chief counselor-at-law, in exchange for a generous salary and a hundred shares of stock which he quietly sold.

The mythical exploits of D. A. Pettifogger provide merely a sampling of the many legal services performed by siliconnected lawyers. In this chapter I relate from both sides of the table real-life experiences with high-tech attorneys. First, let's take a quick tour through some of the territory available to a sharp attorney with a technical mind.

We'll begin our trek by visiting the domestic and foreign computer counterfeiters who have unwittingly generated a good deal of business for attorneys who represent major companies like IBM and Apple Computer. For a time the chief computer counterfeiters were from Taiwan. They specialized in reverse-engineering the proprietary control codes stored permanently in read-only memory chips and then building computers identical in operation to the copied machine. The principal target for the Taiwanese counterfeiters was the Apple II family, one of the earliest and still one of the most popular lines of personal computers. This potentially disastrous invasion couldn't have happened to a more deserving company. Before Steven Jobs and Stephen Wozniak founded Apple they had built and sold illegal "blue boxes," electronic gadgets that counterfeited the dual-tone signals used within the telephone system to steer calls through the long-distance network. With a little practice and some inside information, blue-box owners, known as "phone phreaks," could defraud the telephone company of thousands of dollars in long-distance service.

Heading a Fortune 500 company did to their attitude about defrauding big companies what a bistable electronic circuit called a flip-flop does to a digital signal. When Apple Computer was defrauded by hordes of counterfeiters, it responded vigorously. Armed with copyrights for the Apple II control codes, its lawyers went to battle against the counterfeiters in thirty separate actions, and by 1984 had won stunning victories around the world. First, Lee and Li, a Taiwanese law firm retained by Apple Computer, convinced a Taiwanese court to hand down jail sentences to six computer-company executives charged with counterfeiting the Apple II. In Philadelphia, a U.S. District Court handed down jail sentences to four Americans convicted of smuggling illegal Apple computers from Taiwan. Meanwhile, Apple's busy lawyers fought to keep counterfeit Apple II's out of other countries. In Australia they won a major victory when a federal court agreed that Taiwanese counterfeits infringed valid copyrights.

Apple's battling barristers also tackled a major domestic imitator, Franklin Computer Corporation. Franklin, which had become a significant competitor, openly sold computers containing Apple's copyrighted control codes. Early in 1984 Franklin settled out of court, agreeing to pay Apple $2.5 million and to stop selling computers with copied code. Though Franklin boasted of victory, by the end of 1984 the firm was in bankruptcy.

IBM, too, has had problems with counterfeiters. Thanks in part to precedent-setting decisions won by Apple Computer's legal teams, IBM's lawyers were quickly able to squelch some Taiwanese counterfeiters. In 1983 IBM's attorneys scored a more impressive victory. They arranged a secret $300-million payment from Hitachi Ltd., following a joint IBM-F.B.I. sting operation in which executives from the Japanese electronics giant were filmed offering $600,000 for IBM trade secrets. Later IBM's lawyers settled for $3 million an industrial espionage suit against National Semiconductor, a major Silicon Valley firm.

At the next stop on our tour we peek into high-tech boardrooms and watch greedy executives arrange illegal insider stock transactions. Some cases of alleged insider trading are straightforward. Other suspected insider deals may be perfectly legal. After Apple Computer forecast optimistic sales for its new Lisa computer in late 1982 and early 1983, the value of the company's stock rose dramatically to a high of $63.50. When the stock slid to $17.37 following slow sales and problems with the Lisa, some disgruntled stockholders filed a suit claiming that thirteen Apple officers and directors sold 2,000,000 shares of stock at the same time they were raising public interest by making optimistic claims about the Lisa. According to the suit, Steven Jobs himself sold 500,000 of his 7,400,000 shares for $50 a share. Was this a bonafide case of insider trading? Or were Apple's executives enjoying the rewards of their labors by converting some of their paper stock into greenbacks? Jobs told *The Wall Street Journal* that the stock he sold represented only a fraction of his holdings, and that for a time the shares rose in value after he sold them. Enter the lawyers, the only party guaranteed to win in a complicated case like this one.

Our tour ends on a decidedly low-tech note in the U.S. Patent and Trademark Office as we disperse among seemingly endless corridors lined with cartons containing nearly 4,000,000 categorized and dog-eared copies of patents. Under the terms of a $300-million contract, by 1990 the 25 million documents in the office's antiquated filing system will be accessible through 2,000 computerized work stations. While this will reduce from twenty-seven to eighteen months the average time required to process a patent application, whether the modernized system will enhance the creativity of American inventors remains to be seen. In 1970 225 patents were issued for every million citizens; by 1980 that figure had plunged to 169. More ominous is the rapid growth in the number of U.S. patents issued to foreign nationals, more than 40 percent of the total in 1984. There are many explanations for the sharp decline in the number of patents issued to U.S. citizens, some of them unrelated to any perceived decline in native inventiveness. What follows is a behind-the-scenes account of why a patent was not issued to Bell Labs, the nation's premier research institution, for a new telephone that *Business Week* on December 4, 1978, pronounced "so radically different it may eventually transform American Telephone and Telegraph Co. and the entire telephone industry, with profound effects on data communications, cable television, and every phone user . . . and dramatically alter the basic nature of the phone network."

A Matter of Invention

When Alexander Graham Bell received United States patent 174,465 for his telephone, he learned that a patent is merely a license to sue. The tiny telephone company that eventually became the largest corporation in the world owes its success to its willingness to vigorously defend Bell's patent against dozens of copycats, counterfeiters, and imitators. The legal legacy of the first telephone patent is still very much a priority at Bell Laboratories, the research arm of American Telephone and Telegraph and one of the most productive scientific institutions in the world. Its scientists have received hundreds of awards, seven Nobel Prizes, and nearly 20,000 patents, more than one for every working day.

When I was just beginning to experiment with electronics in the 1950s, I read with astonishment in *National Geographic* about Bell Labs' development of "electronic brains" for missile guidance systems, the solar battery, microwave relay stations, talking motion pictures and, of course, the transistor. One of my ambitions was someday to visit Bell Labs, meet some of its famous scientists, and observe them at work. That goal was fulfilled in 1970 when the Air Force sent me to Bell Labs to visit Dr. I. Hayashi, the physicist who had just invented the first semiconductor laser to operate continuously at room temperature without the need for cooling. In March 1979 I again visited Bell Labs, this time with Peter Purpura, the curator of the National Geographic Society's Explorer's Hall. The principal reason for our visit was to discuss the planned Photophone Centennial, but I had other business at Bell Labs. While Mr. Purpura discussed the technical details of the exhibits Bell Labs was constructing, I was escorted to a private meeting with William L. Keefauver, the eminent attorney responsible for the Labs' 500-member legal staff.

The events leading to the meeting with Mr. Keefauver had their origin in an experiment I conducted as a senior in high school in the spring of 1962. While constructing an analog computer that translated twenty Russian words into English, I became weary of the tedious and time-consuming process of making hundreds of solder connections. After the language translator was completed I decided to pursue some simple experiments with one of the leftover cadmium sulfide (CdS) light-sensitive detectors. Reasoning that the operation of a semiconductor detector of light might be reversible, I tried to elicit light from the CdS cell by connecting its two leads to a battery. When the experiment failed, I assumed that the voltage from the battery was too small. I then connected the CdS cell to the terminals of a 20,000-volt power supply assembled from a discarded automobile ignition coil. This time the entire zig-zag film of cadmium sulfide glowed a soft green and emitted tiny flashes of yellowish-green.

Though I often thought about the outcome of this experiment, and even repeated it from time to time, I could think of no practical use until March 1966. Then I found that silicon solar cells, which are designed to transform light into an electrical current, will themselves emit infrared when a current is passed through them. I managed to send audio tones from a solar cell functioning as an infrared source to an identical solar cell serving as a receiver. The two cells were siliconnected by the invisible stream of flashes passing between them. I hoped to expand this arrangement to send voice in both directions between two solar cells, but the effect proved too weak for any practical purposes. Nevertheless, this simple demonstration was so fundamental to all that follows that an elementary explanation of what took place is in order.

A mechanical siren produces its characteristic whine when the flow of a continuous jet of air is interrupted by holes around the edge of a rotating disk. Though the jet of air is comparatively quiet (*pssssssssss*), the pulsating blasts are exceedingly loud (puff + puff + puff = audible tone). As Professor Bell found during his experiments with the photophone in 1880, a beam of light rapidly interrupted by a chopper wheel produces the familiar siren effect when the resulting flashes strike the surface of a light-sensitive cell connected in a circuit with a battery and telephone receiver. He also found that the mechanical chopper wheel can be eliminated entirely by rapidly switching the current passing through the filament of an electric lamp. If the resulting succession of flashes exceeds about eighteen per second, then the pulsating beam will appear uninterrupted to the eye of an observer. However, if the flashes fall upon a suitable light detector connected to an audio amplifier, a distinct tone will be heard.

This is how I arranged my 1966 experiment. When pulsations of electrical current from a simple transistor oscillator were passed through a silicon solar cell, flashes of infrared were produced. The infrared was not in the form of "heat rays"; instead it was invisible radiation just beyond the red portion of the rainbow of color called the visible light spectrum. When these invisible flashes fell on the second solar cell, a corresponding sequence of minuscule electrical pulses was produced. When boosted by a transistor amplifier, these tiny pulses caused an audio tone to be heard from a small earphone. Keep in mind that the importance of these principles lies in the fact that each solar cell could function as either an emitter or detector of a tone-modulated infrared signal. In other words, bidirectional communications could be established simply by first operating one cell as a source and the other as a detector, and then reversing their roles.

While writing a book on light-emitting diodes in 1972, I found that some diodes that emit visible light and infrared can also function as efficient detectors. Indeed, an infrared diode easily detected the tone-modulated beam from an identical diode located several feet away. I reduced this discovery to practice, as a patent lawyer might say, by demonstrating that a single strand of optical fiber could transport a signal-carrying beam of infrared in either direction by means of a single diode at either end of the fiber. The significance of this scheme was its utter simplicity, for at that time virtually all optical fiber links, experimental or otherwise, used separate fibers for sending and receiving. The only way I knew to send information both ways through a single fiber was to provide a means for a separate light source and detector at each end of the fiber. The simplest method was to attach two short fibers to each end of the main fiber to form "Y" splices. This would provide an optical access port for a separate source and detector at each end of the link.

I measured the sensitivity of some infrared-emitting diodes in the detector mode and was surprised to find they were fully half as efficient as the best silicon detectors (which, like silicon solar cells, functioned very poorly as infrared emitters). Convinced that a simplified single-fiber, two-way lightwave transmission system might comprise a patentable invention, I spent several days searching for what the patent lawyers call "prior art" in the siliconnected journals and books at the library of the University of New Mexico. Since the search turned up nothing, the next step should have been to hire a patent attorney. Unfortunately, I couldn't afford one, or even the expense of preparing and filing a patent application. Since a patent application can be filed within one year of publication of a description of an invention, I decided to describe several versions of the two-way, single-fiber link in my book about light-emitting diodes.

Then I'd submit the invention to one of the major lightwave communications companies before the expiration of the one-year grace period.

Though several companies were then heavily involved in lightwave communications work, the best choice by far was Bell Laboratories. What could be safer? Bell Labs was the most prestigious research institution in the world and an arm of AT&T, a corporation whose worth of $125.5 billion exceeded the combined assets of Exxon, Mobil, and General Motors. On May 29, 1973, I logged the latest results of the experiments in my laboratory notebook, and sent the patent department at Bell Labs a two-page letter describing four applications, including a single-fiber, two-way communications link for diodes that doubled as emitters and detectors. Mr. William Keefauver, Bell Labs' General Patent Attorney, agreed to have the invention suggestion reviewed if I would consent to an agreement that included the following provision: "Should we want to make use of the suggestion, and if it is not already known to us and is not in the possession of the public and is original with the party submitting the suggestion . . . we would expect to discuss the matter with such party in an effort to arrive at an agreement that is mutually satisfactory."

I agreed. The suggestions were reviewed by several patent attorneys and a member of the laboratory's technical staff and his supervisor. The scientist who reviewed the suggestions described at length the different operating principles of semiconductor emitters and detectors of light, and concluded "A single . . . device usually cannot be designed to meet these conflicting requirements." His supervisor then observed, "I think it extremely unlikely that systems considerations would permit a single device to operate as both source and detector. Certainly all of our present thinking has been along the lines of separate fibers for transmitting and receiving." A Bell Labs patent attorney then concluded in a letter to Mr. Keefauver, "it appears that this outside proposal has negligible value to the Bell System, both at the present time and in the foreseeable future. Accordingly, we feel that acquisition of any rights in this proposal is *not* warranted."

At the time I was unaware of the in-house review process given outside suggestions by Bell Labs. I was simply informed by Mr. Keefauver that the letter disclosing my ideas did not "contain any novel features of sufficient interest to us at the present time to warrant our acquiring rights thereunder." Even today I clearly recall the sinking feeling that accompanied the rejection. Nevertheless, I remained convinced the suggestions had merit and continued the experiments. Soon I found that even semiconductor lasers, which are actually highly specialized light-emitting diodes, could double as light detectors. Within a few months I built a two-way lightwave communicator that used an infrared-emitting diode as both an emitter and detector. The communicator could send and receive voice and tone signals hundreds of feet through the air or through an optical fiber. I described construction details of the communicator in the March 1974 issue of *Popular Electronics*. The article concluded, "The fiber-optic mode of operation is a precursor of what telephone systems of the future are likely to resemble."

I continued to write about applications for these diodes. In 1974 I demonstrated some single-fiber communicators for two scientists at the Institute for Telecommunication Sciences in Boulder, Colorado. One of these men, Dr. Robert L. Gallawa, is an expert in fiberoptic communications. Dr. Gallawa was interested in my gadgets, and from that and subsequent encounters arose both a friendship and an invitation to develop for the Institute of Electrical and Electronics Engineers (IEEE) both a text and a short course on lightwave communications. More about that later.

In November 1978 I was startled to learn that Bell Labs had developed a "new device" that doubled as a detector and light source, thus, according to their press release, "greatly simplifying the problem of coupling separate detector and transmitter devices to the same end of a hair-thin fiber." This, of course, was the core of my rejected 1973 suggestion. Bell Labs used this "new" diode in a telephone powered by light sent along a glass fiber. The diode converted the light into electrical power and both received and transmitted voice signals. Thanks to the efficiency of the Bell Labs public relations department, the phone and its new diode received widespread press coverage. *Mechanix Illustrated* in April 1979 reported that "The development was made possible because of a new, highly efficient light detector that doubles as a transmitter." In October 1979 *Electronics* magazine reported, "the new phone could establish AT&T as the No. 1 provider of wideband services to home and industry such as color television, data and computer services and electronic mail." *Electronics* also claimed that "The world's first phone powered by light carried on a fiber-optic cable could probably only have come from a place with the resources of Bell Laboratories."

Remembering the tiny electronics shop in Albuquerque from where I had sent Bell Labs the rejected suggestion whose essence was being hyped as the key to the phone of the future, I didn't know whether to laugh or to cry. Instead, while dozens of articles about Bell Labs' latest triumph appeared in both general-circulation and trade magazines, I exchanged a series of letters with William Keefauver at Bell Labs. Would the scientists involved with the light telephone project acknowledge my publications about the same subject in the technical papers they were then writing about the new phone and its "breakthrough" dual function emitter-detector? Would compensation be provided for what appeared to be the use of the nucleus of the suggestion he had rejected four years earlier? To the request about acknowledgment, Mr. Keefauver responded, "It has always been the practice of our authors to make appropriate reference to the publications of others, and we shall continue to do so." His response about compensation, however, was negative, and several followup exchanges failed to change his mind. My suggestion, he explained, was merely, one of hundreds that recommended such "innovations" as illuminated dials and colored telephones.

In February 1979 Peter Purpura suggested we visit Bell Labs to finalize arrangements for the Photophone Centennial. On the way to join Mr. Purpura at Bell Labs' headquarters in Murray Hill, New Jersey, I stopped in Washington, D.C. to attend a conference on lightwave communications. During a panel discussion, I asked a Bell Labs scientist to expound upon the new light phone. Afterwards, the man seated directly in front of me turned around and said hello. It was Dr. Robert Gallawa, the fiber optics expert I had visited almost five years before to demonstrate some single-fiber communicators.

Before leaving Washington I visited the public search room of the U.S. Patent and Trademark Office. If any of the suggestions in my 1973 letter to Bell Labs had since been patented, I was naively confident of quickly locating the patents. After signing in and receiving a badge, I strode boldly into the vastness of the dimly illuminated search room. Scores of men and women seated at rows of ancient wooden tables were intently poring over enormous piles of documents while others rushed in and out of mysterious passageways carrying stacks of papers. After five minutes of profound bewilderment, I fled from the search room to seek assistance. In a side office at the entrance an understanding civil servant patiently and politely explained the intricacies of conducting a patent search. We went into the search room where he wrote down some numbers retrieved from a big directory. Next we entered an enormous room lined with row after row of compartmented shelves filled with stacks of patents. Two-thirds of the way into the room, the gifted guide plunged down one of the hundred or so narrow aisles, which we followed to the very end. "If your idea has been patented, it will probably be somewhere in this section," he quietly said, motioning toward a wall of shelves that must have contained 10,000 patents. I thanked him for his generous assistance, and he left.

My task seemed doomed to failure. Nevertheless, after breathing a prayer for divine assistance, I reached for a thick bundle of patents and began flipping through them. Incredible as it may seem, in that first stack was a patent issued to Robert G. Hunsperger in 1976 for a diode that sent and received signals through an optical fiber. While the patent didn't precede my 1973 suggestion to Bell Labs, it certainly predated their revolutionary new telephone. After making a copy of the patent, I scrutinized hundreds of others but found nothing relevant. I set off for my meeting at Bell Labs.

Mr. Keefauver began our encounter by politely but firmly insisting that I had no valid claim. He then produced a couple of technical papers by scientists at IBM. Though the papers did not discuss fiberoptics, they disclosed diodes that functioned as both emitters and detectors, the principle underlying both my 1973 suggestion letter and part of the Hunsperger patent. Since the IBM papers held earlier dates, they constituted prior art. Reasoning that a foxy patent lawyer would view as an invention the addition of fiberoptics, as in the Hunsperger patent, I asked whether Bell Labs had filed a patent application on the new phone the press was hyping would transform the telephone system. Yes, Mr. Keefauver responded, much to my great relief. But he then claimed with a straight face that including in the application the concept of a light source that doubled as a light detector, the key ingredient of the new phone, "never occurred" to them. "We want to settle this with you," Mr. Keefauver said. "How much do you want?"

In preparing for the meeting I completely overlooked the possibility Keefauver might actually want to settle the matter. Having no earthly idea how to respond, I stammered about possible options. Keefauver then provided a clue. "It's going to cost us $100,000 to fight you in court," he said. If I asked anything approaching that figure, he declared, they would take me on with full confidence of ultimate victory. I said I would think about it, and get back to him. As the meeting ended, I showed Keefauver the Hunsperger patent. He seemed interested and wrote down the number.

I spent two months trying to pressure Bell Labs to agree in writing to acknowledge my publications and to provide reasonable compensation. Mr. Keefauver at first suggested a payment of $15,000 for my volunteer work in organizing the Photophone Centennial if I would also construct a replica of Bell's original photophone and, of course, agree in writing to drop my claim. Being unequipped with the tools and expertise necessary to duplicate the photophone, I rejected this arrangement. Mr. Keefauver insisted, "We want to make an agreement with you." I foolishly suggested having Bell Labs "sponsor" some of my forthcoming books and articles. This elicited an offer of $25,000, but only if my next three books plus two papers on the photophone were credited to the sponsorship of Bell Labs. I concluded that any such settlement scheme was ridiculous.

By this time I had established contact with Ted Lee, a San Antonio patent attorney who holds a degree in electrical engineering. Ted quickly grasped the essential elements of both the invention suggestion and the controversy. But I was more impressed by the fact that perched on a shelf behind his desk was a copy of my 1973 book about light-emitting diodes, the very book that described how to use diodes that doubled as sources and detectors in an optical fiber communications link. As evidenced by his choice of technical books Ted Lee was obviously an attorney of surpassing wisdom. I listened carefully as he observed that if negotiations collapsed, any legal action seeking relief from Bell Labs would have to be filed before the expiration of the five-year period allowed by the statute of limitations. Since time was rapidly running out, I asked Mr. Keefauver if I could come to Murray Hill to meet with his boss, Dr. N. Bruce Hannay, Vice-President for Research. Hannay was also past president of the Industrial Research Institute, an association of two hundred and fifty companies responsible for most of the industrially funded research and development in the United States.

I arrived early at Bell Labs, and spent half an hour wandering through a museum exhibit in the reception area. The experience was enlightening. The exhibits portrayed Bell Labs as a national treasure, an intellectual fountainhead, and a siliconized cornucopia from which flowed the seminal electronic marvels of our modern age. A few of the exhibits contained placards that made false claims about "pioneering" this and that siliconcocted widget. One placard even claimed Bell Labs made the "first" semiconductor injection laser, an assertion that would have surprised the able scientists at General Electric, IBM, and the Massachusetts Institute of Technology who in 1962 almost simultaneously did just that.

Mr. Keefauver ushered me into what he described as a ten-minute "audience" with the distinguished Dr. Hannay. After flying all the way from Texas at my own expense, I had no intention of spending only ten minutes; I had outlined on ten note cards the highlights of the controversy, and I fully intended to discuss each point. The mood of the "audience" was less than friendly. Twenty minutes into the meeting the discussion became sidetracked, and I suggested returning to the point to avoid wasting their time. "You *are* wasting my time!" Dr. Hanney sniffed. When I observed that there appeared to be a pattern of Bell Labs sometimes claiming for itself the inventions of others, among them the semiconductor injection laser, Dr. Hannay claimed that nobody works harder than they to verify claims. As for the injection laser, he said they had not claimed its invention. When I read him the text from the exhibit in the lobby, Dr. Hannay expressed surprise, said that "might" have to be changed, and then muttered something about an early Bell Labs patent on injection lasers. As for our controversy, they refused to alter their basic requirement that I perform work for hire. The meeting ended after sixty-six minutes, the matter still unresolved. After we made our way through a reception area clogged with people whose appointments with Dr. Hannay had apparently been backed up, Mr. Keefauver displayed a new air of confidence. He said when he retired he planned to write a book about controversies involving priority in invention. I wished him well, impishly thinking he was well equipped for the task.

I next made a fruitless appeal by letter and in a telephone conversation (he answered his own phone) to Dr. Ian M. Ross, the president of Bell Labs. Having exchanged thousands of words of correspondence and participated in two personal meetings and more than a hundred telephone discussions, all to no avail, I felt the admiration I once had for Bell Labs beginning to crumble like Mr. Keefauver's as yet unfulfilled assurances that they would reference my publications. My 1973 suggestion didn't propose painting black telephones pastel pink and equipping them with strangle-proof cords. Instead, it was the essential ingredient in the invention that would one day transform the entire telephone system and revolutionize the communications industry. Under the influence of an overdose of heaping hype emanating from the great laboratory at Murray Hill, I fancifully concluded Bell Labs was no mere ivory tower in the proverbial land of Not Invented Here. In my imagination Bell Labs had become a cloud-piercing castle fashioned from the very tusks brought to King Solomon by the ships of Tarshish.

How would the gentlemanly Prof. Alexander Graham Bell have responded had he found himself in a similar predicament? Hadn't he shared credit for the photophone with his assistant, Sumner Tainter? Didn't his speeches and published papers acknowledge every individual who contributed to the developments that eventually led to the photophone? When Bell's telephone patent was challenged by dozens of imposters, they found themselves in court when negotiations failed. With the statute of limitations set to expire in thirty days, it was time to pay a last-resort visit to Ted Lee. Little did either of us realize what we were getting into when Ted's small Texas law firm agreed to take on the largest corporation in America.

·12·

Mims versus Bell Labs

Order of Battle

LEGAL BATTLES CAN RANGE from quickly settled scuffles to contests having the dimensions of a military confrontation. My clash with Bell Labs certainly fell in the latter category, with a three-ring circus thrown in for good measure. Before the action begins, let's size up the combatants by reviewing what military intelligence specialists refer to as the order of battle, an inventory of troop strength, firepower, and so forth.

My second was Ted D. Lee, the white-suited knight of the Texas law firm of Gunn & Lee, now Gunn, Lee & Jackson. The half dozen or so patriots at Gunn & Lee were bivouacked in a cluster of offices on the seventh floor of a San Antonio office tower within sniper range of a windowless fortress housing the central office of a major enemy field unit, Southwestern Bell. Though few in number, the freedom fighters at Gunn & Lee were gifted strategists who possessed a solid knowledge of legal tactics, excellent timing, and a good sense of humor.

Our adversary was Bell Telephone Laboratories, the research arm of the monolithic monopoly American Telephone and Telegraph. When Gunn & Lee declared all-out legal war against Bell Labs on my behalf in May 1979, the AT&T order of battle included 985,000 regulars and a total annual revenue of $41 billion. The Bell Labs division of AT&T included a corps of 20,000 high-tech engineers and a Patent and Legal Staff of 100 strategists commanded by William L. Keefauver, one of the best-known corporate patent attorneys in the United States. Keefauver's strategists were represented on the field of battle by several mercenaries recruited from two Texas law firms, and a detachment of shock troops supplied by the legal division of Western Electric, another unit of AT&T.

Gunn & Lee's tiny squad appeared to be badly outgunned by an overwhelming force whose revenues alone exceeded those of many countries. Prior to the onset of hostilities, however, those odds didn't faze me in the least, for I knew something the enemy didn't: After graduating from law school in 1970, Ted Lee served a four year hitch as an attorney in the United States Marine Corps. He was a battle-hardened veteran of the legal arena with considerably more trial experience than most patent attorneys. What's more, during must-win engagements with the enemy, fearless Ted reportedly donned a white western-style suit that transformed him into Sir Ted the Invincible. With Ted Lee's help, defeating Bell Labs would be simple. Or so I thought before visiting Ted's office to read the imposing draft of a formal declaration of war entitled FORREST M. MIMS, III, Plaintiff v. BELL TELEPHONE LABORATORIES, Defendant.

Recall for a moment the issue at hand. In 1973 I had sent Bell Labs a suggestion that described how to send communications in both directions through an optical fiber by placing at each end a device called a diode that doubled as both a source and detector of light. After two of its scientists and several patent attorneys reviewed the suggestion, it was rejected. One scientist wrote, "A single . . . device usually cannot be designed to meet these conflicting requirements." His supervisor concluded, ". . . I think it extremely unlikely that systems considerations would permit a single device to operate as both a source and detector." In 1978 Bell Labs announced a new optical-fiber telephone, the key ingredient of which was a diode that doubled as a light source and detector that could communicate in both directions through a single optical fiber. This, of course, was the nucleus of my 1973 suggestion.

Marching Orders

Ted Lee's declaration of legal war against Bell Labs was entitled "COMPLAINT." The complaint included seven specific counts, each of which alleged a grievous violation of my rights by Bell Labs. These included breach of contract, unjust enrichment, detrimental reliance, misappropriation, libel, and fraud.

Within the allotted thirty days Bell Labs responded to the complaint by firing back a document entitled "ANSWER." Not surprisingly, this document denied the specific charges of wrongdoing alleged in Ted's opening salvo. (It also denied such seemingly straightforward statements as that Bell Labs was owned by AT&T and had a working relationship with Western Electric.) Ted shot back a demand for a jury trial, and then the two sides engaged in a skirmish over "discovery," the formal process of reviewing the relevant evidence possessed by each side. The ground rules for the discovery procedures were given in a protective order, an awesome document mutually agreed upon by the combatants and signed by a federal district judge. The protective order provided for the perpetual protection of proprietary and confidential information disclosed by either side. Violating the order by disclosing protected information to unauthorized persons could cause the violator to be held in contempt of court.

The compressed chronology of the events thus far implies a rapid-fire series of actions by both parties. Actually, the proceedings advanced at a snail's pace. From time to time, months of quiet, behind-the-scenes preparation would be punctuated by furious fusillades of hot air and paper bullets. In September 1979, for example, nearly a year after Bell Labs announced its new light phone, Ted and I made our first joint foray into enemy territory to take depositions from several Bell Labs scientists and William Keefauver. Despite Bell Labs' curious denial of a working relationship with Western Electric, this initial confrontation was held in the offices of Western Electric in New York City. After the protective order was signed, several attorneys for the other side surrendered some 2,000 pages of numbered documents from their files, and left Ted and me alone to survey our loot. The documents were provided in response to a formal itemized notice requiring Bell Labs to produce any records, sketches, memoranda, and so forth relevant to the lawsuit.

Aside from some copies of published technical papers, virtually every document was stamped CONFIDENTIAL, and therefore covered by the terms of the protective order. The most notable exception was a file containing the review of my 1973 suggestion by several scientists and patent attorneys at Bell Labs. Didn't they realize that after learning the names of the two scientists, a quick phone call to the Bell Labs operator would reveal the unconfidential fact that their offices were within a few doors of one another and the scientist who invented the light phone? That these papers had escaped the confidential stamp seemed particularly curious since it had been applied to hundreds of documents having considerably less importance. Whatever the reason, the fortuitous absence of the ubiquitous stamp is why quotations from this file can be included in this book.

After an enlightening hour reviewing the booty, the attorneys for the opposing side reappeared and raised a white flag. The gist of the peace talks that followed was that they wanted to discuss settling the lawsuit out of court. Unfortunately, however, a letter I wrote about the dispute that was published in *Spectrum*, a slick monthly sent to members of the Institute of Electrical and Electronics Engineers, had angered Bell Labs' top management. This loss of face, Mr. Keefauver explained, might preclude the possibility of settlement, so he could make no promises. In view of this development, and because we needed more time to review the documents, Ted postponed the taking of depositions, and we returned to Texas. The letter to *Spectrum* apparently had struck a sensitive nerve, for the tentative settlement offer soon vaporized along with Bell Labs' repeated promise to acknowledge my publications.

Silicontentions

Shortly before Ted and I left for New York, Bell Labs filed a lengthy motion asking the judge to dismiss the suit. In retrospect, the then-unknown outcome of this motion rather than the-truth-hurts letter in *Spectrum* probably caused Bell Labs to postpone settlement negotiations. Whatever, Ted Lee assigned Mark Miller, a trusted lieutenant at Gunn & Lee, to prepare a formal response. Meanwhile, Ted formally notified Patrick Leach, the Western Electric lawyer assigned to the case, that he intended to take the previously postponed depositions on November 14, 1979. I left for New York before Ted, and shortly after arriving at the hotel received a message that Leach had unilaterally cancelled the depositions. The best way to convey my reaction is to ask how you would feel if you flew half way across the country, at your own expense, only to learn an important meeting had been called off. Yes, that's how I felt.

Mark Miller eventually assembled a shrewd response to Bell Labs' motion to dismiss the lawsuit. Shortly after it was sent to the judge, Ted rescheduled the meeting to take depositions. For five days Ted took from five witnesses depositions totaling 674 pages. During the testimony there were frequent verbal clashes between Ted and Patrick Leach. The initial fracas was over the presence as counsel of Michael Urbano, the Bell Labs patent attorney who had prepared the then-pending patent application for the light phone. Since Urbano was slated to give a deposition later, Ted objected to his presence. But Urbano stayed. Following two days of fireworks between Ted and Leach, James Curley, another Western Electric attorney, was sent in to replace Leach.

In Leach's absence the depositions proceeded without a hitch. Then Leach reappeared with an older and apparently more senior Western Electric attorney who mumbled a greeting and sat at a far corner of the table. Ted Lee, the lone litigating leatherneck, now faced four Western Electric and Bell Labs lawyers. Fortunately, this time Leach was more subdued and for the remaining few days the proceedings continued with only a few major clashes.

During the depositions, testimony was taken in several different conference rooms in both the former AT&T and Western Electric buildings. Each morning security guards at the door would carefully search our briefcases. Whether the precautions were to detect bomb-equipped terrorists or irate telephone company customers, I cannot say. Whatever the reason, the security procedures infuriated the court reporter who each morning was required to unstrap her transcription equipment from its dolly, open it for inspection, and then strap it back in place. Another ritual that seemed rather odd to a couple of Texans from the hinterlands took place at exactly 5:00 p.m. each afternoon. Before you can say "Gotta catcha train!" the lawyers on the other side of the table scooped up their goodies and made a mad dash for the door. These hasty retreats made Ted and the security guards downstairs a little uncomfortable, since each evening we were left unescorted in enemy headquarters.

Because the testimony taken during the depositions is covered by the protective order, what was disclosed cannot be revealed now or ever. About all I can say is that by the end of the first day I no longer held any idealistic notions about the value of depositions in revealing the truth. Indeed, more enlightening than the 674 pages of confidential testimony was a brief aside with one of the scientists from Bell Labs who reviewed my suggestion in 1973. From the outset I never imagined that he and his coworkers had conspired to "steal" my suggestion. But I did think it reasonable to assume that the essence of the suggestion might have been remembered long after the letter in which it was contained had been forgotten. In any event, I was embarrassed about involving this scientist and his colleagues in the lawsuit, so I apologized for the inconvenience he had been caused. "Don't worry," he responded. "It's not your fault." Then whose fault was it, I wondered. Was he being polite? Did he think my attorneys had overplayed a trivial issue? Did he feel the Bell Labs-Western Electric legal machine had mishandled the affair? Or was there an overall breakdown of common sense during my pre-lawsuit attempts to arrange a settlement and have my papers acknowledged? The scientist's quiet response stayed with me during the rest of the lawsuit and lingers to this day.

Back in Texas, meanwhile, Mark Miller's carefully researched response to Bell Labs' motion to dismiss the lawsuit was being studied by a federal judge. Mark's superb scholarship paid off when the judge overruled nearly all of Bell Labs' weighty motion. Though a deceptive trade practices and fraud count was dismissed, the six remaining counts were left untouched. Bell Labs might have thought the lawsuit groundless, but the judge's action indicated otherwise. So far Gunn & Lee was more than holding its own against the largest corporation in America.

About a month later Bell Labs scored a round for its side when three of its lawyers spent a day searching my office. Although Bell Labs had produced hundreds of documents as part of the pretrial discovery process, they had not allowed us to inspect the famous light phone, nor did they produce several important documents Ted had repeatedly requested. To show the judge that our side had nothing to hide, Ted and I decided to do what we had requested of Bell Labs. Their attorney had sent us a four-page list of requested documents, to include ". . . the original and every copy of every kind of writing or recording . . . letters, memoranda, reports, notes, papers, books, graphs, laboratory notebooks . . ." and some

forty other categories ". . . of the foregoing in the actual or con-
structive custody, care or control of plaintiff." They also requested
the lightwave communications equipment I'd built. Ted responded
that the attorneys for Bell Labs would be free to perform an on-site
inspection of my files to locate the listed items.

On the morning of January 29, 1980, Mark Miller arrived at my
home with a machine for numbering documents. Soon Patrick
Leach and Edward Koziol from Western Electric, and Michael
Urbano from Bell Labs arrived. They marched out to my office and
electronics shop, and began a thorough search of my desk, book-
shelves, and file cabinets. In the process they pulled some 1,800
pages. They easily located all the files pertaining to the lawsuit, as
well as royalty statements, college transcripts, résumés, correspondence, and other personal records that did not appear on their
document list. We had hoped the searchers would examine some of
my homemade lightwave communications gear so we could later
demand an equal opportunity to inspect the famous light phone.
Though equipment was included on their list, they declined our
invitation and merely took a quick look at the gear.

My major complaint about the search was the examination of the
eight laboratory notebooks I've kept since college. I had no objec-
tion to the Western Electric lawyers looking through the notebooks, particularly since I had placed them under the protective
order by labeling them CONFIDENTIAL. I did, however, object to
Michael Urbano inspecting them since he was a Bell Labs patent
attorney and my notebooks described many possibly patentable
inventions. Nevertheless, Urbano sat at my desk and reviewed
every page in each notebook. The on-site search, which had seemed
like such a good idea to demonstrate openness, was not a pleasant
experience.

Near the end of the day while Urbano was still reading the
notebooks, Leach and Kozoil asked about other locations where
documents might be stored. I remembered a large box of book
manuscripts in the attic and offered to give Leach a light if he
wished to examine them. Instead, he insisted that the box be taken
down from the attic, promising it would be replaced before they
left. Mark and I then watched the fun as the two well dressed New
York lawyers wrestled the heavy box through the small opening in
the attic. After they inspected its contents, none of which they

wanted, Mark reminded Leach about his promise to return the heavy box to the attic. Leach turned away and announced, "The box will not be returned." Having spent an entire day watching Leach and his crew shuffle, crease and otherwise disrupt my files and records, I wasn't at all pleased by the prospect of having to replace the box. Though I was supposed to communicate through Mark, I told Leach he had promised to replace the box and I expected him to do so. "The box will not be replaced," droned Leach, as he stared out a window. "The box *will* be replaced!" I ordered. "The box will *not* be replaced!" Leach retorted. After a few more exchanges I gave up and announced, "None of the documents will be provided if the box is not replaced." My ultimatum quickly got Mark Miller's attention since failing to provide the documents would give Bell Labs the opportunity to tell the judge we were uncooperative. Leach, on the other hand, realized his failure to cooperate would give us an opportunity to complain about the way the search was conducted. Without saying a word, he motioned toward Koziol and began shoving the box toward the ladder.

About the time Leach and Koziol climbed down from the attic, Urbano finished reading my notebooks. Then without a goodbye the trio hustled through the house and out the front door. Just as they reached their fancy rental cars parked by the street, the clock in the living room chimed out five.

On February 19, 1980, three weeks after the search, my wife and I were in Washington for the opening of the Photophone Centennial exhibit. A few days earlier an AT&T publicist had called to ask if he could interview me for a film they were making about the event. Apparently Bell Labs got wind of his plans, for the interview was later cancelled. Fortunately they didn't cancel the exhibit. Thanks to the efforts of James Lowell, a bearded Bell Labs exhibits coordinator who bears an uncanny resemblance to Alexander Graham Bell, the photophone exhibit in Explorer's Hall was first-rate.

Victory

During the summer and fall of 1980 the attorneys representing Bell Labs issued at least ten deposition notices to people and companies in seven states. They took a deposition from Dr. Robert Gallawa, my friend from the National Institute of Telecommunications in Colorado. In Dallas they deposed David Gunzel, the chief technical editor at Radio Shack. In New York they took depositions from Arthur Salsberg and John McVeigh of *Popular Electronics*. Meanwhile, Ted Lee served notice that he intended to take the depositions of several top executives at Bell Labs. He also fired off a flurry of interrogatories, and both sides exchanged broadsides of motions, answers, rebuttals, briefs, affidavits, and notices.

Finally, Bell Labs sent notice to take my deposition. The discovery procedures required me to bring to the deposition every relevant document (". . . letters, memoranda, reports, notes, papers, books . . .") generated in the ten months since the search of my office, so I decided to have a little fun with the other side. I had recently completed writing a text and short course on lightwave communications for the IEEE, and had accumulated enough new documents to fill a briefcase and a large carton. The document request specified "every copy of every kind" so I included everything from used typewriter ribbons to an envelope stuffed with a thousand or so holes punched from the margin of the IEEE manuscript so it could be placed in a three-ring binder. A second briefcase contained lightwave communications equipment I'd built plus a camera.

On November 10, 1980, I rolled a dolly loaded with the new documents into a conference room high in an Austin office tower and took a seat opposite a large window that framed the picturesque Texas state capitol building. A few moments later a fellow wearing a sports shirt strode in and introduced himself as Richard Keeton. Bell Labs had hired Mr. Keeton, a notable trial lawyer from Houston, to represent them in the upcoming trial, and it was he who would take my deposition. Keeton said he enjoyed visiting his Austin office because of the spectacular view it provided of the capitol building. In fact, he observed, I was seated exactly where he liked to sit. Wouldn't I prefer to move to the other side of the table? The books on the art of negotiation I'd read before the first meeting with William Keefauver at Bell Labs stressed the importance of seating arrangements during a meeting. Since Mr. Keeton preferred the seat I had selected, it seemed only prudent to stay put. "No thanks, this is just fine," I replied.

After Ted Lee and the familiar trio of Leach, Urbano, and Koziol arrived, the court reporter administered the oath and the deposition began. After an hour of routine questions about educational background, military service, and technical experience, Keeton quizzed me at length about six pages of notes from my files that I'd labeled "Telephone Artifacts." Shortly before the lawsuit was filed, a scrappy Texas lawyer who had taken on Southwestern Bell in a highly publicized lawsuit told Ted and me to assume my telephone was bugged. Whether it was or not I do not know, but between March and November 1979 there occurred a rash of strange clicks, pops, taps, disconnects, volume changes, and interruptions unlike anything I'd ever heard before. Often these artifacts were noticed by the other party, and I jotted down some of their comments. For instance, on March 14 while I was briefing a reporter for *Electronics* magazine about the Bell Labs dispute, he commented, "You're not going to believe this, but you're voice disappeared for the last ten seconds." Later that same day my paranoia index soared an order of magnitude when I spotted a man wearing a telephone lineman's kit climbing a utility pole down the street from my house. He was driving a blue pickup, not one of the vans used by the privately owned telephone company in my town.

The notes about the telephone anomalies were in a file that also contained several papers entitled "Bell Labs Action Plan." This was a guerilla law arsenal of "actions to be undertaken should Bell Labs fail to settle my claim against them." It listed such goodies as complaining about Bell Labs' conduct to the Justice Department, the American Bar Association, and the American Association of Patent Attorneys. After I learned that the action plan would have to be produced during the discovery process, I added more ammunition to the list—names of congressional committee staffers, magazines and TV networks to contact. Probably the most potent document was an annotated copy of the Canons of Professional Ethics of the American Bar Association. Ted Lee considered the action plan a hot potato, and I could hardly wait for the other side to see it. Richard Keeton was certainly interested in the action plan, for he asked lots of questions about it. Later I learned Bell Labs had marked the papers in the action plan with a special set of serial numbers different from those applied to the remaining 1,800 papers they selected during the search of my office.

Halfway through the morning of the first day, Mr. Keeton decided to inspect the new documents I'd brought along. After an hour of sorting, sifting and stacking, the other side gleaned what they wanted of the paperwork. I then opened the briefcase containing lightwave communications gear and removed my camera. Since Leach, Urbano and Koziol had not objected when I took pictures of them when they searched my office, I planned to photograph them examining the equipment. But suddenly Leach dove under the table and Urbano fled the room. There followed a lengthy and lively exchange between Keeton and Ted about whether or not I would be allowed to take pictures. Eventually the other side said they didn't want to inspect the equipment so I agreed to put the camera away.

Ted and I had been concerned that Bell Labs had made a wise move in selecting a smooth-talking Texan to represent them before a jury of his fellow citizens. But after the flap over the camera, Keeton and I got along just fine. Though he was a tough interrogator, after two long days of questioning I developed considerably more respect for Keeton than for his northeastern clients. Even though he was a product of the University of Texas and I was a graduate of arch-rival Texas A&M University, we were tuned to the same wavelength. He appeared interested in the books I'd written, respected my request that Urbano not view my notebooks, and asked about the Photophone Centennial. He even seemed sympathetic when I explained that Bell Labs had refused to acknowledge my publications in their light phone papers.

On the third day the depositions were moved to San Antonio. When I returned to the conference room after a break for lunch, Keeton and his clients were clustered in a corner discussing strategy. When I arrived they began whispering, but Urbano could still be clearly heard coaching Keeton about how to ask a very technical and crucial question regarding my 1973 suggestion. When Keeton asked the tricky question an hour or so later, I was ready with the correct response. Urbano scribbled some followup questions for Keeton to ask, and they, too, were easily answered.

On the fourth and last day of the depositions Ted Lee donned his white western-style suit and cowboy boots for the first time since the lawsuit was filed 18 months earlier. His uniform was soon to have the intended effect. Near the end of the day when the Bell

Labs people collected their materials and prepared to leave, Keeton asked them "What are you turkeys [going to do]?" Leach and Urbano looked uncharacteristically sheepish and didn't appear nearly as pleased as I was by Keeton's fowl appellation. After they left, Mr. Keeton continued the interrogation for another half hour, then plaintively observed for the record that all his colleagues had gone, and ended the deposition. Then he leaned back in his chair and propped his feet on the table. He announced that Bell Labs was prepared to fight the lawsuit in court, and that he was their "cannon" and was fully able to "shoot" us down. However, Keeton continued, in his judgment it would be better for both sides to settle the lawsuit out of court. Ted now propped his cowboy boots on the table, and quickly worked out the terms of a tentative agreement with the laid-back interrogator. Keeton even agreed to ask Bell Labs to include in the final settlement an agreement to reference my relevant papers in their light-phone papers. Not surprisingly, Bell Labs refused. A week before Christmas 1980, Ted and I met in San Antonio to sign the settlement papers and pose for pictures with a sizable check from Bell Labs.

With a little help from my action plan and a white cowboy suit, Ted Lee, Mark Miller, and I had successfully taken on the largest corporation in America. I have no idea what has become of Bell Labs' ambitious plans for the light phone. Their scientists published several technical papers on diodes that double as sources and detectors of light during 1979–80, but since the settlement I've seen no additional papers on the subject by Bell Labs authors. In September 1980 they suddenly abandoned their U.S. patent application for the light phone, but a few years ago I learned they had also filed at least one foreign patent application. Thanks to prior art requirements of Dutch patent law, the foreign application cited my 1974 article for *Popular Electronics* that concluded that a single-fiber lightwave link using dual-function source-detectors "is a precursor of what telephone systems of the future are likely to resemble." Despite their obstinance about referencing my papers, someone in that siliconized ivory tower eventually saw the light.

·13·

The Silicon Press, B.A.*

"Breakthrough!"

SINCE ITS EMBRYONIC INCEPTION in the papers and patents of Alexander Graham Bell in 1880 describing the use of selenium to detect voice-modulated light beams, the silicon press has blossomed into a vast array of high-tech publications. They range from instruction booklets for solid-state consumer products to highly technical reference and engineering books about telecommunications, computers, fiberoptics, radio, and quantum electronics. The silicon press also includes manufacturers' news releases, product brochures, integrated circuit data books, catalogs, conference proceedings, dissertations, in-depth market reports that sell for $1000 or more, and hundreds of periodicals.

The periodicals are the message centers and bulletin boards of the silicon press. At the most fundamental level are a dozen or so journals that carry scholarly papers by the physicists, metallurgists, crystallographers, chemists, and other scientists who are exploring the cutting edge of semiconductor research. The field is broad and the topics range from new kinds of exotic semiconductor alloys to the precise milling by means of electron beams of microscopic structures in solid silicon. Next are journals that describe in precise detail the fabrication and operation of working electronic devices made possible by applied semiconductor research. This is the territory of device physicists, the scientists who conceive and fashion new kinds of microscopic transistors, memory cells, laser diodes, and the like.

Then there's a rich assortment of engineering journals that describe the practical applications made possible by the device physi-

* Before Altair.

cists. Here are found papers about the latest integrated-circuit microprocessors, fiberoptic systems, balloon-borne atmospheric research probes, and remote imaging systems for earth satellites. The electronics trade magazines are next. Many of them are highly specialized and cover specific topics such as fiberoptic communications, lasers, computers, or military weapons and systems. Sometimes they cover the same topics as the research and engineering journals, in simplified technical articles. They also emphasize news of recent developments as well as practical articles that describe specific classes of commercial and industrial products ranging from light-emitting diodes and power transistors to microprocessors and computer-controlled test instrumentation.

Finally, there are magazines for high-tech consumers, computer enthusiasts, and electronics experimenters. Like the trade magazines, these periodicals are financed by advertisers. The consumer magazines cover everything from electronically controlled cameras and home video recorders to citizens band radio and digital audio systems. Computer magazines and books form by far the largest group of silicon-based publications. Some cover the entire computing field while others are "machine-specific" and describe a single computer or family of computers. They range from limited-circulation newsletters to 500-page monthlies that resemble a mail-order catalog more than a conventional magazine.

Though magazines for electronics experimenters are comparatively few in number, they have made an impact on the entire semiconductor electronics industry. Many of the scientists and engineers who made the discoveries in modern solid-state electronics now taken for granted were influenced in their youth by these magazines. Moreover, magazines for experimenters and hobbyists have in the past been a spawning ground for new high-tech products in the form of projects that could be assembled into working devices by savvy readers. The "breakthrough" electronic projects published as cover stories by one such magazine, *Popular Electronics*, reads like a high-tech wish list: low-cost digital counting units, digital test equipment, a helium-neon laser for under $100, an infrared communicator, a telephone speech scrambler, do-it-yourself holograms, an electronic heartbeat monitor, and the first kit electronic calculator. Comparatively few of these projects were authentic technological breakthroughs. Nevertheless, many of them demonstrated that high-priced scientific and engineering equipment could be made available to the everyday user at an affordable price. Certainly the most far-reaching "breakthrough" project ever to appear in a hobbyist magazine was the two project articles about the MITS Altair 8800 microcomputer project in the January and February 1975 issues of *Popular Electronics*. The inventors of the microprocessor had not foreseen for their brainchild the product developed by Ed Roberts. Even Ed himself had no idea that his Altair would launch a multi-billion-dollar industry and profoundly influence the way many people work and play.

Magazines for electronics experimenters have their origins in the fertile mind of Hugo Gernsback. Today Gernsback is well known to science fiction aficionados since the prize given each year for the best novel in that genre is called the Hugo. In 1926 he began *Amazing Stories*, filling its pages with what he called "scientifiction," and establishing himself as the father of science fiction. But more important than Gernsback's science fiction magazines were his periodicals for radio and electronics hobbyists. Science fact was on his mind in 1904 when the 19-year-old Gernsback arrived in the United States with a patent for a new battery he hoped to sell. Two years later he and a friend started the Electro Importing Company, the first business to specialize in radio parts and supplies. Since radio was so new, the company's catalog had to include lengthy technical explanations alongside many of its items. By 1908 the catalog had evolved into what Gernsback billed as "The electrical magazine for everybody," *Modern Electrics*.

Prior to beginning *Modern Electrics*, Gernsback had secured several thousand paid subscriptions simply by circulating a letter to which electronics hobbyists today can readily relate. "The publishers of the new magazine," Gernsback wrote, "*know* what young men want. The thousands of inquiries asking for all kinds of information show that the amateur is in need of knowledge which cannot be found in our best text books." In an editorial in the premier issue entitled "To Our Friends," Gernsback echoed his conviction about the worth of the amateur experimenter: "It is surprising to find how many young men in these days are the proud owners of well-equipped little shops and the editor knows quite a number of young people who are conducting at the present writing experiments of which many professors would not be ashamed." Among the articles in that historic 34-page first issue were "How to Make an Electric Whistle," "Experiments in Static Electricity," and "Recharging Dry Cells." Also included were two pages of "Technical Notes" with tips about working with glass and metal, and "Electrical Patents of the Month." But it was the lead article, "Wireless Telegraphy," that most clearly reflected the major interest of Gernsback and his readers.

Radio brought about the golden age of hobby electronics, an era when thousands of experimenters built crystal sets and radios on kitchen tables and in garage workshops. Gernsback capitalized on the trend by following *Modern Electrics* with a series of hobbyist magazines that were eventually to have a profound impact on many young experimenters. These included *Electrical Experimenter* (1913), *Radio-News* (1919), *Radio-Craft* (1929), and nine other amateur radio and television magazines. Gernsback livened up his magazines with predictions about the future of electronics, many of which eventually became true.

Eventually *Modern Electrics* was merged with several other magazines to form what is now *Popular Science*. *Radio-Craft* is still published as *Radio-Electronics*. After some changes in ownership, *Radio-News* evolved into *Electronics World*, a Ziff-Davis magazine that was later merged with the most innovative of the siliconnected hobbyist publications, *Popular Electronics*. The first *Popular Electronics* magazine I saw was on a magazine rack in a Weingarten's grocery store in Houston in 1956. I was twelve; the 35-cent magazine was two. An editorial by Olliver Read in the October 1954 premier issue described the mission of the new magazine: *"Popular Electronics,* as its title implies, is devoted to the science of electronics at a how it works, why it works, how to do it and how to use it level." For nearly three decades the magazine faithfully fulfilled Read's aspirations, publishing thousands of construction projects and feature articles about electronics. Since many of the projects used hard-to-find parts and required printed circuit boards, the magazine encouraged its writers to find companies that would offer kits containing the necessary parts and circuit boards. Many of these small companies were silicon garages operated by the writers themselves.

Besides construction projects, tutorial pieces, and articles about the latest electronics developments, *Popular Electronics* featured several columns on such subjects as shortwave radio and high fidelity.

During my teenage years my favorite column was Louis E. Garner, Jr.'s, "Transistor Topics." Since the mid-'50s magazines like *Science and Mechanics* had presented simple one-transistor radio construction projects, a frequent subject of Garner's column. But "Transistor Topics" went farther, and included details about how to make transistorized metronomes, beepers, light-activated relays, and midget transmitters. I read "Transistor Topics" faithfully, thinking of trusty Lou Garner as my personal guide in the world of solid-state electronics.

In February 1968 *Popular Electronics* ushered in a new era in hobby electronics. The magazine's cover proclaimed "KEEP THIS ISSUE. Introducing a New Series of Projects Utilizing This— BREAKTHROUGH PROJECT: Decimal Counting Unit for $12!" Adjacent to the "breakthrough" proclamation, as if it had been punched through the magazine's cover, was a circuit board festooned with integrated circuits and transistors. On one end of the circuit board were mounted two staggered rows of ten lamps numbered 0 through 9. Several of the counting-unit circuits could be connected and mounted in a row to form a multi-digit digital display. Imagine, for the first time electronics hobbyists could build sophisticated projects with digital readouts: timers, clocks, voltmeters, frequency counters, and the like. Indeed, the next month *Popular Electronics* again amazed its readers with a construction article that used three of the decimal-counting units to form a precision electronic stopwatch capable of counting up to ten million events per second. The article showed in detail how to use the stopwatch to "easily time a speeding bullet in flight!" Kits containing parts and circuit boards for the stopwatch circuit and the individual decimal-counting units were available from Southwest Technical Products, a small electronics company in San Antonio.

The man responsible for these two articles was Don Lancaster, an Arizona electrical engineer. Don's articles elicited an unprecedented outpouring of mail and phone calls from readers. A university student working on a master's thesis in ballistics summed up the views of most readers when he wrote, "I really do not believe there is a word in the dictionary that can adequately express the quality of Mr. Lancaster's 'Low Cost Counting Unit' and 'Electronic Stopwatch.'" When both articles were later reprinted by *Popular Electronics* in an annual project issue, the editor wrote, "Stuffy electronics engineers who think hobby electronics is beneath their dignity received a severe blow to their pride when *Popular Electronics* published plans for an in-line decimal counting unit. Adding insult to injury, the cost of building one DCU reached a rock-bottom price of $12—about $40 less than the major manufacturers of electronic equipment had been able to offer for a similar item of much less flexibility." Almost as important as its counting capability was the decimal-counting unit's liberal use of integrated circuits. In 1968 the high cost of IC's had prevented many experimenters from using them. When prices finally began falling Don Lancaster became the first hobby electronics writer to use them widely in his magazine projects.

Don Lancaster's articles postponed my goal to become an electronics writer. He was a real engineer; my degree was in government. He wrote about analog and digital integrated circuits; I was still using transistors and had barely begun experimenting with IC's. Besides, building miniature model rocket-guidance systems left no time for writing electronic construction projects. In the summer of 1969 I accompanied the teenaged members of an Albuquerque model rocket club to a conference at Eastern New Mexico State University, where I met George Flynn, the editor of the now-defunct *Model Rocketry*. Flynn became interested in one of the transistorized flight flashers I had made to track night-launched model rockets, and asked me to write an article describing its construction. Nothing was said about payment, so it came as a surprise when Flynn sent me a check for $93.50. This article led to a monthly column in *Model Rocketry*, and restored my ambition of becoming a full-time writer. The flasher article also led to the formation of Micro Instrumentation and Telemetry Systems, or MITS.

Meanwhile, *Popular Electronics* continued publishing articles about "breakthrough" projects considerably more complex than two-transistor light flashers. In 1970 the Smithsonian Institution mounted a special exhibit to celebrate the tenth anniversary of the invention of the laser. While visiting the exhibit in Washington that spring, I wasn't at all surprised to find that a sophisticated laser communicator on view was a do-it-yourself model that had graced the cover of *Popular Electronics*. Roused into action by the laser exhibit, that summer I finally sold the magazine that taught me about solid-state electronics a feature article about light-emitting diodes. This article led both to MITS's decision to move out of the model rocketry field and to Leslie Solomon's 1970 visit to us in Albuquerque. As will be recalled, Les was the technical editor of *Popular Electronics*, and he often combined his summer vacations with visits, at his own expense, to the magazine's freelance project developers and writers. In November 1970 *Popular Electronics* published as its cover stories the light-emitting diode feature and a construction article describing how to build the MITS Opticom infrared voice communicator. MITS, of course, offered a kit version of the Opticom.

Our intention at MITS was to emulate the Southwest Technical Products–*Popular Electronics* siliconnection, but with more emphasis on "breakthrough" projects. A year after the Opticom, I published a pair of articles about a semiconductor laser, with MITS selling a kit version of the laser and a receiver. A month later Ed Roberts's 816 calculator was featured on the cover of *Popular Electronics*. It was immeasureably more successful than either the Opticom or the laser, and was more advanced than any of Southwest Technical Products' projects. Thanks to MITS, the digital age introduced so effectively to the electronics hobbyists by Don Lancaster and his low-tech decimal-counting units had become decidedly high tech. The 816 calculator was indeed a breakthrough project.

MITS published additional project articles in *Popular Electronics* during the early 1970s. But then the magazine's management decided to devote full attention to subjects that attracted more advertising revenue, such as citizen's band radio, audio, and so forth. Much to the displeasure of the editorial staff, the electronic construction projects that had been the magazine's mainstay were now banned. The vendors of electronic parts like transistors, diodes, and integrated circuits couldn't afford the fancy four-color ads the magazine wanted them to buy. During this low period Lou Garner moved his famous monthly column to *Radio-Electronics*. MITS and Don Lancaster began submitting articles to *Radio-Electronics*, and so did I. Now it can be told that even articles by Les Solomon were published in the rival publication under the pseudonym "B. R. Rogen," his wife's maiden name. Ever loyal to the experimenter, it was Les who surreptitiously encouraged many of *Popular Elec-*

tronics's project developers to send their material to Larry Steckler, the editor of *Radio-Electronics*. Like Hugo Gernsback before him, Larry never lost touch with the experimenter.

The nostalgic "breakthrough" days at *Popular Electronics* were over, at least for a few years, and *Radio-Electronics* became the leading electronics hobbyist magazine. I would like to think my semiconductor laser and infrared viewer projects, which were featured as cover stories, were among its major breakthroughs. And they might have been had not Don Lancaster been hard at work in his Arizona workshop on what became his famous TV typewriter. The cover of the September 1973 issue showed a typewriterlike keyboard atop a clumsy enclosure placed before a television set that displayed: "BUILD THIS TV TYPEWRITER AND DISPLAY MESSAGES ON YOUR SET'S SCREEN. DON LANCASTER." Don's TV typewriter, a computer terminal without the computer, was a year ahead of its time. In many ways its design was far more complex than the hobby computers that followed, since their most complicated circuits were neatly packaged into the integrated circuits called microprocessors. The TV typewriter used no microprocessor.

In July 1974 *Radio-Electronics* again scooped its uptown rival with the first digital computer–construction article, Jonathan Titus's article on the Mark-8. By then the management at *Popular Electronics* had seen the error of the project ban, and Arthur P. Salsberg, the magazine's new editor, renewed the project competition with *Radio-Electronics*. Art stayed aware of the latest solid-state developments via the pages of *Electronics*, a high-quality trade magazine. Art knew that a microprocessor could form the key ingredient to a small digital computer, and he had been looking for a project article on the subject. When the Mark-8 was featured in *Radio-Electronics*, Art scrubbed a similar article he had planned. How Les told Art about Ed Roberts's more advanced computer project at MITS, thereby giving *Popular Electronics* its biggest "breakthrough" project ever, is now microcomputer history.

The Altair Era

When the Altair 8800 appeared on the cover of the January 1975 issue of *Popular Electronics*, the experimenters who had been introduced to the digital era by Don Lancaster's decimal-counting units and Ed Roberts's calculators were only just beginning to peek through the expensive fence surrounding the ivory towers inhabited by the computer priesthood. With the advent of the Altair, the experimenters had rushed through the gates. For a few short years hobby electronics enjoyed a golden age that surpassed even the radio boom of the 'teens and '20s as thousands of nonhobbyists joined the Altair revolution. Want to save $100 on an Altair? Buy the kit version, learn to solder, and build it yourself. How about cheaper memory boards than those sold by MITS? Build them too. *Popular Electronics* printed a few articles describing do-it-yourself circuits that could greatly expand the capabilities of the Altair, but they didn't begin to satisfy the voracious appetite of the computer hobbyists. Newsletters sprung up around the country to fill the void. *Computer Notes*, a tabloid begun by MITS in June 1975, also helped.

Though there were several computer trade and professional magazines, they at first largely ignored the Altair phenomenon. Only a few visionaries then recognized the vast, untapped potential of the market for personal computers and magazines and books about them. Chief among them was David Ahl. A few months before the first Altair article appeared, Ahl, a former Digital Equipment Corporation employee who had grown up building projects in *Popular Electronics*, had begun *Creative Computing* magazine. By the end of 1976 *Creative Computing* had evolved from an ad-free, newsprint serial intended for educators to a slick magazine complete with advertising and plenty of microcomputer articles.

In May 1975 in the mountains of New Hampshire, less than six months after the *Popular Electronics* Altair story, Wayne Green began organizing a magazine for computer hobbyists. Green, an outspoken ex-submariner and a fanatical amateur radio enthusiast, had started *73 Magazine* (73 means "best wishes" in amateur radio parlance). He selected as editor Carl Helmers, a bright computer hobbyist in Boston who published a microcomputer newsletter for a few hundred subscribers. The new magazine was named after the term for the ubiquitous pattern of eight binary bits familiar to every computer user: *Byte*. While Green secured advertising for *Byte*, Helmers began looking for writers. I had never heard of Carl Helmers when he called to ask if I would be willing to contribute articles to the new magazine. Though intrigued by the prospect of writing for the first hobby computer magazine, I was then heavily involved in electronic project books for Radio Shack. Also, for more than a year I had been trying to talk Art Salsberg, the editor of *Popular Electronics*, into allowing me to write a column for his magazine. That summer, after I poured on his desk a dozen circuits that flashed, counted, bleeped, and transmitted, he formally assigned the column. We decided to call it "Experimenter's Corner." The chance to write for the unknown *Byte* just didn't measure up to the opportunity to write a column alongside Lou Garner's, the man whose articles I had faithfully read for nearly two decades. Write for *Byte*? Maybe later, I told Carl Helmers. Meanwhile, instead of becoming a *Byte* writer, I became a charter subscriber.

"COMPUTERS—the World's Greatest Toy!" proclaimed the cover of the first issue of *Byte* in September 1975. Inside were articles by Carl Helmers and microcomputer pioneer Hal Chamberlin. MITS had two full-page ads plus the back cover. But what really caught my attention was an article by digital hobbyist guru Don Lancaster. In a trailer to his first editorial entitled "The Impossible Dream or, 'Wouldn't it be neat to have a computer all one's own without being rich as Croesus?,'" Helmers observed that, "The art of home brew computing has come a long way in the past few years. . . . It's almost getting to the point where a basement tinkerer can put together a manufacturable robotic device and plant the economic acorn which will grow into an industrial oak tree."

Back then even the guys at *Popular Electronics* who were the first to recognize the potential of the Altair didn't hold out much hope for *Byte*. There's just not enough advertising out there to support it, one of the editors told a visiting columnist. If only he could have seen the explosion taking place at MITS in Albuquerque. Though I had a personal window on the Altair boom, the computer that Ed Roberts gave me in return for writing the machine's operating manual gathered dust on a shelf while I wrote "Experimenter's Corner" for *Popular Electronics* and electronic project books for Radio Shack.

Because the project books were sold in enormous quantities, many of them to youngsters, I flagged them with safety tips and warnings and powered most projects with batteries instead of household current. With good reason, too, for a few years before I had experienced the power of raw electricity when a network of eight capacitors, each charged to 600 volts, slipped off my workbench. There was a loud pop and a violent contraction of my leg muscles that catapulted my body from the chair and slammed it soundly against the wall. The discharging capacitors had blown a quarter inch hole through my jeans and left a sooty crater in the flesh below. Had I not followed the customary practice of pocketing one hand while working with high voltage, I would have grabbed the capacitor chain, possibly receiving a lethal jolt.

The first installment of "Experimenter's Corner" appeared in the October 1975 issue of *Popular Electronics,* just one month after *Byte* premiered. Each month I described several electronic circuits that I had usually designed and always built and tested. This approach, and the column's hand-drawn circuit diagrams, proved popular with readers, so Art Salsberg asked for a second column and then a third. Though writing three columns for *Popular Electronics* required a week out of every month, I thoroughly enjoyed sitting at the workbench concocting color-uncoordinated tan or green circuit boards stuffed with candy-striped resistors, golden brown capacitors, and raisinlike transistors. Most of the circuits were sprinkled with chocolate-colored microchips, and sometimes they were stopped by a tiny golden can capped with a glistening lens that meant an infrared-emitting diode was installed inside. After the boards were done, the combined scents of molten solder flux and phenolic circuit board sweetened the air while a battery was connected and the circuits were "powered up" for the first time. Building circuits was, well, just like cooking.

My *Popular Electronics* columns and Radio Shack books attracted hundreds of letters from school boys, high school teachers, college professors, inventors, doctors, engineers, and company presidents. Scientists and engineers in communist-bloc countries sent letters. So did scientists at Bell Laboratories (though none have written since Mims vs. Bell Labs). Some readers sent thank you notes, but most letters asked technical questions. Some were simple ("Where can I buy a SN76488 sound synthesizer chip?"). Others were multiple-page lists of questions or requests for custom circuit designs that would have required hours or even days to answer. Many letters came from students building science fair projects ("Please reply right away since my project must be ready in one week.").

Others came from university students ("Please reply right away since my paper must be ready in one week."). Still others came from foreign countries ("Mi gran amor es la electronica. De todos los libros el mejor el suyo conel titulo de 'Getting Started in Electronics.' ").

Though I sometimes fail to catch an error in an article or book, their readers do not. Sometimes they even find errors where none exist. Like the angry letter sent to Radio Shack's president that charged the firm with fraud because the writer, a university professor, believed a light flasher circuit in one of my books would not work. "It's theoretically impossible," he wrote. That flasher circuit was the one I had used for years to make tracking lights for model rockets. It was the subject of my first magazine article, and it was MITS's first product. Nevertheless, when a copy of the letter arrived from Radio Shack, I dutifully rebuilt the circuit, and it worked. The irate professor, it turned out, had never built the circuit.

Then there's the correspondence I save in a special file labeled "Strange Letters." This is where I keep letters that suggest perpetual motion machines, U.F.O. detectors, laser handguns, and the like. Also in this file are a few disturbing letters, like the one from a man who reported he was bugged, literally. He claimed his jaw had been implanted with a tooth containing a tiny radio transmitter which sent his conversations to a malevolent dentist. Only one letter in my Strange Letters file is from a computer enthusiast. It arrived under the letterhead of AIBMUGO and was signed by "The Shadow." AIBMUGO is the Anti-IBM Underground Guerrilla Organization, a California-based group that urges technical writers to, ". . . do something about IBM before IBM does something about all of us." For $5, AIBMUGO will send its supporters a lapel pin and a automobile window sticker consisting of the red international symbol for stop superimposed over the blue IBM logo.

Only three percent of the engineers in the United States are women, a gender gap that is reflected in the mail to hobby electronics writers and publishers. Indeed, of the many hundreds of letters I have received from readers since 1970, fewer than 10 came from women. Even after the old *Popular Electronics* became a computer magazine, virtually all the mail was from male readers. Little had changed since 1908 when Hugo Gernsback referred to the first installment of *Modern Electrics* as "the maiden issue" and its readers as "young men" and "boys." In the late 1970s a significant change seemed to be in the offing when an excellent technical article about microprocessors appeared in a trade magazine under a woman's byline. So surprising was this development that I rushed into the house to share the good news with Minnie and a neighbor who happened to be visiting. It later developed that the author of the article was once a male engineer who had renounced his gender but not his profession.

Computer Connections

By the late 1970s hobby computers had evolved from the Altair and its imitators into true personal computers complete with all the golly, gee-whiz features only dreamed about when Carl Helmers wrote his first *Byte* editorial. *Byte* was eventually joined by a few other magazines devoted to the do-it-yourself side of computing. Then, in January 1977, David Bunnell, the former editor of *Computer Notes* at MITS, began a new kind of general computer magazine called *Personal Computing*. Bunnell left the hobbyists and hackers to *Byte*, and emphasized home and business computing. Before there was an Apple II, Radio Shack TRS-80, or IBM PC, *Personal Computing* printed articles about computer stores, interviews with personalities, and colorful ads for computers made by MITS, Processor Technology, Southwest Technical Products, Cromemco, and other pioneers. The magazine's best articles were about going into business with your own personal computing system. This concept, which *Personal Computing* dubbed the "Lemonade Computer Service Company," attracted many letters to the editor, including a snooty retort from the high priesthood of computers in the September/October 1977 issue:

"Many of the things you say and imply in your magazine are very upsetting to me. . . . Your lack of respect for the institutions we have established is both rude and shortsighted. You should be grateful that the industry is making personal computers available to private individuals, instead of pretending that just anybody should be allowed to use computers any way he wants to. You should know that a strong movement is under way to establish legal standards for licensing computer programmers. . . . The shabby Lemonade operator will become a memory of the past unless he learns his work properly, shows authorities that he deserves professional standing, and can really contribute to society. Cancel my subscription."

That profoundly priggish pronouncement, and the fact that the magazine printed it, was proof that people like Wayne Green, Carl Helmers, and David Bunnell were on to something big. I promptly resolved to renew my subscriptions to *Personal Computing* and *Byte*, and to begin writing about computers. In the summer of 1977 Don French, the electronics parts buyer at Radio Shack who had faithfully provided the components for the two dozen or so project books I'd written, had been placed in charge of his company's infant computer marketing program. Hardware-hacking Don, who had built a computer on his kitchen table, had prodded Radio Shack's management into entering the computer business. One of my first chances to write about microcomputers since doing the Altair manual for Ed Roberts came with Don's assignment to write some introductory material for Radio Shack's first computer catalog. Shortly before the catalog project, David S. Gunzel, Radio Shack's director of technical publications, had assigned me to write a short booklet about computer basics, *Radio Shack Introduces the World of Computing*. Soon thereafter Dave Gunzel produced the missing ingredient that enabled me to grasp the fundamentals of digital computers well enough to design and build PIP-1, a simple but working computer. Since microprocessors are much more powerful and sophisticated than PIP-1, I never wrote an article about its construction. Nevertheless, that mess of wires, chips, and lights called PIP-1 was a "breakthrough" project for me.

·14·

The Silicon Press, A.P.E.*

Inscrutable Dave

YOU WON'T FIND David S. Gunzel's name listed on a magazine masthead or in a library's card catalog. But his influence on the silicon press extends far beyond his office high in one of the twin Tandy towers in downtown Fort Worth, Texas. When I first met him in 1972, Dave single-handedly edited all of Radio Shack's books, instruction brochures, and service manuals from a windowless office buried deep in an old warehouse that then served as Radio Shack's corporate headquarters. After Radio Shack's first TRS-80 personal computer was introduced in 1977, Dave received permission to hire George Stewart, the first in a series of assistant editors. George eventually left Radio Shack to become an editor for *Byte,* and now he's a freelance writer of computer books and articles. Stan Miastkowski came next. He eventually left Radio Shack to write books and a computer column in *Esquire.* Stan now manages eight other technical writers for Rising Star Industries, an electronic cottage software development company. Then there was Harry Helms, a first-rate writer and editor with a gift for spotting both good authors and coming trends in the personal computer industry. Harry left Radio Shack to become a senior editor at McGraw-Hill and then Prentice-Hall and to write books of his own. Harry is a latent entrepreneur; someday he'll probably start his own publishing company. While Harry was at Radio Shack he and Dave joined forces to transform Thomas R. Powers from an avid electronics hobbyist experimenter and author of pulp science fiction stories into a prolific compiler of books about electronics and computers. Jonathan Erickson succeeded Harry and Tom, and

* *After Popular Electronics*

then went on to become a senior editor at Osborne/McGraw-Hill and a writer of books about computers. Though their personalities sometimes clashed with Dave's, all these writers attribute much of their current success to the training they received from Dave Gunzel. Dave wasn't merely hiring editorial assistants; he was running a school for new computer writers financed by scholarships from Radio Shack.

Dave Gunzel influenced more than his editorial assistants. Take Dr. David A. Lien, the founder of Compusoft, (TM) Inc., and the author of several bestselling books about BASIC. It was Dave Gunzel who hired Lien to write the instruction manual for Radio Shack's first TRS-80 computer, and who helped him develop the widely acclaimed "user-friendly" style that has since characterized Lien's books. Then there's William Barden, Jr., an established computer programmer and writer who has the rare ability to design and program circuits that use microprocessors and then write a book telling others how to do the same. Dave began assigning books to Bill early in his career, greatly expanding Bill's popularity.

While David Lien was writing the first TRS-80 manual in 1977, Dave Gunzel and Leon Lutz, Radio Shack's book buyer, asked if I would like to write a technical book to be called *Understanding Digital Computers*. Even though I was an Altair veteran, I didn't understand digital computers well enough to write an in-depth book about them. Analog computers, binary numbers, digital logic, and BASIC were straightforward enough, but fully grasping the operation of a digital computer's central processing unit (CPU), its siliconnected nerve center, was something else. Though Dave knew about this knowledge gap, he didn't object when Leon assigned the book to me. Picking experts to write books for beginners just wasn't his style. Dave once said a writer who first learns a subject well enough to practice it is better equipped to write about it for beginners. He had used this approach in 1972 when he asked me to write about integrated circuit projects when I had barely progressed beyond transistors. Dave's strategy worked well then, but digital computer CPU's are much more complicated than simple integrated logic chips.

Work on the early chapters of *Understanding Digital Computers* progressed nicely, but the project ground to a halt at the CPU chapter. A time-consuming search through hundreds of computer books at two university libraries failed to yield a straightforward explanation of the inner workings of the typical CPU. Those sili-confounded books explained what the CPU did in terms of moving instructions and data around inside a computer's memory, but they didn't reveal how all this was accomplished electronically. Some compared a computer's memory to the boxes in a post office, and its CPU to a lightning-fast worker who sorts the mail and loads it into the boxes. Others compared the CPU to a traffic cop or signal directing eight or sixteen lanes of traffic racing along data highways at millions of bytes per second. To some readers those analogies may have seemed clever, but I found them confusing. Besides, I rationalized, there are no lightning-fast postal workers, and police directing traffic on an expressway usually signify the presence of an accident up ahead.

The frustration brought about by the nagging CPU question affected more than the unfinished computer book. During the 1970s many articles in trade electronics magazines stressed the importance of learning about the miniature CPU on a chip known as the microprocessor. Sometimes these articles included reminders about what happened to the careers of engineers who didn't make the transition from vacuum tubes to transistors in the 1950s, and those who didn't advance from transistors to chips in the 1960s. I had finally learned to design reasonably complex logic circuits using integrated circuits, but had yet to fully grasp the electronic operation of the CPU. Would I miss the microprocessor revolution? Understand how the circuits in a microprocessor work, I told myself or face the prospect of eventually becoming a low-tech anachronism in a high-tech age.

The deadline for *Understanding Digital Computers* approached and I still hadn't written the crucial CPU chapter. I remembered an earlier deadline when a public relations company hired me to write two booklets about Hewlett-Packard's scientific calculators. The deadline was so close they flew me to their headquarters in another state where they plucked pages of rough draft out of the typewriter before I had a chance to read them. When an understanding staffer told me that the first writer they hired for the job had to be institutionalized for a nervous breakdown, I asked to work on the manuscript in a motel room. After the first booklet was completed, they flew me to Silicon Valley to see the still secret Hewlett-Packard calculator that was to be described in the second booklet. The environment at H-P was much like that of the Air Force Weapons Laboratory, and I felt right at home until the man responsible for the booklet project began discussing his primal scream therapy sessions. I asked to finish up the project in the peace and quiet of a motel room.

Writing for Radio Shack's Dave Gunzel was the antithesis of that crazy Hewlett-Packard project. Dave was born in China just before the outbreak of World War II and grew up there with his Baptist missionary parents. Harry Helms described him perfectly when he said, "Dave Gunzel is the most Eastern Westerner I've ever known." Dave never ordered his writers how to write. Instead, he guided them by inference and intuition. A conventional editor might tell the author of a book about computers, "Be sure to include a chapter about business graphics because we're going to use a picture of a computer-generated pie chart on the cover." Dave would ponder the black logo on his yellow pencil and carefully say, "This book wants to have a chapter about business graphics." After a moment or two he might lean back in his chair with his hands behind his head, glance toward the Japanese calendar on the wall and ask, "What do you think?" When the book was complete Dave would ask, "Is it the best you can do?" To those who hesitated and replied, "I think so," Dave might probe, "Why aren't you sure?" He was satisfied the book was ready to be published only when the writer confidently responded, "It's the best I can do."

Dave Gunzel's Chinese-American School of Sublimely Intuitive Technical Writing is what kept *Understanding Digital Computers* from being just another book about computers. During a meeting in his office in the old warehouse, Dave listened patiently as I worried about not being able to write the key chapter. Then he plucked from a shelf heavy with books a flat black volume by Albert Paul Malvino that had recently arrived from McGraw-Hill. Dr. Malvino's book, *Digital Computer Electronics*, possessed the key to the mystery; it neatly unwrapped the electronic secrets of the CPU and made them crystal clear. After Malvino, the CPU was no longer an intangible and mythical electronic post office or traffic signal. Instead, it seemed more like the synchronized machinery of a bottling plant or the precisely methodical mechanisms of an ordinary music box.

Although I really didn't have time to spare, I became captivated by the prospect of designing and building a CPU that would work. The Altair used a ready-made microprocessor for its CPU. My plan was to design from scratch a CPU made from the standard integrated circuits that, when fabricated by the hundreds on a single silicon chip, form the basic building blocks of every microprocessor. Within a week the circuits for a simple 4-bit CPU were designed as was a set of binary-coded instructions that would tell the CPU what to do. A few weeks later a working version was assembled from a dozen integrated circuits and a few hundred connection wires installed on several plastic breadboards. I called it PIP-1 for Programmable Instruction Processor. Though primitive by comparison with real microprocessors, PIP-1 understood half a dozen binary machine language instructions like those in real computers. And it worked! Instructions and data were encoded as patterns of holes punched into strips of black paper. The information was entered into the 16-word memory by pulling the punched card past a row of light-sensitive phototransistors installed behind a slot in a small block of wood. Watching that rat's nest of colored wires and buglike chips process half-byte chunks of data and primitive instructions, and then flash out the cryptic results on a row of red-light-emitting diodes, was a thrill worth a shelf full of Altairs.

Thanks to Dave Gunzel's strategy and the homemade PIP-1, *Understanding Digital Computers* was published in 1978, and more than 130,000 copies were sold before Radio Shack, following its usual practice, dropped it when sales fell below around 20,000 copies per year. Many readers wrote that the book had for the first time helped them understand the totally logical fetch-instruction-from-memory and do-what-it-says operation of a CPU. Simply by assigning that book, Dave forced me to grasp the elusive secret of the CPU, and pass it on. *Understanding Digital Computers* became my master's thesis for Dave Gunzel's technical writers' school. I had survived the transition from transistors to integrated circuits to microprocessors. Would *Popular Electronics*, the magazine that triggered the personal computer revolution, do the same?

Popular Electronics, R.I.P.

The twenty-fifth-anniversary issue of *Popular Electronics* was published in October 1979. Lou Garner reminisced about experimenting with transistors in the 1950s, and I described how to make voltage-to-frequency converters in "Experimenter's Corner" and a tri-state tone generator in "Project of the Month." There were only three articles about computers; *Popular Electronics* was still very much an electronic experimenter's magazine. But over the next few years the personal computer explosion came to dominate the magazine. By November 1982 the magazine's name was changed to *Computers & Electronics.* The first issue of the revamped magazine contained nine articles and columns about computers. In his editorial, Art Salsberg assured readers that the magazine would continue "the editorial tradition of covering the broad field of electronics technology."

A few months earlier Art had called to discuss the new format and to assure me of his continued interest in my columns. Therefore, I had prepared a special three-part series for "Experimenter's Corner" about inexpensive ways to take aerial photographs by flying radio-controlled cameras from kites and balloons. Art mentioned the first installment of the series in his first *Computers & Electronics* editorial. "Experimenting with electronics is, naturally, at the forefront of our readers' interests," Art wrote. "In this respect I'm eagerly following Forrest Mims's three-part column on experimenting with Kodak's new disk camera. . . . Forrest tells me that the applications resulting from his electronic modification work on the camera are among the most exciting work he's ever done."

And it was; especially when a large helium-filled balloon burst in my face and when a kite-borne camera crashed in a fenced pasture filled with curious cattle. The tethered balloon-borne camera couldn't be safely flown unless the air was perfectly still. On the other hand, my big, brightly-colored nylon delta kites wouldn't reliably lift the half-pound camera payload in anything less than a steady 15–20 mph breeze. Nevertheless, after many heart-stopping moments spent helplessly watching the delicate camera system nearly crash into treetops, fields, tall buildings, and the Gulf of

Mexico, I had a good collection of aerial photos and Art published several of them.

While I was telling readers of *Computers & Electronics* to go fly a kite, the magazine's management was watching the revenue from computer-related ads soar above that from ads for electronic parts. The new format of *Computers & Electronics* was designed to capitalize on this trend, a dramatic reversal of the criticism Art received in 1975 for publishing the Altair articles. To give the magazine more of a computer look, my three columns were consolidated into a single giant column called "The Electronics Scientist." In an editorial introducing the reformatted column, Art announced, "When Mims writes, people read! Proof of this is that columns by Forrest Mims III have never failed to win top rank in our editorial readership studies over the years." Pleased as I was by Art's editorial, something seemed amiss. The magazine was trying to flip-flop from electronics to computers since computer companies bought more and bigger ads than electronics parts dealers. But during the transition the management didn't want to lose its traditional readership of electronics hobbyists, which I later found out was the only reason my columns weren't eliminated.

I was puzzled by the changes. Despite the computer boom, electronics experimenting seemed to be as popular as ever. At least basic books about how-to electronics were doing well. For instance, Dave Gunzel at Radio Shack had years before taken an interest in my laboratory notebooks. He said that someday he hoped to convince one of the buyers to publish a collection of hand-drawn circuits just like those in my notebooks, so I drew up a formal proposal. Gary Burkhart, who succeeded Don French as Radio Shack's parts buyer, eventually agreed to buy the proposed book. It was called *Engineer's Notebook*, and its two editions sold nearly 700,000 copies between 1979 and 1982. As *Computers & Electronics* seemed to move irrevocably away from hobby electronics, I shared the sales figures for *Engineer's Notebook* with Art Salsberg. But Art's days at *Computers & Electronics* were numbered, and by the end of 1983 he was gone.

Seth Alpert replaced Art. I came close to dropping "The Electronics Scientist" when Art was let go, especially when my column was changed to "The Computer Scientist," and I was required to write about only computer-related subjects and eliminate projects for those who some at the magazine now referred to as "the wires and pliers crowd." But Seth Alpert turned out to be a real gentleman, and it was a pleasure to write for him. I continued the column, transitioning from do-it-yourself lasers, lightwave communicators, high-flying radio-controlled cameras and the like to computer-related hardware and software projects. The computer projects were as fascinating and challenging as anything I had ever tried, especially those involving those pen-wielding, deskbound robots known as plotters. But the magazine insisted that any electronic circuits designed to be connected to computers be very simple. I missed the smell of solder and tinkering with chocolate-colored microchips and candy-striped resistors. But at least I could include electronic circuit diagrams; much to the displeasure of Les Solomon, the magazine's long-time technical editor, electronic circuits were banned from the rest of the magazine. An ominous sign of things to come occurred when Les tested the ban and a couple of his columns were kicked back.

Boom Times

The identity crisis at *Computers & Electronics* was not helped by the simultaneous explosion in the number of computer-related publications. In 1974 there were *Creative Computing* and only a handful of computer trade magazines. By 1983 hundreds of magazines were trying to satisfy the computer-buying public's appetite for information about personal computers for homes and businesses. In 1984 the tenth edition of *Microcomputing Periodicals* listed 843 magazines, newspapers, and other serial publications. A few of the computer magazines became so sated with advertising they began to resemble mail-order catalogs. Consider *Byte*, the magazine started by Wayne Green with more vision than cash back in 1975. *Byte* evolved from the hardware-hacking computer hobbyist's best friend to a sophisticated McGraw-Hill trade magazine crammed with advertisements. In November 1983, when many readers complained about late delivery of the current issue, the editors learned that mail carriers were complaining about having to deliver that month's record 728-page issue. The October 1984 *Byte* contained some 300 pages of paid-in-advance, $6,000-per-page advertisements. Controversy accompanied the unprecedented growth in the computer magazine field. Major computer companies courted magazine editors and writers with elaborate press conferences and "controlled leaks" designed to titillate the public about "unannounced" new products. Apple Computer became an expert at the hype-and-hoopla game, spending $15 million to introduce its new Macintosh computer. According to *The Wall Street Journal* Adam Osborne, the founder of the company that introduced the first transportable computer, boasted: "Certainly I used the press. But then the press wanted to be used."

Readers and pundits complained about magazine "fluff pieces," friendly product reviews that pleased advertisers. Some of the connections between ads and articles became so obvious that one wondered who was in charge. The April 1984 issue of *Personal Computing*, for instance, included a 2-page, 4-color Macintosh ad sandwiched between the pages of an exclusive interview with Steven Jobs. Some ads were misleading. One for IBM's PCjr computer cleverly concealed the brick-sized power pack attached to the machine's electrical cord. Other IBM ads claimed its PC used a 16-bit microprocessor when Intel, the chip's maker, had specified it as an 8-bit unit. Apple ads claimed its Lisa and Macintosh used a 32-bit microprocessor when Motorola, the chip's maker, had specified it as a 16-bit unit.

The magazine boom was matched by a similar phenomenon in the book publishing industry, and in 1983 the Department of Commerce estimated that from 20 to 30 new computer books were published each week. Computer books had become the fastest-growing segment of the publishing industry. During the first five months of 1984, fourteen major publishers released a torrent of 500 new computer books. The traditional silicon press watched helplessly as their turf was invaded by mainstream publishers anxious to cash in on the boom.

In a mad scramble to find writers, magazine and book publishers offered payments and royalties substantially higher than ever before. Traditional publishers of electronics books like Howard Sams & Co. and Tab Books typically paid their authors advances of a few thousand dollars. During the peak in 1983 good writers commanded advances of $25,000 and up. Suddenly anyone who owned a microcomputer was a potential writer. Meanwhile, to comply with postal regulations that defined the minimum ratio of editorial to advertising pages, some magazines fat with computer ads inflated scarce editorial copy with blocks of white space, oversize margins, and huge photographs.

The computer publishing boom of 1983 collapsed in 1984. Customers became bewildered by the glut of titles that filled bookstore shelves. They also became disillusioned by publishers and authors whose books were little more than rehashed and dressed up computer company technical brochures and news releases. Bookstores cut back the number of periodicals they carried, and magazine-saturated subscribers often failed to renew their subscriptions. At the beginning of 1984 the top ten computer book publishers planned to release 1,500 new titles during the year. But that was before bookstores began returning a flood of unsold computer books. At the end of 1984 a senior editor at one of those publishing houses confided that he had been assigned the task of cancelling fully two-thirds of his company's computer book contracts.

Though the silicon-press shakeout cost publishers millions of dollars in cancelled projects and lost revenues, some of the old timers who saw it coming are glad it happened. I welcomed the shakeout, hoping it would end the publication of fluff books, and drive nontechnical publishers back to their cookbooks, biographies, and novels. I didn't realize that I would become one of its casualities.

The End of an Era

The cover of the February 1984 issue of *Computers & Electronics* displayed a new logo, with *Computers* printed in bold red letters, and *& Electronics* in tiny black print below. Simply by changing its emphasis from electronics to computers, overnight the magazine became what it boasted above the new logo: "World's Largest Computer Magazine." Meanwhile, many of the alumni of the old *Popular Electronics* rebelled at the final transition of their beloved publication into just another computer magazine. Eventually most dropped their subscriptions, but their numbers were rapidly replaced and even exceeded by hordes of latter-day computer enthusiasts.

By the end of 1984, even Les Solomon, the go-between for dozens of "breakthrough" projects, was gone. A few days before he retired, the zany character who claimed to practice levitation in his spare time told me, "They said I'm an anachronism around here." With both Art Salsberg and Les Solomon gone, any chance for the revival of the old *Popular Electronics*, the experimenter's "breakthrough" magazine, had vanished. Though its circulation had ballooned to 600,000, only a tenth of the readers remained from the old *Popular Electronics* days. Somehow my column survived the transition from electronic circuits to computer programs and projects. I was the only remaining writer from the pre-Altair days.

Before Les retired there were rumors that *Computers & Electronics* might again change its format, this time to emphasize business computing. Something had to be done; advertising revenues had flattened, and *Computers & Electronics* was now losing money. But would there be a place for "The Computer Scientist" in the revamped magazine? I suspected my column's days were numbered when Seth told me to stop sending installments more than a month in advance. What Seth couldn't tell me was that Ziff-Davis had much bigger plans. On February 15, 1985, the staff was told the April issue of the magazine, which was already prepared, would be the last. Within a few days, the entire editorial staff was let go and custodians began transferring the contents of their desks and file cabinets to trash dumpsters. Bob Lascaro, the magazine's art director, reluctantly stayed an extra week to supervise the carnage. He mailed me a rare copy of the famous January 1975 Altair issue of *Popular Electronics* he had saved from the doomed files and an early MITS calculator he had retrieved from a trash can.

Subscribers received the final issue of *Computers and Electronics* in late March. "The Computer Scientist" described how to make stencil characters with a pen plotter and a computer. Ironically, the two plotter-drawn words I had selected to illustrate what became my final column were MIMS and EXIT. *Computers & Electronics* had fallen victim to an identity crisis brought about by the computer revolution begun by *Popular Electronics* in January 1975. Its passing ended an era. Would the "breakthrough" days at the magazine have continued if MITS had not developed the Altair? Have ready-to-run computers and canned software eliminated do-it-yourself electronics and computer experimenters? Is there a place in today's computer magazines for a fortyish Altair veteran who likes to tinker?

·15·

Siliconclusions

Flakes of Flint

ON A HOT AUGUST AFTERNOON in 1984 two anthropologists at Southwest Texas State University stood at the end of a long wooden table covered with flattened paper bags on which big black numbers had been scrawled. Flakes and larger pieces of flint were piled atop each bag. "Take a look at this," the man with sandy-colored hair said to his colleague with the thick mustache, offering what appeared to be a pretty ordinary piece of bone. "Think those scratches might be tooth marks?" Dr. Tom Gray peered intently at the specimen through a ten-power magnifying loupe as he rolled it around with his fingers. "Could be, but it would take lots more study," he replied.

I had no idea what to expect when Dr. Gray invited me to visit the anthropology laboratory at his university. But having worked in and visited high-tech, siliconnected laboratories, and having a fairly well-equipped electronics shop, I was unprepared for the austere setting. Take away the electric lights and the air conditioning and Charles Darwin himself would have felt right at home seated at the flint-stacked table surrounded by wooden specimen cabinets and drawers.

Tom Gray and I had agreed to meet following an exchange of guest columns in a local newspaper on whether creationism should be taught alongside evolution in public schools. Tom was a worthy opponent, for as a graduate student he and Donald Johanson discovered the fossil hominid in Ethiopia known as "Lucy." Though our views sharply differed, we eventually became good friends. Reflecting on our initial meeting in that rustic anthropology lab, I remember the quartz hammerstone Tom handed me more vividly than our discussion about evolution. While fondling that chunk of glistening white rock that had long ago been fashioned into a crude but useful tool, I realized that the quartz in my hand and the flint flakes on the table were silicon dioxide, a mineral from which pure silicon can be refined. People have been fashioning silicon into tools and weapons since the Stone Age. It's as if the mysterious monolith in the films *2001* and *2010* was a slab of silicon. There was enough raw material in that quartz hammerstone to make thousands of microprocessors, each the size of a baby's fingernail and every bit as sophisticated as the one inside my digital watch that doubled as a precision timer and a multiple-function scientific calculator. What's more, even if all those microprocessors were identical in design, each could be programmed to perform a unique task. One might be instructed to count cars at an intersection to control a traffic light in the most efficient manner. Another might be programmed to control the fuel-air mixture in an automobile engine to provide high efficiency and low emissions. Still another might electronically simulate aerial combat in a fast-moving video game or send control signals to the steering vanes on a real air-to-air antiaircraft missile.

Hundreds of diverse functions can be performed by identical versions of the same silicon chip simply by changing the instructions encoded in the microscopic switches of a silicon memory array. That's because the operation of a microprocessor resembles that of a player piano. Both have been carefully engineered to perform a task in accordance with a list of precise instructions prepared by a human being. Just as the player piano can play any tune encoded as patterns of holes in a roll of paper, the microprocessor sequentially fetches instructions from its memory and then acts on them. Unlike the player piano, however, the microprocessor is interactive. It can be instructed to respond to signals from the outside world and then modify its operation accordingly. For many of the uninitiated, and for some of those who should know better, this decision-making capability transforms a lifeless flake of silicon into a system having seemingly lifelike intelligence.

One of the chief values of personal and home computers is that they have helped remove the "electronic brain" mystique from computers in general. Unlike the traffic light, gasoline engine, video game, and guided missile applications, the microprocessor in a small computer is not dedicated to a single task. It can be programmed by the user, or by means of instructions prepared by others, to accomplish thousands upon thousands of different tasks. Personal computer users take this capability for granted. Some even denounce and ridicule the makers of machines that fall slightly short of the performance standards they deem necessary. Critics might temper their complaints if they would first remember the personal computer's do-it-yourself days in the mid-1970s and reflect on how far the technology has come.

Imagine the reaction of Archimedes or Galileo to a $5.98 solar-powered calculator with square root and memory keys. Now peak in on my two children the day after Christmas 1984. Fifteen-year-old Eric is seated at one of two computer tables in his bedroom busily typing something into the keyboard of his CoCo, a Radio Shack Color Computer II he bought with his own money the preceding summer. On his right is a Coleco Adam and on his left is an IBM PCjr. Plugged into Eric's CoCo is a white module called a sound/speech cartridge. He received it for Christmas along with some other attachments, including a printer, a touch pad for making drawings on the computer's screen, and a "mouse" that rapidly positions to any point on the screen a symbol called a cursor. Nine-year-old Vicki is seated before the Texas Instruments 99/4A computer in her bedroom. She received it for Christmas of 1983 after T.I. announced it was leaving the home computer business. The earliest versions of the 99/4A sold for $1,000; Vicki's cost $79.95. Two modules called a terminal emulator and a speech synthesizer are plugged into the machine.

Though Eric and Vicki are silent as they type into their keyboards, they are carrying on a lively discussion. The computers are not wired together so that their messages appear on each other's screen, though this is certainly possible. Instead, the words Eric and Vicki type are automatically transformed into clearly recognizable male speech by the voice synthesizer modules plugged into each of their computers. Eric's computer suggests in its ubiquitous siliconnected accent, "Let's try words that start with vowels to see whose machine talks best." Vicki's responds, "Okay. You go first." The CoCo speaks with more tenor than the deeper sounding and somewhat raspy TI 99/4A. But the TI machine adds some inflection to its words; the CoCo speaks in a monotone. I'm more amazed than Eric and Vicki by their computers' speaking abilities, even though I first heard a speech synthesizer in the 1970s. But back then I'd just turned thirty. Kids today are products of the high-tech generation. They react like Kevin Washington, one of Eric's friends who dropped by while the computers were engaged in a lively conversation. "What did you think?" I later asked. "Well," Kevin replied, "I suppose they sounded okay."

Minnie enjoys listening to the electronic banter emerging from the kids' rooms, but she isn't into computing. She says she wants to learn how to use the PCjr or the Tandy 1000 for business applications. Maybe. But she'd rather balance the accounts with a miniature calculator equipped with a built-in printer. Minnie is fascinated by computer graphics, but she's never accepted my invitation to sit before the keyboard of one of our dozen computers and learn how to transform a glass display into a colorful butterfly or a spiral rainbow. She would rather look through the latest needlepoint magazines. After a morning preparing graphics programs for *Computers & Electronics*, I happened to flip through one of Minnie's magazines while having lunch. In it were needlepoint patterns in the form of grids of thousands of tiny, color-coded boxes almost identical to the computer graphics worksheets in my office. I used to think Minnie should join the computer revolution with the rest of us. But in her own way she already has. Her car has a microprocessor-controlled carburetor. She has to show me how to use some of the more exotic digital timer functions on her microprocessor-controlled microwave oven. As for learning to use a keyboard computer, Minnie will do okay when she's ready because she exhibits a couple of classic computer programmer traits: she enjoys solving crossword puzzles and assembling jigsaw puzzles. Meanwhile, she's taking piano lessons. The language of notes and symbols in her music books is as meaningless to me as the printouts of BASIC programs and HPGL plotter codes on my desk are to her.

Our children have grown up with computers; Eric played with the switches on the Altair when he was five. The Altair was a year old when Vicki was born. Eric and Vicki will be well prepared for the increasingly computerized society that lies ahead. But what about children whose families can't afford the electronic machines Eric and Vicki take for granted? You don't have to own a computer to know what computers can do. What matters more than the ability to program a computer or even having access to one is that today's children will enter adulthood viewing computers as tools, appliances, office machines, and games rather than incomprehensible "electronic brains." That's especially beneficial considering the mischief that big computers can perform for both government and business. New kinds of computer memory systems can give rapid access to vast quantities of information about one's personal history, including credit rating, income, arrest record, education, and so forth. One such system developed in the Netherlands stores 600 gigabytes in a unit about the size of a home washing machine. That's enough storage capacity for a one-page dossier about every resident of the United States. This system and others like it store information by means of a laser that produces microscopic patterns on a specially prepared tape or disk. A similar technology is used in digital video and audio disk players.

Big Brother computer systems are the dream of despots. On the other hand, the Soviet Union has been reluctant to join the small computer age, probably because of fear as much as primitive technology. The commissars' high-tech nightmare is thousands of Russian computers interlinked by telephones and exchanging passages from Solzhenitsyn and Pasternak, tidbits from Voice of America, scripture verses, and, even worse, news about newer and better computers. Forbidden political thoughts could be launched into such a computer-telephone network with no way of detecting their origin. A single floppy disk in a thin envelope less than six inches square marked "CCCP Komputer 100-Year Plan" could easily contain the entire text of "One Day in the Life of Ivan Denisovitch" plus some commentary by previous readers. Should a computer-savvy KGB agent drop by for a visit, the prohibited disk could be easily concealed between the pages of Marx or the latest five-year plan. Or the contents of the disk could be quickly erased by either a computer or a strong magnet. The commissars and their fellow tyrants face a high-tech predicament. They must train their people to design, program, operate and repair computers if they are to meet the siliconnected military, scientific and economic challenge from free countries. But if this is done on a scale that matters, the population will become electronically if not physically free. Imagine the mischief waiting to be worked by Soviet counterparts of the young computer enthusiasts in the United States who get an electronic thrill by illegally penetrating corporate and government computer systems. Jerry Pournelle best summed up this happy dilemma when he wrote in the April 1984 issue of *Popular Computing* that, "The microcomputer will do more to make the world an open society than any previous invention."

The computer's potential for both good and evil is a dual-personality trait shared by many other siliconnected developments. Consider electrostatic copiers that reproduce in full color. Some of these machines work so well that they produce credible copies of paper money, thereby providing a potential tool for forgers and counterfeiters—whose machines can literally pay for themselves. Communications satellites transmit news of floods, famines, droughts and wars from far off lands. They broadcast dramas, comedies, concerts, and religious services. And they electronically spew violence and pornography upon every square centimeter of the United States. Ultra-transparent filaments of silica provide such vast information carrying capacity that they can simultaneously carry television signals and thousands of telephone conversations. The infrared waves coursing through such a fiber can at the same instant transport the tender coos of two absent lovers and the sickening message of a dial-a-porn service called by a curious nine-year-old child. Remarkably sophisticated guidance and control systems steer airliners across oceans and place satellites into precise orbits. The same technology enables a silicontrolled ballistic missile to place a nuclear bomb within a hundred yards of a target on the other side of the earth.

Inventors and engineers and the companies for which they work are often surprised, or at least claim to be, by some of the applications to which their silicontraptions are put. When an electronics writer called Western Union to ask if pornographic movies were being bounced into the country's living rooms by its communications satellites, a nervous official bounced the question to higher-ups. His superiors ignored the reporter's written questions. So did the President of the United States and assorted government officials. Perhaps the space shuttle was on their collective minds. What might become of the clean-cut image of American astronauts if the communications satellites they carry into orbit become part of the ever expanding pornography network? Pandora's silicon box has been partially opened, and we've just begun to see the malevolent surprises lurking inside.

Good Old Days

The personal computer would eventually have appeared without Ed Roberts. But Ed's Altair 8800 moved up the arrival date by two years or more at a time when some new microchips become obsolete the year they're introduced. I think back to the pre-Altair days at MITS and wonder what would have happened had the circumstances been different. Could the Altair have sparked the revolution without the *Popular Electronics* connection? What might have happened four years before the Altair had Ed, Stan Cagle, and I followed up on our plans to design and sell analog computers? After *Computers & Electronics* assigned me to write an article commemorating the tenth anniversary of the Altair cover story in *Popular Electronics* Ed Roberts, Stan Cagle, Art Salsberg, Les Solomon, and I reminisced about the early days at MITS. We had often discussed the future: unforeseen applications for a new chip, upcoming readout technologies, the next generation of high-speed logic, and our personal goals. But as 1984 ended we turned to the good old days. We mourned the passing of the "breakthrough" era at *Popular Electronics* (Art was no longer editor; we didn't know that Les would soon be gone). We reflected on the amazing advances in the personal computer industry since the build-it-yourself days of 1975, and bemoaned the distortions and errors about the history of MITS that had begun to appear in articles and books.

What I remember most about this nostalgic conversation was Ed's observation about the state of the personal computer art. Yes, Ed agreed, small computers had come a long way since the introduction of the Altair. But MITS didn't stop there. "I've been very disappointed in the speed of the technology," Ed said. "When we sold MITS to Pertec [in 1977], you could have bought an Altair that would have done essentially anything that can be done today." When Ed wants to emphasize a point, the pitch of his deep voice rises along with his rate of delivery. That's how he spoke as he concluded, "It's a little disappointing that the technology hasn't moved any further than that."

Ed was right. The silicon press demanded that the industry produce personal computers more powerful than the outdated equipment made by IBM. Then when IBM's competitors announced new and more powerful machines, the silicon press ridiculed those which weren't IBM compatible and, therefore, unable to use software developed for the IBM PC. A classic example was Radio Shack's super computer, the Tandy 2000, a machine that significantly outperformed the PC. Though the Tandy 2000 drew praise for its sophisticated design, reviewers complained about the machine's incompatibility with the PC. Radio Shack then designed a PC-compatible clone called the Tandy 1000, which promptly broke Radio Shack's sales records.

IBM's dominance of the personal computer market is exactly what the computer hobbyists of the 1970s hoped would never happen. The PC and its many clones use an advanced version of the BASIC first developed for the Altair. Commercial software, add-on memory boards, disk memories, speech synthesizers, printers, plotters, graphics tablets, joysticks, and modems were all available from MITS or other companies before Ed sold the company. Now these products are more affordable, and there are many more choices, but where are the *Popular Electronics*–style "breakthroughs" like the one that launched the Altair? Recently I told Ed it's time for a couple of siliconnected guys with some good ideas to start another MITS. Yet as I reflect back on what's happened since the Altair, it seems there may not be another MITS in our lifetimes. Ed's Altair was a technological giant step on the same scale as the popularization of the automobile by Henry Ford and the camera by George Eastman. At least for the foreseeable future, substantial developments in the state-of-the-personal-computer-art will be determined by an industry far mightier than the silicon garage that gave birth to MITS.

Though personal computer technology hasn't advanced as far as Ed anticipated, and has even begun to stagnate under IBM's imposing dominance of the market, there has been no shortage of positive developments since the Altair days. Computer prices have tumbled, and memory capacity now deemed commonplace would have staggered an Altair pioneer. You can buy a computer that fits into a shirt pocket yet has a miniature typewriter-style keyboard, understands BASIC, plugs into a miniature battery-powered printer, has sixteen times the memory of the original Altair, and costs a fourth the price. Even if computer hardware were to freeze at today's level, an army of programmers could work for a generation without exhausting the capabilities of existing equipment. Best of all, the old computer priesthood is gone forever. Today anyone can become a computer priest simply by memorizing a few buzzwords and hanging out at the corner computer store.

Now that the pace of personal computer technology has slowed, renewed emphasis is being given such long-sought goals as the reliable and economical recognition of speech and images. It's been estimated, for instance, that a computer must make ten billion computations to reliably recognize a 10,000-word vocabulary as spoken by a single person. And even then it will require incredibly complicated software to distinguish between such identical sounding words as here/hear, piece/peace, son/sun, and so forth. Then there's the electronic nervous breakdown that might ensue should the operator catch a cold, thereby siliconfusing the computer so painstakingly trained to recognize the operator's normal voice.

The most elusive of the unfilled high-tech siliconnected goals, "artificial intelligence," is the objective of the so-called fifth-generation computer programs. At the annual conference of the Association for Computing Machinery in 1984, Herbert Grosch, a former president of that organization, cast some much-needed light on the status of "state-of-the-art" fifth-generation research. "The emperor is naked from the waist up," Dr. Grosch declared. "[Fifth-generation systems] are expert systems, and we've had them for thirty years. All the AI [artificial intelligence] boys did is relabel them." Dr. Grosch urged his audience to resist "journalists with crazy stories" and predicted that some of the advanced technologies supposedly ready for development won't be ready for decades.

In these heady, high-tech times, realists like Herbert Grosch are just who the scientists and engineers need as a healthy reminder to ignore the hype emanating from their companies' public relations departments and to avoid taking themselves too seriously. *The Wall Street Journal* learned a lesson in this regard after it printed in its

"Notable & Quotable" feature for May 15, 1984, the following excerpt from a speech at Stanford University by Ian M. Ross, president of Bell Laboratories: "After 20 years of doubling the number of components on a silicon chip every year, we are still doing so every 18 months. At the same time the equivalent cost per transistor has become 1,000-fold cheaper. Today at AT&T Technologies we are . . . close to achieving a manufacturable 'megabit chip'—one containing a million components. As a result, the single-chip processor has surpassed the capability of a mainframe computer of 15 years ago. . . ." A few weeks later, *The Wall Street Journal* printed a letter from a Mr. Harry Lee Smith about Dr. Ross's speech: "Mr. Ian Ross of Bell Laboratories has the right to be proud of the miniaturization accomplishments of the silicon chip industry. . . . But let us be humble in the light of nature's accomplishments. A sperm contains the blueprint for a complete and growing human being. If all the sperm responsible for conceiving all humans since the race developed were accumulated in one spot, they would fill a small thimble."

There's a message in Mr. Smith's letter for dreamers who for years have forecasted the eventual development of robots having lifelike intelligence. Consider, for instance, the nocturnal aerial feats of the incredible bat, the flying mammal whose head contains a sonar system smaller, lighter and more precise than any such system devised by modern technology. The next time you swat a pesky fly, remember that this remarkably agile aviator is equipped with a sophisticated inertial guidance and control system. Look behind a fly's two wings and you can see the two vibrating knobs, called halteres, that accomplish the same functions as accelerometers and gyroscopes in high performance aircraft and guided missiles. The fly's tiny brain processes the mechanical signals from its halteres and the complex video signals from its compound eyes and then passes precise instructions to the creature's flight control muscles. This engineering marvel is faster, smaller, more powerful and uses less energy than any comparable siliconnected system. The capabilities of the bat and the fly, to say nothing of other living creatures put Bell Labs' megabit memory chips and IBM's PC to shame. What's more, the earliest bats and flies in the fossil record possessed sensory, guidance and control capabilities apparently identical to those of their present day descendants.

Often I reflect upon the remarkable abilities of living systems, especially when an engineer acquaintance or friend becomes too enraptured by some super-sophisticated project and develops high-tech siliconitis, a highly contagious state of mind known also as HTS. The typical HTS victim can be recognized by an excessive use of jargon, an acute tendency to vicariously identify himself with a particular silicon chip, and an inflated view of his work's impact upon society. The disease is not to be confused with HT$, an incurable malady that attacks high-tech entrepreneurs, venture capitalists and investors. Nevertheless it is essential to recognize that both HTS and HT$ can strike simultaneously. HTS spreads rapidly within the scientific and engineering community, and out-breaks have often swept through Bell Laboratories and Silicon Valley. It can be easily transmitted to members of the press who swallow news releases infected with the HTS virus and be passed from them to the general public.

Having suffered numerous brief but virulent attacks of HTS, almost always while working on a "breakthrough" project for an electronics magazine, I'm well aware of its mind-altering symptoms. Now that I'm an HTS carrier, to protect myself from relapses and to help curtail the spread of this highly infectious malady, I always keep nearby a pouch containing a miracle remedy that has never failed to work. Inside the pouch are several ancient specimens of fossilized resin exuded from primeval trees and known in the English-speaking world as amber. I begin an HTS treatment session by handing the victim a nodule of glistening amber, and telling him the word electronics is derived from *elektron*, the Greek word for amber. Then I give the patient a ten-power magnifier and instruct him to examine the perfectly pre-served fossil flies encapsulated within the golden nodules. While the patient ogles the ancient insects, I administer a subliminal dose of HTS purgative: a brief lecture about the carbon-based parallel microprocessor and the video-augmented, inertial guidance and control system possessed by the fossil flies and how their capabilities and design are apparently identical to those of their modern descendants. Soon the HTS symptoms disappear, and the patient regains a more rational and humble view of his place in the grand scheme of things. At least until he's visited again by the HTS virus.

Silicontinuations

Shortly before *Computers & Electronics* was closed, I received a phone call from a fellow electronics writer whom I've never met, Steve Ciarcia, author of *Byte*'s popular column, "Ciarcia's Circuit Cellar." For several years I had been thinking about contacting Ciarcia, so his call came as a happy surprise. Steve had also wanted to establish contact, and after reading "Setting the Record Straight," a piece I wrote for the Altair tenth-anniversary issue of *Computer & Electronics*, he finally decided to call. During our conversation, which lasted more than an hour, we discussed how we had both been influenced by high-school science fairs and "The Amateur Scientist Column" in *Scientific American*. We talked about the dramatic shifts at *Byte* and *Computers & Electronics* from build-it-yourself "breakthrough" projects to features and reviews about computer software and equipment. Both of us were the last of the project writers for our respective magazines. "To the publishing executives, we're just 'The wires and pliers guys,'" I said. "We're the fellows who check under the hood when they roll up to the service station in their new Mercedes." Steve agreed. We were definitely on the same wavelength.

After telling Steve that Les Solomon had retired from *Computers & Electronics*, I passed on some good news: Art Salsberg had started a new magazine called *Modern Electronics* to compete with Gernsback Publications' *Radio-Electronics*. Did Art realize, I wondered aloud, that Hugo Gernsback's first magazine back in 1908 was called *Modern Electrics*? Steve had already seen *Modern Electronics*, and knew that Art had recruited Don "TV Typewriter" Lancaster and me to write monthly columns. Imagine that, my column alongside Don Lancaster's, the engineer who introduced digital electronics to the readers of *Popular Electronics* back in the late 1960s. My column, "Electronics Notebook," was like my old "Experimenter's Corner"; Don's was a question-and-answer column. After Steve and I agreed Art's new magazine could become another *Popular Electronics*, Steve asked, "Aren't you worried about your professional reputation, writing a column for *Modern Electronics* after being associated for so long with *Computers & Electronics*?" "What 'professional reputation'?" I responded. "My degree's in government."

To be able to admit to an electrical engineer and writer of Steve Ciarcia's caliber that I lacked his formal training was a personal "breakthrough." It was reinforced, coincidentally, the day before Steve called when I learned of a study by the Massachusetts High Technology Council that concluded, "engineers are beyond their prime at age 37." The study was cited in a letter from a Max. J. Schindler in the January 1, 1985, issue of *Electronic Products*, a trade magazine. Mr. Schindler quoted a professor at M.I.T. as having said that because of rapid advances in technology the "effective professional life" of an engineer today is only fifteen years. Schindler attributed the problem to an overemphasis on specialization in fields having a limited lifetime. Having successfully and easily made the transition from vacuum tubes to solid-state devices to computer software, Schindler is an engineer whose views count. To what does he attribute his success in a time when engineering graduates are obsolete in fifteen years? ". . . I largely credit the spartan facilities and dedication that prevailed at my [bombed-out] alma mater. Said one professor: "We'll teach you how the world works through physics, chemistry, metallurgy, math. Above all, we'll teach you how to learn.' . . . An engineer who knows his physics, and knows how to learn, never becomes obsolete."

Mr. Schindler's enlightening letter laid to rest the last vestige of doubt about my decision to take the easy way out during the siliconnected window of opportunity in the early 1960s. Had I majored in electrical engineering in college I might have become obsolete by 1981. And what with those long hours engineering students must devote to their studies, there wouldn't have been time to experiment with state-of-the-art light-emitting diodes, design travel aids for the blind, build and launch miniature guided rockets, transform in-the-ear hearing aids into in-the-ear radios, and communicate by light beams across the campus. In my case, far more valuable than an engineering degree were all those high-school science fair projects, especially the analog computer that translated Russian into English. Designing, building, troubleshooting, programming, and operating that silicontraption provided valuable lessons in how to learn, the essential ingredient of Max Schindler's formula for avoiding engineering obsolescence.

Experimenters who know how to learn never become obsolete; they just keep on experimenting. Why, just the other day, Dave

Wolf called from Radio Shack and assigned a new book that will provide several happy months of experimenting. I can hardly wait to start. Dave Wolf is the corporate buyer of the hand-illustrated electronic circuit books I produce for Radio Shack. The computer book industry may have fallen on hard times, but the demand by fellow experimenters and science fair savants for those circuit books is apparently insatiable. Dave understands this phenomenon better than a roomful of computer-crazy publishing executives, because he's an experimenter himself. When Dave and I get together the conversation is likely to be about the latest new analog chip, a new speech synthesizer, a midget piezo-electric beeper, or a touch-sensitive switch. Even though Dave owns a computer, the computer-mania bug has succeeded only in taking a few bytes out of his wallet. He's still a rational human being; instead of spouting out a stream of boring buzzwords about the latest of the jillion or so spreadsheet programs now available, Dave would rather tell funny stories about his adventures managing Radio Shack stores.

Like the dozens of project and circuit books I've written for Radio Shack since 1972, this new book was assigned Texas-style; there'll be no incomprehensible contracts to haggle over. In a week or so I'll just climb in the pickup, and drive up to Fort Worth to iron out the details and shake Dave's hand. Of course I'll take along some new parts and circuits I've been tinkering with to show the guys at Radio Shack. Working on the book will be an experimenter's dream. I can already hear the sizzle of moist fingertips cooling fresh solder connections, feel the spinning wire-wrapping tool twisting a new connection on a rainbow-striped resistor lead, and see the thin blue squiggles dancing across the oscilloscope screen. Just like the good old days.

Index